ROCK SOLID

TWO COPS' OBSESSIVE MANHUNT
FOR ONE OF AMERICA'S MOST
DANGEROUS CRIMINALS

Frank Bose
and
Bob Barchiesi

As told to Dolph LeMoult

G. P. PUTNAM'S SONS
New York

The following is a true story. In some instances names have been changed to protect the innocent or to safeguard the identities of informers. Maria Salazar, Anna Ruiz, Natalia and Benito Torres, Jorge Romano, Leonardo Carreon, and Ricky Truck have been given new names and identifying characteristics to obscure their identities. Other individuals whose names have been changed are Anthony Quinones, Mary Rodriguez, Lucy Conigliaro, Tony Oliveri, Eduardo Guzman, Amanda Savinon, Lily Santana, Elaine Figliusi, Sonia Perez, Toni Menendez, Bram Carper and Raymon Salizar. Wherever possible, actual events and conversations have been taken directly from undercover audio and video surveillance tapes. Where such taped material is unavailable, or when its use would compromise ongoing criminal investigations, the authors have drawn upon eyewitness testimony to the incidents portrayed.

G. P. Putnam's Sons
Publishers Since 1838
200 Madison Avenue
New York, NY 10016

HV
8148
N52
B67
1992

Library of Congress Cataloging-in-Publication Data

Bose, Frank, date.
    Rock solid : two cops' obsessive manhunt for one of America's most
dangerous criminals / Frank Bose and Robert Barchiesi as told to
Dolph LeMoult.
        p.   cm.
    ISBN 0-399-13659-2
    1. Police—New York (N.Y.)—Case studies.   2. Drug traffic—New
York (N.Y.)—Investigation—Case studies.   3. Lower East Side
(New York, N.Y.)   4. Bose, Frank, date.   5. Barchiesi, Robert,
date.   6. Lopez, Alejandro.   I. Barchiesi, Robert, date.
II. LeMoult, Dolph, date.   III. Title.
HV8148.N52B67   1992
364.1'77'097471—dc20   91–18738 CIP

Printed in the United States of America
1 2 3 4 5 6 7 8 9 10
This book is printed on acid-free paper.
                ∞

This effort is dedicated to the most forgiving person I have ever met:

Candace Mary Gaccione.

It's for you I made sure this one dealer will never claim another John.

Love you,
Frank

To Mom and Dad for teaching me to stand by my convictions, thereby making this all possible.

To my wife, Linda, and sons James and Robert II for all your understanding and all the lonely nights you endured.

All my love,
Bob

Acknowledgments

The authors wish to acknowledge J.R., one citizen who stood up and took notice.

. . . and all who worked on this case, too many to name. Without your help we would have been lost.

. . . and all police officers who are willing to risk it all; and sometimes fall.

Frank and Bob

"I do solemnly swear to support the Constitution of the United States and the Constitution of the State of New York, and that I will faithfully discharge the duties of Police Officer in the Police Department of the City of New York to the best of my abilities."

Foreword

ALONG the street called Delancey in the shadow of the Williamsburg Bridge, a cold wind blows in from the East River, probing the narrow side streets and alleyways beneath the massive granite pillars, propelling gusts of soot and scraps of refuse across the flattened cobblestones like tumbleweed rolling across a dry mesa. Centuries-old wooden joists groan before the wind, and steel stanchions shudder. Beneath the ancient overhangs, stray dogs huddle near the wheels of idle garbage trucks parked in front of the Department of Sanitation, and fifteen-foot-high metal fences cordon small, empty enclosures of hard-packed dirt, suggesting the possibility that someday, something of significance might be built here, but it is not likely. This is a grim, empty, loveless place; a place where nobody with any sense at all would want to be. It is a place of leftovers; leftover garbage, leftover architecture, leftover people, rising out of the pavement as toneless as a fading tintype.

Beyond Delancey and Houston streets on the Lower East Side of Manhattan, an area encompassing Delancey north to Fourteenth Street between Avenues A and D in lower Manhattan has come to be known as "Alphabet City." Here, block after block of squat, crumbling tenements hug the earth tenaciously, spread flat along the narrow litter-strewn avenues as if they had been squeezed out from the center of the glistening metropolis and left there to decompose. There is graffiti everywhere, scrawled in "Day-Glo" marker and spray paint, attesting to the deeds and masculinity of the young Hispanic men who make this place their home. They are fourteen- and fifteen-year-old youths with street names like Chepo and Spanky, Shorty and Campeon. They spend their afternoons on icy streetcorners, steering, running, and acting as lookouts for the drug merchants of the area, waiting for their turn to move up in the hierarchy, hoping someday to become rich and powerful druglords themselves.

On East Eleventh Street between Avenues B and C, a corrugated steel shutter covers the exterior of El Continental Cafe y Restaurante. Emblazoned across its front is an inexpert rendering of a naked female in streaks of orange and black. Someone has added the inscription SAY NO TO CRACK beneath it, with an arrow pointing to the figure's grossly enlarged genitalia. Further down the block, the former Hombres Social Club is corseted with a metal grillwork, its rusted padlock attesting to the fact that there has been no socializing there for some time. Inside a twelve-foot chain-link fence topped with coils of razor wire, choking weeds and piles of uncollected garbage fill what once had been a children's playground, and empty backboards rise out of the buckled concrete where sweating, barechested youths once slam-dunked in the sun.

Sixty-seven-year-old Elizabeth Calabrese has lived in the building at 512½ East Eleventh Street between Avenues A and B all her life. Now partially disabled, she stands uncomfortably on the second-floor landing and supports herself with a wooden cane. "It was like a circus," she responds when asked about the building across the street. "They were lined up around the block to buy drugs twenty-four hours a day." She pauses, her eyes rake the dingy, poorly lit hallway that reeks of mildew and heating oil. "I don't want to say too much, you never know who's around.

"My family moved here when I was two," she finally goes on. "I went to P.S. Sixty-one right around the corner and later I was transferred to the Catholic school, Mary, Help of Christians, because my father wanted me to learn respect. I guess I was a little wild in those days." She giggles self-consciously then hastens to add, "But not like what they do today. There were no drugs or nothing like that when I was growing up. This was a good neighborhood then.

"I married my husband, Mr. Calabrese, when I was eighteen and we opened an import-export business downstairs a few years after that; fans, carvings, mostly Oriental things; and we stayed in business until he died three years ago. We stayed in business even through the worst of what was going on across the street, the drugs, the killings . . ." Her voice trails off.

"How can I explain?" She presses the heels of her palms together and extends her arthritic fingers to form a bowl. "It was like the building there was the center and all the fingers were leading down to it. You could look out in the snow and see the footprints coming into the middle—north, south, east, and west, everyone came here and lined up to buy drugs."

She becomes distracted by a splintered bannister that is coming loose from the wall, then her focus returns. "This was a real nice neighborhood once," she repeats defensively. "Even 507 across the street was okay until the city took it over, then all sorts of terrible people moved in." She drops her voice to a whisper. "Puerto Ricans, you know."

Pressed to speak about the killings, she shrugs. "What I didn't know couldn't hurt me, right? Sure I saw things, ambulances pulling up to the front of the building at all hours of the night, carrying out bodies. Were they dead? Who knows? We heard about some of them; that little Daisy, you heard about her, God rest her little soul. What was she, two, three years old? That didn't make no difference to them. They killed her just like they killed all the others."

She shifts her weight painfully on the cane and shakes her head. "Sure we were scared; wouldn't you be scared with all that going on right across the street? I just don't know what this city is coming to when people like that can sell drugs like it was a supermarket or something, right out in the open like they did, day after day, and nobody lifted a hand to stop them. Not the police, not nobody . . ."

Suddenly she becomes agitated. "And you know what was the worst thing? That awful music they played all the time late at night. It got so you couldn't even watch television it was so loud." She rattles the loose bannister. "I don't know, I just don't go out anymore."

PART ONE

"When bad men combine, the good must associate; else they will fall one by one, an unpitied sacrifice in a contemptible struggle."

—EDMUND BURKE

Chapter One

"There's a sick joke around the precinct that if you want to get rid of somebody, tell them to move to East Eleventh Street."

—LIEUTENANT MARTIN KENNEDY,
NINTH PRECINCT DETECTIVE SQUAD

RALPH Rodriguez died hard, even by the standards of his downtown drug associates who saw violent death as the cost of doing business; six slugs pumped into him point-blank, three in the middle of his face where it would show the most. They drove his body across East Eleventh in Manhattan to Bowery Street, over the Manhattan Bridge to Brooklyn, where they dumped him in the middle of nowhere like the shitbag he was. They sprinkled glassines of cocaine on his chest to show the world he had fucked with them and that would not be tolerated. Then they departed, leaving his body twisted grotesquely on the concrete while his final traces of inner warmth escaped through the bullet wounds in his head, like tiny geysers steaming gently in the frigid night air.

They dumped Ralph in Bushwick; in front of a fringe of ugly brown tenements. The next morning, a coating of sooty snow shrouded the streets and alleyways of Bushwick, aggravating beleaguered residents on their way to work, and delighting neighborhood schoolchildren. The children chased each other along slippery sidewalks and threw rock-hard snowballs at automobiles in the clogged roadways, unaware that nearby a young man had oozed his last few drops of blood on the frozen pavement.

Nobody mourned.

An anonymous call was placed to 911 Central shortly before midnight. Officers Ed Delano and Don Straub were winding down their four-to-twelve shift in Bushwick when the notification came over the radio of their sector car: male shooting victim on the street in front of 1343 Halsey; possible DOA. It was a lousy break on a lousy night in a lousy part of town. Working Bushwick was shit duty to begin with, gloomy and squalid. They counted the hours and, as the end of their tour approached, the minutes and the seconds. Another few minutes and they would have been safely out of it, drinking mugs of bitter black coffee with the guys back at the precinct. Somebody else would have had to deal with the no-name homicide out on Halsey Street.

Ralph Rodriguez was very dead when they arrived. They examined his corpse by flashlight, recording their initial impressions of the scene for later reports: A Hispanic male, twenty-five to thirty years of age, fully dressed in jeans, black-and-red high-top sneakers, and a heavy woolen mackinaw. The body was on its back, arms extended upward, right leg twisted unnaturally backward under the left. There were multiple gunshot wounds to the head and chest. They notified EMS as a matter of form, then radioed it in to 911 Central.

What followed was the inevitable jumble of police, bystanders, and emergency vehicles that routinely descended on a crime scene: haphazardly parked radio cars with staccato flashing lights; an EMS ambulance; a blue-and-white Emergency Services truck; a Crime Scene van; the Coroner's wagon. A throng of curious spectators gathered behind tape barricades in the freezing mist; harsh, flat silhouettes caught in the reflective glare of enormous halogen lamps that spotlighted the scene. Inside the flimsy plastic enclosure detectives scanned the street for shell casings and other bits of discarded evidence while clusters of uniformed patrolmen milled about the periphery of the crime scene, exchanging information and speculation, shooting the shit. Somebody from the Crime Scene Unit chalked an outline of the victim on the street.

Finally the body of Ralph Rodriguez was covered with a plastic sheet and placed inside the waiting Coroner's wagon. Police and medical personnel packed up and abandoned the crime scene one by one, until all that remained was a single patrol car left to guard the area against the improbable prospect that someone might desecrate it in some way.

The next morning, word of Ralph Rodriguez's murder spread throughout the East Eleventh Street community where he had lived and worked. Along the block stretching from Avenue A to Avenue B just two blocks north of Tompkins Square Park, clusters of Hispanic men and women gathered and spoke in hushed tones, solemnly affirming to one another that Ralph had been killed because he spoke to the police. The liquor had been his downfall, they all agreed. The liquor greased his tongue and turned him into a braggart. There was no telling what he might have said to the police that day he had been spotted leaning into their car window and blabbing like a fool, but it was certain his death would serve as a clear, unambiguous message to anyone else on the block who felt like getting friendly with the cops. Talk to the police and you're dead.

Police Sergeant Bob Barchiesi and Officer Frank Bose were informed of Ralph's death by two women from the neighborhood as they drove slowly down the block in a four-year-old confiscated taxicab and paused briefly at the corner. "Ralph was shot dead," a woman named Maria Salazar whispered into the cab's open window as she rushed past. "They killed Ralph," a second woman, known to them only as Lourdes, repeated before hurrying away. The officers looked at one another then continued on down the block heading west. Rodriguez was a scumbag and he died the way scumbags usually died on the Lower East Side. It wasn't the worst news they had gotten in a while, but it brought them no great comfort either. Without actually saying it to one another, each of them felt partially responsible.

Bob Barchiesi leaned back in the passenger's seat of the taxicab and let his mind drift off in the familiar sounds of traffic; back to a time only a little more than a week ago when they were driving on Eleventh Street and Ralph had approached them in front of number 507.

"Hey, what's with you two?" he had asked in a voice resonant with booze-induced bravado.

"What're you trying to be, a fucking smart guy?" Bob demanded. "You trying to tell everybody on the street we're here?" He had eyed Frank Bose ruefully. The dilapidated taxicab was no deception to anyone, they knew, least of all to seasoned drug dealers in the area, who knew them by sight and passed the alarm whenever they approached. *"Feo bajando,"* the cry went up. *"The ugly ones are coming down!"*

Ralph leaned into the car. His breath came at them in pungent waves of whiskey, garlic, and unwashed teeth. "I gotta talk to you guys," he whispered conspiratorially. "Go around the corner, okay?"

They had driven the cab around the corner, double-parked along Avenue A, and waited until Ralph arrived. Their revolvers were drawn and resting between their legs on the vinyl seat. Nobody was taking any chances. Cops who let their guards down in this area could end up dead cops. Twelve years ago, in May of 1973, two New York City patrolmen, Greg Foster and Rocco Laurie, had been gunned down on the sidewalk by members of the Black Liberation Army less than two blocks away.

"This better be fucking good, Ralphie," Frank Bose warned when Ralph arrived and again leaned in the window. "We're gonna drag you in if we find out you're jerking us off here."

"Listen, you guys've always been straight with me," Ralph slurred, his eyes darting up and down the avenue. "I'm no rat, you know that; but I gotta draw the line when it comes to certain things." He paused, surveying the area. "You guys know Tito. You know his people; you know they got a lot of Uzis, shit like that . . ."

"What shit? What the hell are you telling us?" Bose asked impatiently. "Either get to the fucking point or get your ass outa here!"

Ralph took a deep breath. "Next time you come up the street you better watch out. They're looking to spray the two of you with an Uzi."

The officers' eyes met in a nervous moment of awareness. Ralph Rodriguez was a flyspeck, little more than a stooge in the cocaine organization they had been investigating for almost six months, but they took his warning seriously. They knew that murder was a serious business on East Eleventh Street. "Who's *they*?" Bob Barchiesi pressed. "Who are we talking about here?"

"You know . . ." Ralph shuffled nervously.

"No, we don't!" Bose objected. "How do we know you're not fucking us around here? Where did you hear shit like this?"

"I heard it. I was in the apartment, man."

"What apartment? You're not telling us what we want to hear, asshole!" Frank Bose leaned across the front seat and stuck his chin into Ralphie's face like a Marine Corps drill sergeant confronting a terrified recruit. His hand reached beneath him and felt the reassuring bulk of the revolver on the seat. "We want it straight, Ralphie. No bullshit."

Ralph paused, measuring his words. "They're not fucking around. They know you both got kids . . ."

"They know *what*?" Barchiesi interrupted.

Ralph looked at Frank Bose. "They know you got a little girl. They're gonna chop her up in little pieces and mail her to you in shoeboxes."

He turned to Bob Barchiesi. "And you, they know you got a kid, too. They're both in for it if you don't cut out what you're doing."

Bose felt his throat tighten. He wanted to reach out the window, grab Ralph by his scrawny neck, and squeeze the life out of him with his massive, calloused hands. Bob Barchiesi, a serious weight lifter for years, felt an almost irresistible urge to lift the drunk bodily into the car and crush him like a bug with one of his enormous forearms. Neither of them acted on the impulse. Infuriated as they were, they knew Rodriguez was only the messenger, and killing the messenger was not going to help them, or their children.

"How the fuck does Tito know I have a little girl?" Frank Bose demanded, referring to Alejandro "Tito" Lopez, the man they both knew was behind the message.

"Tito's 'The Man.' Tito knows everything," Ralph replied reverently, falling into the trap and revealing the source of the threats. "Nobody is stronger than Tito."

Ralph's assessment was chilling but both Bose and Barchiesi knew that he echoed the belief of everyone on the street, everyone who had ever dealt with Alejandro Lopez. They had watched the druglord rise to power on a tidal wave of high-grade cocaine and over the murdered bodies of anyone who had dared to oppose his organization or simply got in its way. They had witnessed the almost supernatural aura of invincibility and mystique he had woven around himself, and the climate of cold fear he inspired among neighborhood residents who lived in the shadow of his Alphabet City drug citadel.

But until this very moment it had just been business. Until this moment Alejandro Lopez was just another piece of street scum to be followed and observed, and if the opportunity presented itself, arrested and sent to prison where he could no longer sell his poison to the residents of the Lower East Side. The fact that his cocaine organization was one of the largest single street operations in the history of New York narcotics enforcement had only excited them, heightened the enjoyment of the chase and strengthened their resolve. But it was business, and as best they could, they put it aside at the end of the day and entered another world where the cruelty and squalor of Alphabet City melted into quiet tree-lined streets and children's laughter.

Now Alejandro Lopez had turned it into something very different. Now they could never again think of Lopez as anything less than the man who had threatened to take their children and cut them into pieces. They could never again follow him with the professional detachment of law enforcement officers who simply had a job to do. Where before they had wanted Alejandro Lopez for what he did and what he was, now they wanted him for what he threatened to do and threatened to become. It had gotten personal. Now their mission came from the bottom of their very souls as police officers and as men. It had to do with life given and life preserved, and that elusive thing that takes ordinary human beings and turns them into heroes. It had to do with obsession.

Chapter Two

I T had begun for Frank Bose and Bob Barchiesi five months earlier in March, when a peripatetic New York City Council-woman named Marion Friedlander telephoned the Seventh Police Precinct, headquarters for a much-heralded anti-drug task force known as Operation Pressure Point, to report her constituents' concerns over drug activity in their Lower East Side neighbor-hood. Although Friedlander was known to the police as somewhat of a gadfly and publicity hound, her complaint warranted investi-gation. Bose and Barchiesi, partners in Pressure Point for only a few months, responded to the call, along with a third officer named Frank Katan.

Inaugurated amid much media hoopla in January of 1984, Operation Pressure Point had combined police officers and detec-tives from the Fifth, Seventh, and Ninth police precincts into a task force designed to apply unrelenting pressure on street-level narcotics dealers and purchasers throughout the troubled down-town area. For Bob Barchiesi, a policeman since 1979, assignment to Pressure Point seemed a natural outgrowth of a career that had been notable for an abundance of high risk, high visibility assign-ments. As one of the earliest members of the police department's newly organized Street Narcotics Enforcement Unit, and later as an officer in the Street Crime Unit, he had distinguished himself by assisting in more than four hundred arrests and winning fifty-two commendations for bravery and meritorious service. Pro-moted to Sergeant in 1984, he was asked by his superiors to supervise Operation Pressure Point and gladly accepted.

Frank Bose was appointed to the police force in January of 1982 at the age of thirty-two. A latecomer to the department, he quickly earned a reputation for being a tough, aggressive police officer and soon found himself assigned to the Seventh Precinct on the Lower East Side of Manhattan, one of the most volatile and high-

17

est crime areas in the city. In September of 1983 he was transferred to the Seventh Precinct Street Narcotics Enforcement Unit (SNEU), where he participated in hundreds of street narcotics arrests before being assigned to Pressure Point. The recipient of twenty-four departmental citations as well as numerous civilian awards, he saw the assignment as a chance to help the beleaguered Lower East Side recover from the scourge of illegal drugs that had become its hallmark. Like Bob Barchiesi, he believed Operation Pressure Point could make a real difference.

Bose and Barchiesi did not know each other well, and although each of them suspected they shared a common philosophy about police work and a similar enthusiasm for the job, their earlier encounters had not always gone smoothly. In fact, as Frank Bose remembered it, he wasn't very impressed by their first meeting:

"I was riding with a guy named Benny Ayala. It was before Pressure Point. I was in the Seventh Precinct SNEU [Street Narcotics Enforcement Unit] at the time. Benny was in the SNEU with me and we carpooled every once in a while. One night we were on our way home and stopped along Essex Street to take a leak in Seward Park; you know how it is when you've been riding all day in a sector car. So we're standing there relieving ourselves behind a bush when this taxicab pulls up behind us and Bobby and his partner try to arrest us.

"I turned to Benny and asked, 'What the fuck is going on here?' Benny said, 'Oh, it's just those jerk-offs Walsh and Barchiesi from Street Crime.' These guys had the reputation of being a couple of gung-ho go-getters, gun collar guys. I guess I figured at the time they knew we were cops and were just busting our balls. Anyway, I thought Bob was kind of a jerk back then. Given another two or three seconds, we probably would have ended up in a shoot-out with each other."

Bob Barchiesi remembered the incident and recalled his first impressions of Frank Bose: "Once I got to know him a little bit I saw him as a hardworking guy, a good cop. He was older than most of the guys new in the job. I knew he had a military background in Vietnam and that he liked guns. I guess I saw him as being a bit crazy, but that's okay, because I consider myself crazy, too. I have a tendency to hook up with crazy people."

On a warm July evening in 1985, Bose, Barchiesi, and Katan parked their sector car on East Eleventh Street and made a sweep of the building at 517-519. Finding nothing incriminating inside, they returned to the street and were approaching their vehicle when a small voice summoned them from the curb.

"Hey cops, *inside*! They're dealing rock in the back of the hallway!"

The officers looked quizzically at one another, then at the frail six-year-old boy seated at the edge of the sidewalk, barefoot and dressed only in a frayed pair of cotton shorts. "What's that?" Bob Barchiesi queried.

"They're dealing rock in there . . ." the boy responded in a reedy, childlike lisp, lightly inflected with Spanish.

"The building we just left?"

"Uh-uh." He pointed behind him. "*Number 507.*"

They shrugged, grinned at one another and cautiously entered the run-down tenement building. Inside they were met with the redolent smells of vomit, stale urine, and decay as they accustomed their eyes to the dank, semi-lit foyer. "Smells like a fucking sewer in here," Bose whispered, adjusting his eyes to the darkness.

Simultaneously, the three spotted the figure of a young Hispanic male standing in the hallway, the dull wooden handle of an automatic stuffed into his waistband, barely visible in the dim light. The figure ran and the officers unhesitatingly followed him. There were no words between them; no commands or warnings or shared insights. They understood the danger at the end of that blackened hallway, but they also knew they could waste no time worrying about it. Pursuit is a split-second thing and you never get a second chance. In that frozen moment, each of them had to put his life in the hands of an untested partner.

The suspect fled into apartment number 2 and the officers plunged headlong after him. Screaming at the top of his lungs, Frank Katan hurled his body across the small room like a seasoned linebacker and tackled him from the rear, while Bob Barchiesi turned his attention toward a surprised female who had bolted upright from a chair inside the apartment, spilling almost two hundred glassines of cocaine onto the floor.

The male lunged from Katan's grasp, but Frank Bose hit him full-force with a 220-pound full body block and sent him crashing into an ancient iron radiator, where he continued to struggle. "*You motherfucker!* If you don't stop I'm gonna run your head through this thing like it was a bread slicer!"

His prisoner slumped to the floor.

"What's your name, scumbag?" Bose demanded as he subdued and cuffed the sweating youth.

"Anthony," he panted.

"Anthony what?" Bose tightened the cuffs.

"Anthony Quinones." He grimaced in pain.

"What about you, what's your name?" Barchiesi restrained the female prisoner who was struggling toward the open door.

"Mary Rodriguez," she replied sullenly.

"How old are you, Mary?"

"Sixteen."

"How about you, Quinones?" Bose asked the male, who remained resolutely silent.

"He's old enough to carry this," Katan observed, holding the prisoner's confiscated double-action .380 automatic pistol aloft. "This cannon's fully loaded with hollow points; one already in the chamber ready to go."

The officers' eyes met fleetingly in a nervous, shared response. They knew the power of the handgun. They also knew the hollow-nosed bullets were designed to blow apart and rip a person up inside. They knew it took a long, agonizing time to die.

Cops would rather pull an illegal gun off the street than a thousand pounds of dope. It is a matter of priorities, a matter of survival. Drugs kill thousands, and policemen know that they are saving lives by keeping them out of the hands of users. Fundamentally, they understand that every confiscated glassine of heroin or cocaine could be the one that pushes a desperate, trembling addict over the edge and stills his overburdened heart forever, but that is in the abstract. Illegal guns kill cops, and in a city where junkies die daily as a matter of course, dead junkies do not tug at the heart like dead policemen. There is not the same feeling of loss, the same hidden sense of relief among cops that this time, at least, they themselves have been spared. They understand the tragedy of a junkie's death in moral and sociological terms. They feel the death of a cop in their gut.

The inside of the small apartment was dirtier and more cluttered than the reeking hallway: Everywhere, garbage and clothing were heaped carelessly on the floor. A filthy foam mattress rested against the crumbling plaster wall. A rusted metal faucet dripped incessantly into a chipped enamel sink crusted with food and black sludge, then leaked through the ancient drainpipe onto the floor. A frayed electrical cord trailed from the open window to the single ceiling outlet, where a bare bulb provided the room's only illumination. Searching for weapons, Frank Bose opened the door to a small refrigerator and reeled backward as it came alive with the stench of rotting food and the sight of thousands of crawling cockroaches. He eyed the obviously pregnant sixteen-year-old female. "Is this the kind of life you want for your baby?" he asked.

Her eyes swelled with tears, but she did not answer.

Bob Barchiesi opened a Styrofoam cooler next to the weeping female and discovered a plastic shopping bag full of cocaine. Packages containing two hundred sealed glassines each, totaling more than fifteen hundred in all; plus more than a thousand dollars in loose currency. Bose examined one of the glassines, rubber-stamped with the word ROCK on one side and SOLID on the other in black ink. It was common practice for street narcotics dealers to label their product, offering at least the illusion of quality, strength, and safety in a business where unscrupulous dealers could package talcum and sell it as dope, and a bad load of the real stuff could mean death. "Rock Solid; now there's a brand we haven't seen out here yet," he commented, replacing the glassine in its bag.

Barchiesi examined an index card appended to the bag of glassines. "Whatta you make of this? It has the number twenty-five stenciled on it here. How many more like this do you think are floating around?"

Bose and Katan checked the card. "Do you suppose there's a number fifty out there someplace?" Bose wondered.

"What do you say, scumbag?" Barchiesi confronted the male Hispanic. "Where do they keep the rest of the coke?"

The prisoner set his chin and stared into space.

Barchiesi and Bose eyed one another wordlessly. Both of them realized that what they had uncovered was bigger by far than anything Pressure Point had yet seen.

"They sure as hell aren't keeping the stuff in this shithouse," Bose commented, glancing around the debris-strewn apartment. "They probably bring it in from an intermediate drop as they need it."

"You wanta tell me where you're getting this shit?" Barchiesi again asked the young male. "I can make it easier for you if you help us out."

It was obvious they would receive no further information from the prisoners. The officers knew that despite their youth, the two were seasoned drug dealers, fully cognizant of their rights and the limitations of their captors. The pair knew that they would be handled leniently by the courts because of their age, and that they would soon be free to resume selling cocaine to the insatiable clientele of Alphabet City. Sixteen-year-old Mary was pregnant and she cried a lot. Both of them knew she would be treated compassionately by a system she held in utter contempt.

"Let's get the hell out of this shithole," Bob Barchiesi told the others after they had completed their search of the apartment. "I could use a breath of fresh air."

Outside on the sidewalk, a cool evening breeze drifted across Eleventh Street and they inhaled it gratefully, cleansing themselves. They watched as their prisoners were led away by the backup unit they'd requested, each winding down in his own way from the turmoil inside. There'd been a lot of screaming and a lot of threats, most of them empty. They'd screamed because that was what they did at times like these. They knew the shouted threats frightened perps, intimidated them and set them off balance, made them less likely to do something violent. The shouts were like a pressure valve when things became hot and heavy, muting the fear they all felt, making their adversaries believe they were brave even if they doubted it themselves.

The descending sun crept between buildings, imprinting shafts of yellow light on the darkening pavement of East Eleventh Street. The sidewalks were less crowded as nightfall approached and residents disappeared behind bolted doors, fearful of the explosion of drug-induced violence that always came when daylight ended. Bose, Barchiesi, and Katan felt the pressure lifting, the screaming that continued inside each of them being carried away in the discordant sounds of salsa music and the rhythms of traffic.

They breathed deeply, relieved that it was over and confident that they had functioned effectively as a team. For Frank Bose and Bob Barchiesi, the operation at 507 was the first of its kind they had worked on together and it had turned out well. Nobody had gotten hurt. They'd taken a weapon off the street. They'd seized fifteen hundred glassines of cocaine. They'd busted two perps. And they'd managed to do it all by the book, without violating anyone's rights, breaking any laws, or getting in each other's way.

Not bad for a night's work.

Chapter Three

"Partners have to function as one person. They have to become closer than husbands and wives because their lives depend on each of them covering the other's back with no questions asked, every day of the week. A wife has to be willing to share her life with her husband. A partner has to be willing to sacrifice his."

—FRANK BOSE

I T would be hard to imagine two more unlikely partners than Frank Bose and Bob Barchiesi. Born at Saint Joseph's Hospital in Brooklyn, New York, on September 3, 1949, Frank Bose seemed determined to live a life filled with tumult and adventure, perhaps attempting to emulate the exploits of his father, who died when Frank was just seven years old. At the time of his death, Francis Salvatore Bose, an official of the Seafarer's International Union of North America, had traveled around the world several times as a merchant sailor. At the start of World War II he enlisted in the Merchant Marine, served aboard various allied tankers, and was torpedoed a total of five times, enduring periods of as long as fourteen days bobbing helplessly in lifeboats in the hostile North Atlantic.

Young Frank was raised by his mother and grandmother, and admittedly gave them a rough time. Restless and adventure-seeking, he was constantly in and out of trouble with the police and with his teachers in elementary and high school. He played hooky when it suited him, which was often, studied little if at all, yet managed to scrape by with a quick, facile intelligence, guile, and an abundance of wit and bluster. Even those qualities, which were later to serve him well in the New York City Police Department, were not enough to sustain his academic interest. He quit high school before graduating and took a job with his father's old

Seafarer's Union prior to enlisting in the Marine Corps. When the war in Vietnam broke out, he was among the first to volunteer, graduating first in his class at Parris Island. At a ramrod straight six foot one and an exercise-hardened 220 pounds, with dark brown hair and hazel eyes, Frank could have been any casting director's idea of what a United States Marine should look like.

"I couldn't wait to get there," Frank recalled. "There was an attitude of integrity among the troops. It was an ideology we really believed." His enthusiasm and belief as well as his performance under fire earned him numerous combat decorations and a promotion to the rank of Sergeant in only thirteen months, one of the first meritorious promotions to that rank awarded since the Korean War.

"You get there and you're thrust into that horrible destruction . . . all that noise," he remembered. "I learned the true meaning of two words in the English language. One was 'dark,' because I've never seen such darkness in my life. The other was 'frightened,' because I was really scared. You start out with an attitude of 'God, Corps, and Country,' but after a while its strictly a matter of surviving. You do what you have to do to stay alive, no flags, no bands. I wouldn't have missed it for a million bucks. I wouldn't do it again for five."

For Frank Bose, the early glow of police work did not come until he had exhausted a string of lackluster jobs and business ventures. Owning and operating several successful restaurant franchises taught him all about working well under pressure but failed to arouse his restless spirit. He obtained a high school equivalency diploma and attended the College of Staten Island where he studied Engineering Electronics, Physics, and undergraduate Law. Still he found himself facing an uncertain and uninspiring future. "When I got home from Vietnam at age twenty I missed the jungle, missed the action. And I remember thinking to myself, 'Where the hell do I go from here?' I took the police department test in '78 or '79, knowing that if I was sixty-five some day, sitting at a job someplace never having tried this, I would regret it all my life. I was trying to get back that feeling I had in Vietnam, getting as close to the edge as possible without falling off, and I believed the nearest I could get to that feeling as a civilian would be as a police officer."

Bob Barchiesi had been a cop for three years when Frank Bose became a patrolman in January of 1982, and unlike his future partner's, his early life seemed free of turmoil. Born Robert Clayton Barchiesi at Polyclinic Hospital in Manhattan on February 19, 1955, the youngest of three children born to the former Joan Hummel and James John Barchiesi, he was raised in a stable, supportive environment. "I was brought up to be my own person," he relates. "I was taught to do something because it was what I wanted to do, not because someone else wanted me to do it."

He was an above-average student in Holy Rosary grade school and Saint Peter's High School on Staten Island, where his family lived first in city-owned projects and later in a private house on Hylan Boulevard. School appealed to him, and the discipline imposed by Catholic school education has undoubtedly contributed to his personal manner of conduct and present style. A big man at six foot three, 230 pounds, with blue eyes, sandy hair, and a steel-hard body honed from playing a variety of sports and years of serious weight lifting, Barchiesi is not given to lavish discourses. Quiet and respectful almost to the point of shyness and taciturn with new acquaintances, his speech often drifts unconsciously into the cryptic, shorthand vernacular of his childhood, but it quickly becomes apparent that he's a thoughtful man. His responses are reasoned and conservative. Bob Barchiesi is no hip-shooter.

After receiving an Associate's degree in Liberal Arts from Staten Island Community College, he graduated with a Bachelor of Science degree from John Jay College of Criminal Justice in 1977 and became an agent in the U.S. Customs Service. "I was disillusioned," Bob recalled. "It was a law enforcement job but it wasn't what I had pictured law enforcement to be. We made a lot of Narcotics arrests, some of them resulted in significant seizures, and I suppose that experience paid off for me later in the NYPD. But to be honest, I never really felt like a cop, so I took the test for NYPD in 1979. I guess I felt I could find some excitement there. Maybe a kind of adrenaline high, thrill of the chase sort of thing.

"When I went to work for the police department the station houses were dingy. There weren't many typewriters and the radio cars were falling apart. Only sergeant's cars had air-conditioning. In most precincts you couldn't find any toilet paper. Even today most cops store toilet paper in their lockers. One of the things I remember most was when I graduated from the police academy and got my shield, it came without a pin to attach it. When I asked for a pin they gave me one, and charged me twenty-five cents for it.

"Still I loved the job. I loved walking a foot post, calling my own shots. When I got transferred to the Street Crime Unit, I loved going to work every day and if I took a vacation, I missed it. It was what I envisioned a cop should be. The excitement was there, just what I was looking for. I was out there on the front line with my partner, Mike Walsh, and we both felt like what we were doing was making a difference. We got a reputation for making gun collars and robbery busts, we won a lot of awards. It was a really good time in my life, and I was proud to be a New York City cop. My family was proud that I was on the force."

Brought together for the first time by Operation Pressure Point, the two made an improbable pair. But despite their differences in background, style, and temperament, it worked. As the weeks and months passed, Bose and Barchiesi began to realize that they shared the same outlook on things. They saw the job as more than a way to get a little respect and a guaranteed paycheck, and each of them saw qualities in the other that they felt they lacked themselves. Today they like to call it "the mesh." They found they had respect for one another, and in the virile corridors of police stations it is an unspoken axiom that respect must come before friendship. Bose and Barchiesi were friends before they knew it.

As a sergeant, Bob Barchiesi was given the chance to fill in for supervisors from various SNEU teams on their days off. More and more, he found himself working the streets with Frank Bose and liking what he saw. More and more he found himself asking that Bose be assigned to his team. It was an assignment that Bose relished. In the three years he had spent on the street, he had worked under sergeants who were strictly low-key, guys who did not share his enthusiasm for aggressive law enforcement. The chance to work with Bob Barchiesi, who he knew to be an energetic and action-oriented supervisor, was what he believed police work was all about.

"It was real teamwork," Bose recalled. "We were both there to catch drug dealers so that was what we did. There was this one case where we got three fully automatic weapons and a handgun off the street, and busted a couple of really bad guys. It was a tremendous bust for a SNEU team."

"I was a supervisor in the Seventh Precinct SNEU," Bob Barchiesi remembered. "One of my teams arrested two guys who were wanted for a shooting in Brooklyn and while they were taking the perps' pedigrees, I noticed that one of them, an Albanian, had given an address that was different from the one listed on his driver's license. That led me to believe that he was hiding his true residence for a reason. Frank and I have this good guy–bad guy routine, and we used it on them. We told them we had a search warrant for the location listed on the Albanian's driver's license and that if anything illegal was found inside we would arrest everyone there, but if they cooperated with us we would only confiscate the illegal merchandise and make no arrests. It was a long-shot bluff but it worked.

"The Albanian admitted to having a machine gun in that apartment and when we bluffed some more, he caved in and told us there were actually three illegal machine guns and a handgun hidden there. He even drew us a map of the place pinpointing their exact locations, so when we went up there in uniform all we had to do was pick them up. It was a rewarding experience. We used brains, ingenuity, and we got a significant arrest out of it. We got instruments of death off the street."

Bose and Barchiesi became partners in early July 1985, a few weeks before their arrest of Anthony Quinones and Mary Rodriguez. Those arrests, along with the seizure of more than fifteen hundred glassines of "Rock Solid" cocaine, had convinced them both that they would make a good team. The fact that the seizure pointed to the probability of an even greater cache of illegal drugs somewhere else in the city piqued their interest, and one of their first operations as partners was to set up surveillance of the building at 507 East Eleventh Street.

On the afternoon of August 8, less than a month after the Quinones bust, as they drove slowly by number 507 in one of the condemned New York City taxicabs Pressure Point command had provided to its street operatives, they observed an attractive female Hispanic standing in front of the building. Seeing them, she hurriedly threw a small packet of what appeared to be drugs on the sidewalk. Frank Bose screeched the car to a halt, approached her, and retrieved the discarded glassine of cocaine. "What do you think we are—assholes?" he asked. "Don't you think we saw you drop this bag, and don't you think we saw you dealing to the guy who just went around the corner?"

The last was a lie, but an acceptable lie. Possession of a single glassine of cocaine is a misdemeanor in the city of New York, but dealing drugs is a felony. Faced with the possibility of doing real time for dealing drugs, suspects can become sweetly reasonable during their interrogations, often implicating friends, loved ones, and fellow dealers. It's a tough world out there, cops say. All's fair in love and dope busts.

"Hey, man, I don't sell this stuff," she protested.

"We saw you when we drove by, plain as day," Bob Barchiesi repeated.

"Don't take me in. I got a kid to take care of," she pleaded. "She don't got no way to eat unless I'm there."

"You should've thought about that before you started doing this shit," Bose told her, gentling her into the backseat of the taxicab. "You're busted. You'll see your kid if we like what we hear from you."

Back at Seventh Precinct headquarters, Bose and Barchiesi took their prisoner into the tiny first-floor room that served as the Pressure Point operations center. The windowless room was steamy and oppressive, holding the heat from almost two weeks of record temperatures like a pressure cooker with no release valve. They sat the trembling female at the room's only desk and began to question her.

"Anna," she responded when asked her name and age. "Anna Ruiz. I'm twenty-three."

"Well Anna, it looks like you got a big problem here. I don't see where we have any choice but to lock you up for sale," Barchiesi told her. "That is, unless you want to cooperate with us."

Her large brown eyes darted nervously about the room. Beads of sweat began to form on her upper lip. "I gotta get out."

"What are we supposed to do?"

"I gotta get out and be with my kid. I'll cooperate if you promise you'll let me go."

Barchiesi nodded. "Well, I guess it all depends on what you tell us. I have the authority to issue you a desk appearance ticket and let you go home, but my bosses don't like me to do that. They want you people off the street. They want you to spend the night in jail at the very minimum."

"I can tell you something really big," she blurted.

"How big?"

"I can tell you where they're keeping twenty or thirty shoeboxes full of rock cocaine."

The officers shot a fleeting glance at one another. It was a staggering amount. Frank Bose activated his portable tape recorder and set it on the desk in front of her. "Do you want to tell us how a street kid like you would know about amounts like that?" he asked.

"I used to deal for these guys," she reported. "I stopped doing it awhile back because I didn't want to get hooked. Now I only do it every now and then."

The admission that she had once been a dealer was significant. One of the primary rules of determining credibility in a witness was whether they were willing to implicate themselves in a crime greater than the one they were being charged with. Bose rolled the tape.

"There's a place over by the river, by the Ones Discotheque, a big place upstairs where Tito lives and keeps the stuff . . ."

"Who's Tito?" Barchiesi broke in.

"Tito Lopez, he's a real big man up there." She eyed them incredulously. "You don't know Tito? Everybody knows Tito. He's called 'The Man.' "

"Tell us about 'The Man.' " Bose urged.

"Tito is big," she said reverently. "He's got airplanes, he's got places all over; even a house in Puerto Rico where he raises horses and pit bulls. He's got lots of pit bulls; he walks them all over the West Side. He's a legend, man. Ain't nobody ever going to get Tito. He's too smart, too big." Her eyes grew wide. "And you know what else he's got up in that place? He's got a projection TV, can you imagine that?"

"How about the shoeboxes?"

She paused, searching her memory. "When you come up to the place there's a flat dock where the trucks pull up . . ."

"A loading platform."

"Yeah, and outside on the fire escape there's a TV camera so The Man can see who's coming in and out of that place. He's got microphones so he can hear people, and more cameras inside so he can see them coming up the stairs . . ."

Bob Barchiesi shot a penetrating glance across the desk at his partner. This did not sound like any nickel-and-dime operation.

". . . There's a hot tub in the bathroom and a punching bag hanging from the ceiling," she rambled on in almost perfect English. The recollections seemed to have eased her nervousness, and she related her thoughts effortlessly, almost with relief, as if she was going to confession. "There's a mirrored wall behind the punching bag that opens up, and there's a big safe in there with all the rock in it."

"What's this *rock*?" Bose asked.

"Cocaine," she explained. "It's solid, man. Not broke down or nothing."

"And you say there's thirty or forty shoeboxes full of it in there?"

"Sure, and there's another room behind that where he keeps even more."

The officers looked at each other. "Do you have any idea how much dope you're talking about here?" Barchiesi asked her.

She shrugged. "A lot of keys, I guess, but they get rid of it quick. They bag it and cut it up and ship it off all the time."

"To where?"

"I guess it all ends up at The Rock sooner or later."

"The Rock?"

"You know, the building you busted me in front of."

"We're talking about number 507 here, right?" Bob Barchiesi clarified.

"Yeah, 507," she affirmed. "Tito calls it The Rock 'cause it's like his personal fortress. They cut the dope and bag it and stamp it and bring it down there to deal it."

Frank Bose looked at the plastic evidence bag containing the glassine of cocaine they had confiscated earlier. "Is that the same stuff we caught you carrying before?"

"Sure, it's Tito's brand. It's called *Rock Solid*."

Chapter Four

A FIREBALL sun stood directly above East Eleventh Street and the heat rose up from the sidewalks as the sheen of recent rain evaporated. The block between Avenues A and B was lined with people who had fled their suffocating apartments as soon as the rain ended, hoping to find the temperature slightly lowered outside. They clustered in doorways and lounged on front steps, staring languidly into the yellow press of air, tapping their feet to the dissonant sound of salsa rhythms blaring from ghetto blasters. Brown-skinned teenage boys dressed in torn jeans and gaily colored body shirts danced to the music in spite of the heat, and young Hispanic girls strutted in skintight miniskirts and cotton tube tops, mimicking the obsessive Latin beat with swaying hips and giggling at the shouted obscenities that followed them down the sidewalk.

Bob Barchiesi and Frank Bose drove by 507 East Eleventh Street for what seemed like the hundredth time. They had been circling the block for several hours, observing an empty van parked in front, waiting for a male and female suspect to appear. The female was named Irma Garcia, her husband, Raphael Martinez; and according to information supplied by Anna Ruiz, they dealt a brand of cocaine called "Pony-Pak" out of apartment 6 in the building. Her hair was bleached streaky blonde giving her hardbitten features a waxy, jaundiced look. He was slumped and overweight, marginally imbecilic. On the street she was called "Blondie" and he was nicknamed "Juahito," Spanish slang meaning "country boy." To look at them one might surmise that she was perpetually angry and he was perpetually bewildered.

Anna had been vague when Bose and Barchiesi pressed her as to why Blondie and Juahito were allowed to operate a splinter faction out of the stronghold controlled by Tito Lopez and his own brand, "Rock Solid." They were some sort of partners, she guessed, but she wasn't sure. What she was sure of was that Blondie was the meanest, most treacherous bitch on the Lower East Side. Everybody hated her. If Tito Lopez had ever been afraid of anyone in his life it would have been Irma Garcia.

Frank Bose stretched uncomfortably behind the wheel of the radio car. At six foot one and more than two hundred pounds, he was cramped in the driver's seat even under the best of conditions, and these were far from the best of conditions. Outside the car a peddler hawked snow cones from a pushcart bearing the crude inscription HILADO DE COCO that was piled high with mounds of glistening shaved ice and multicolored bottles filled with sweet syrup. It looked tempting to the sweat-drenched officers. Their car had no air-conditioning but that was par for the course.

Bose and Barchiesi passed the oppressive, uneventful hours getting to know each other better. Frank Bose talked a little bit about his first marriage to the former Patricia Louise McKeegan, and the bitter court struggle that resulted in Patricia getting custody of their two sons. Frank was still bitter after almost eight years. He allowed that the hurt and anger were eased somewhat by the success of his second marriage, and the warm, caring relationship that had developed between him and his stepdaughter, Edith, but the custody battle was still a painful subject for him. He got emotional just thinking about it.

Bob told Frank about his wife, Linda, a former member of the Pennsylvania Ballet Company; and about how she had introduced him to the world of dance when they were dating back in the late seventies. He recalled some of his experiences as an officer in the U.S. Customs Service and his earlier postings in the police department. The talk was general, neither of them wanting to get into specifics this early in their partnership. As a rule cops are wary of giving too much of themselves away until they are certain the confidences will be respected. Most importantly they need to know that they share a common philosophy when it comes to the job. All policemen do not see it the same way. There are shadings in perception and in performance, and those can be determined only by working closely together over a period of time.

It was beginning to happen for Bose and Barchiesi. The debriefing of Anna Ruiz told them that they operated on the same wavelengths. Both of them believed her story, as much for what she hadn't said as for what she told them. She had not tried to defend herself or to embellish her position, readily admitting complicity in crimes more serious than the charges against her. They had given her opportunities to lie, but she'd refused to take advantage of them to save her skin. Lastly, her disclosures had remained consistent from beginning to end; disclosures so revealing and dangerous to her that both officers feared for her safety when she returned to her old neighborhood.

They knew Anna's arrest would have been observed by anyone in or near the building at 507, and that they would become suspicious when she was released from custody with nothing more serious than a desk appearance ticket. What little they were beginning to learn about Tito Lopez told them he was brutal and sadistic, that he had no tolerance for informers. Finally, Bose and Barchiesi had invented a cover story for her to tell when she returned to the street: She had AIDS, she was supposed to have told the gullible police, who were notoriously reluctant to hold AIDS carriers and risk contamination themselves. It remained to be seen whether the ruse had worked.

As Pressure Point members operating out of the Seventh Precinct SNEU, Bose and Barchiesi themselves could not pursue an investigation of the cocaine warehouse she had described. The area was a section of lower Manhattan known as TriBeCa, and that was outside their territory. Her account of Blondie and Juahito and the building at 507 East Eleventh Street was closer to home. It was something they could use to keep the ball rolling while they figured out a way of penetrating the Lopez organization without exceeding their authority or stepping on a lot of tender departmental toes.

"Somebody's in the van," Barchiesi rasped as they approached the vehicle from the rear. "See if you can get a make on the guy in the driver's seat."

"It looks like Juahito to me," Frank Bose replied, observing the puffy face of the driver reflected in the van's side-view mirror.

Bob Barchiesi craned his neck and looked into the van as they drove slowly past. "There's a blonde woman in the front seat next to him, probably Irma Garcia. Pull up and let's see what they do next."

What the driver of the van did next was screech away from the curb without signaling, a violation of vehicular traffic law. "Gotcha," Bose exclaimed. "Do you believe those dumb assholes? They had to know we were sitting here and they still can't help breaking the law."

The van turned southbound on Avenue A, running a red traffic light. "That's *two*, asshole." Bose grinned. It was almost too good to be true. "Okay, let's take him," Barchiesi said.

"Where do you want me to tag him?" Bose asked, taking up pursuit.

"Let him clear the intersection."

Bose activated the car's siren and roof rack, pulling them to the curb. Cautiously they exited their vehicle and approached the van from behind, Frank on the driver's side, Bob on the passenger's side. Reflected in the van's large side-view mirror, Frank Bose saw Juahito suddenly bend forward in the front seat and disappear from view. He cracked his holster. "License, registration, and insurance card!" he demanded.

Simultaneously, Bob Barchiesi pounded the other side of the van with his fist, creating a diversion and allowing Bose to survey the inside of the vehicle. He could see three additional males seated in the back, and the handle of a pistol partially jutting from beneath the driver's side floor mat. Both officers drew their service revolvers, ordered the occupants of the van out onto the sidewalk and spread-eagled them alongside the van.

"I got a weapon here," Frank reported as he retrieved a fully loaded .32-caliber revolver from the van, unloaded it, and placed it in his belt.

"What the fuck are you people doing here?" Barchiesi demanded, beginning to pat the suspects down.

"Delivering flowers," Blondie replied.

A quick, thorough search of the van revealed no flowers, but a shopping bag in the rear was filled to overflowing with cocaine paraphernalia. Flat and bundled as if they had just arrived from the printer were thousands of empty wrappers called "pyramid papers" in the drug trade; each had the image of a rearing black stallion printed on one side and the brand name "Pony-Pak" imprinted on the other. Also in the bag were rolls of Scotch tape and rubber bands, the unmistakable apparatus of the cocaine merchant.

Now they had a violation of Penal Code Section 220-50, possession of drug paraphernalia, a B misdemeanor punishable by up to six months in prison. The confiscated pistol was probably illegal and that would mean additional charges against the occupants of the van, who by now had been cuffed and searched with the help of a second radio car that had arrived at the scene. A curious crowd of twenty to thirty people had gathered around the periphery of the van. Among them, a teenage youth listened intently as

Blondie muttered several words to him in Spanish, then turned and headed across the street. Although his knowledge of Spanish was imperfect, Frank Bose clearly heard her utter the words *perico*, meaning cocaine, and *basura*, meaning garbage. "I think the kid's going to dump some cocaine," he told Bob Barchiesi.

"Okay, go after him and see what he's up to," Barchiesi directed.

Bose followed him, walking at a fast trot. Suddenly the youth turned, saw he was being shadowed, and broke into a run. Bose sprinted after him, through the entrance of number 507 East Eleventh and up a narrow stairwell to the second landing. He drew his revolver and paused briefly to catch his breath. "Thirty-five's a bitch," he thought ruefully before picking up the chase. The stairwell was eerily silent. Frank could hear the staccato sounds of footfalls on the metal steps as he continued upward, the exaggerated thump of his heartbeat and the labored rasp of his own breathing as he pushed himself beyond the pain barrier in pursuit of the faster, younger man.

His mind flashed back to the police academy, where he had watched disgustedly as kids barely out of their teens dropped panting from the compulsory two-mile run while he propelled his thirty-two-year-old, pain-wracked body onward. He would have dropped dead on the spot rather than admit he couldn't hack it in front of a bunch of kids back in those days. Now he was three years older and if anything the pain was worse, but that stubborn pride persisted. No teenage slimeball junkie was going to show him up, here or anywhere else.

The youth fled into apartment number 6 and Bose followed, raking the inside of the flat with the point of his service revolver. A rough-hewn handmade staircase led to a hole in the ceiling where the young Hispanic bolted into an upstairs apartment. By the time Bose negotiated the rickety stairs he had disappeared entirely. "He's gone," Frank reported to Bob Barchiesi, who was by now close on his heels.

They went back and made a cursory check of apartment 6 to satisfy themselves that no other individuals were hiding on the premises. "Those two look familiar to you?" Barchiesi asked, pointing to a computer-generated photograph tacked to the wall of the apartment.

"No doubt about who lives here, is there?" Bose grinned. It was unmistakably a likeness of Blondie and Juahito rendered in thousands of tiny numerals and letters, the kind of portrait taken at carnivals or amusement parks.

There was a mirrored valet dressing table in the hall by the front door. On it they found an open shoebox stuffed partially into a brown paper bag. Fifteen hundred to two thousand packets of cocaine were crammed into the box, the wrappers marked the same as the confiscated Pony-Pak pyramid papers they had recovered earlier. A .25-caliber automatic pistol and a fully loaded .30-caliber carbine clip were lying on a lower shelf.

By now, Anna Ruiz's story was beginning to look better and better to Bose and Barchiesi. She had given them solid information about Pony-Pak and that made her description of the cocaine warehouse in TriBeCa all the more credible. It remained to be seen whether Blondie and Juahito would be able to corroborate her account in any way, but however their interrogation turned out, both officers were now certain that they were onto something big. They could feel their adrenaline pumping as they exited the apartment and descended the staircase to the street.

Chapter Five

BOB Barchiesi stood in an airless telephone booth on the corner of Avenue A and Tenth Street after the prisoners had been secured and transported to the Seventh Precinct, waiting for a district attorney to come on the line and issue them a warrant to enter the building at 507 and conduct a search. "The only one working is a duty DA named Roy Sweetgall," he told Frank, angry at the delay and the lassitude of the DA's department. "They're beeping him now, so we gotta stay by here and wait for him to call back."

It took DA Sweetgall an hour to return the call. "I'm in a restaurant in Jersey having dinner with my wife," he groaned when Barchiesi filled him in. "Can't this thing wait until tomorrow?"

Barchiesi tried to control his voice. "I got two thousand glassines of cocaine sitting in the apartment. I got a pistol and a machine gun clip in plain view!"

A low moan. "Okay. I gotta come into New York to write it up. Call me there in about an hour." Sweetgall slammed down the phone irritably.

The wait seemed interminable. The officers soon found themselves alone in a sea of pinched, hostile faces that skimmed past them on the slowly darkening street. They understood that they were not well loved by the drug merchants of Alphabet City, who saw them as a detriment to the orderly flow of commerce, and that they could expect to be ignored by most of the remainder. To the upstanding citizens of the area, becoming too closely identified with the police was like asking for an ice pick in the ear. For Bose and Barchiesi, it was a long, lonely vigil.

Finally the hour was up and Barchiesi dialed the DA's office once again. Assistant DA Roy Sweetgall came on the line and began to take the information. "By the way, what unit are you guys from?" he asked casually.

"The SNEU team," Barchiesi replied.

"*Oh, Jesus*, why the hell didn't you tell me that before I humped my ass all the way in here from Jersey?" Sweetgall howled. "I can't issue you a search warrant. Only the Narcotics Division is allowed to have search warrants."

"What are you telling me? Doesn't my shield say 'Police Officer of the City of New York'?" Bob demanded.

"It's the rules," Sweetgall shot back.

"*Rules*? A Port Authority cop can get a search warrant in a goddam bus terminal. A guy who stands in a toll plaza can get a fucking search warrant, for chrissakes! You're telling me that I'm standing here with every legal right under the CPL to obtain a search warrant and I can't get one?"

"Those are your own job rules, pal," Sweetgall snarled. "You want a warrant, you go through the Narcotics Division and let them ask me for the warrant. Without them, you're shit out of luck."

Barchiesi remained silent for a moment, afraid he might explode into the telephone. "I can't waste another four or five hours going through Narcotics," he told Sweetgall finally. "Now here's the way it's going down. My partner and I are going in there with or without a warrant, and we're seizing everything there that's in plain view, and I don't give a fuck what you do with it. You want to throw it out, throw it out. At least one of us will be doing the job the city pays us to do!"

It was a frustrating moment. Rules were rules, and in the Byzantine world of New York City Police politics, rules predominated. For the most part they worked, they kept people from tripping one another up with too much zeal or bravado, but there were times when they simply got in the way of energetic law enforcement, and the process seemed to grind to a screeching halt. This was one of those times. Bose and Barchiesi realized that the evidence they had uncovered in apartment 6 was crucial to unraveling the secrets of the cocaine stronghold and its enigmatic kingpin, Tito Lopez. Without hesitating, they made a protective sweep of the apartment, confiscated the illegal drugs and weapons, and returned to the Seventh Precinct to debrief their prisoners.

All five were brought upstairs to the Pressure Point administrative office, where they were seated side by side in wooden chairs, read their rights again, and asked if they were willing to make any statements. To their surprise, Blondie volunteered to speak, and from that point on it became a one-woman, dog and pony show.

She had lived in apartment 6 at 507 East Eleventh Street with the prisoner, Raphael Martinez, and her two children for four years, she told them without prompting. Her last legitimate employment was in 1982, and she had been on public assistance since that time, receiving about $90 every two weeks.

Blondie told them that the building at 507 East Eleventh Street was a cocaine distribution center run by Alejandro "Tito" Lopez, and that he had approximately twenty people working for him, most of them having emigrated from a village in Puerto Rico named Aguadilla. When she was asked to describe Lopez, her face twisted into a mask of hate and she spat the words out like mouthfuls of tainted meat:

"One of his guys named Raul came to me in January or February of 1985 and told me I had to store cocaine in my apartment for 'The Rock' or else they would kill Raphael, me, and my children. I did it once, then they told me if I didn't keep on doing it, they would turn me in to the police."

She related that on May 29, 1985, she had been seated in her dining room with Martinez and her two children when two men knocked on her door. Before she could answer, one of them, Nelson Alphonso, who she identified as Lopez's hit man, shot through the door with a pistol, hitting her in the shoulder and narrowly missing the others in the room. When the two men had left, Martinez drove her to Beth Israel Hospital, but seeing both men parked in front waiting to finish the job, he took her instead to Beekman Downtown.

Despite her professed fear and hatred of Lopez, Blondie spoke of him with a reverence bordering on awe, confirming many of the things Bose and Barchiesi had already heard from Anna Ruiz, including an almost identical description of Lopez's cutting-and-bagging warehouse in the TriBeCa area. Tito Lopez was bigger than life, she affirmed: a modern-day hero to many who knew him, and a terrifying ogre to others. He was more powerful than any of his rivals, more powerful than the police. He had made millions from the sale of Rock Solid cocaine. He had killed many people himself and many more had been killed on his orders.

From what Bose and Barchiesi were hearing, Alejandro Lopez's Rock Solid organization might have been one of the largest and most brutal street cocaine enterprises in the history of New York drug enforcement, and virtually nobody outside of his immediate circle of operatives and customers knew about it. They were not surprised. Both of them understood that the police department was so compartmentalized that one arm of law enforcement rarely knew what the other arm was doing. Patrol units, who were authorized to arrest street-level dealers only, were not encouraged to share information with Narcotics units who had the authority to conduct more probing investigations. Patrol could bust street mopes all day long and that was as far as it went. Nobody had bothered to follow the trail any higher.

Blondie's narrative lasted for almost a half hour and was a classic performance. Refusing to admit complicity in any way, she portrayed herself as a victim of life, her environment, and the ruthless machinations of Tito Lopez. She spoke nonstop while the others nodded assent, making only occasional comments of their own. Her one-sided diatribe was self-serving, the officers knew, but it added greatly to their knowledge of the size and scope of the Rock Solid organization as well as to the emerging portrait of terror and mystique surrounding Lopez himself.

"How much stuff are we talking about here?" Barchiesi demanded when she was finished. "How many bags do they push out of 507 in, say, a week?"

"They drop ten thousand bags at a time," she replied. "Tito has guys from the Bronx bring them there. They cut and bag in the loft and bring it down to a place on Ninth Street before it goes to The Rock."

"And how often do they make a drop at 507?"

"All the time, at least every day."

Bose and Barchiesi exchanged glances. At that rate the operation would have to be pushing as much as $50,000 a day in illegal cocaine out of the Eleventh Street address alone. If that was true, how much more could they expect to find at Ninth Street and TriBeCa?

One by one, Irma Garcia enumerated apartments in the building at 507 East Eleventh Street that were controlled by Lopez and actively involved in the sale of Rock Solid cocaine: number 6, number 7, numbers 8, 9, and 10; the list went on. Downstairs, apartment 2 was a sealed fortress where rock was dealt openly through a barred window in the back. A roster of major players began to unfold: Nelson, the enforcer, Raul Garcia Feliciano, Jorge Romano, a man called "Mello," Lopez's girlfriend, Vivian, who watched after his pet pit bulls, another woman named Maria Salazar, whose function was to see after the members' sexual and emotional needs. Lopez even owned a social club called "Barcelonita" in the building, where his workers could wind down after a day on the job. Nothing was overlooked, nothing left to chance. What Blondie described was a complete, vertical, free-enterprise operation that took good care of its own, maintained its control over the neighborhood with violence and intimidation, and eliminated its competition by killing them.

Bose and Barchiesi had a dilemma on their hands. They had uncovered what seemed to be one of the largest street operations in the history of New York drug enforcement. The deeper they became involved, the more they found themselves bumping up against an impenetrable wall of departmental regulations and prohibitions. Their hands were tied. As SNEU members they were powerless to conduct an investigation into Tito Lopez's operations at TriBeCa, Ninth Street, or The Rock at 507 East Eleventh. Drug investigations were strictly the function of the Narcotics Division, and in this case that meant Manhattan South.

Reluctantly they decided that they had no choice but to turn it over to Detectives Larry Oleaga and Don Schwally of Manhattan South Narcotics, whose office was just down the hall. They hated to give it up. More than anything in the world they wanted a piece of Lopez. They wanted to be a part of the investigation and the collar. They wanted to see their hard work rewarded. Still, the choice was clear. If they couldn't get Lopez, somebody had to. His arrest and the destruction of the Rock Solid organization were, after all, what really mattered. This way at least somebody would get the collar. At least somebody would put these bastards out of business and lock them up behind bars where they belonged.

Chapter Six

"I guess you could call it naive, but I really believed these guys were going to do something about this."

—BOB BARCHIESI

O N the afternoon of August 20, Bob Barchiesi drove home from the day shift at the Seventh, parked in the driveway of his Staten Island condominium, and climbed the front steps. Inside, the house was filled with the rich smells of a meal cooking, roasted chicken he thought, one of his favorites. His wife, Linda, was busy in the kitchen when he slammed the front door.

"Aren't you even going to say hello?" she chided.

"Sorry, it's been a shitty day," Bob walked up behind her and kissed her neck.

"Why don't you take a shower and try to relax," she suggested. "Your mother and father will be here in fifteen minutes."

He'd forgotten they were coming for dinner today. Resignedly he went into the bedroom and began to undress. The last thing he felt like was company after what he'd learned that afternoon back at the precinct. It would be almost impossible for him to remain pleasant during dinner, almost impossible for him to pretend everything was just fine feeling as pissed off as he did, and there was just no way he could stop being pissed off. When he'd asked Manhattan South what progress had been made in locating Lopez's TriBeCa warehouse, they'd told him it was a dead end. They'd checked it out and had been unable to find any trace of it, they said. By now the trail was probably cold, Bob decided. Lopez and his people had probably figured out that the location was under scrutiny and moved the operation someplace else.

Both parents would spot his mood, he knew; especially his father. Like Bob, sixty-two-year-old James Barchiesi was slow to anger. He brooded about things, let the fury build up until it was ready to explode. He could spot that in his son, sometimes even before Bob knew it was happening himself. In the Barchiesi family the apple didn't fall far from the tree.

He stood in the shower and allowed the stream of hot water to caress his sore muscles, hoping it would ease the tension he felt; it didn't. His anger swelled, rose in waves like the clouds of billowing steam that surrounded him. He was talking to himself, clenching and unclenching his fists, arguing points with unseen adversaries that should have been argued that afternoon. Finally he turned off the water, toweled off hurriedly, and dialed Frank Bose from the telephone by his bed.

"What's up, Bobby?" Frank asked when he came on the line.

"I just heard that Manhattan South hasn't done shit with that information we gave them about the warehouse at TriBeCa."

"You're kidding me! They've had almost a week, for chrissakes!" Bose fumed. "We gave them everything we had on that scumbag, Lopez. We told them where to look, told them it was near the Ones Discotheque. What the fuck do they need, a goddam road map?"

Bob took a deep breath. "Look, if we want the place found, we're just going to have to do it ourselves. I want to locate it, get a photograph, and shove it down their fucking throats."

It was Frank's day off and his wife, Candy, would not be happy if he took off on an unauthorized search, but both he and Bob knew that every additional day's delay in locating the warehouse gave the cocaine dealers more time to clear the premises. "How soon do you want to leave?" he asked.

"Give me a half hour, I'll pick you up. Do you have a good camera?"

Frank laughed. One of the things Bob hadn't yet learned about him was that he was an electronics nut. He had more cameras and equipment than Panasonic.

Bob dressed hurriedly in jeans, a T-shirt, and a shoulder holster containing his 9mm Beretta, a legally registered weapon but not an authorized one for police officers. His father and mother had arrived and were waiting for him when he emerged from the bedroom.

"Where are you going?" his mother asked when he hugged them both perfunctorily and went to the hall closet for his windbreaker.

"Gotta go out and meet Frank," he muttered.

"What for?" his wife, Linda, asked.

"A case we're working on."

"You getting paid for this or is it on your own time?" his father queried.

"It's just something I gotta do . . ."

James Barchiesi was tough and feisty, and he'd had it with Bob's single-minded obsession with his job. As a former union machinist in the Brooklyn Navy Yards, he abhorred the concept of work for no pay. As a navy man who had survived underwater demolition duty in World War II and Korea, it seemed doubly unthinkable when his son was risking his life.

"What's the matter with you? Isn't fifty-two department commendations good enough for you? Don't you know you have a family here?" he demanded.

"This won't take long. Keep a plate warm for me." Bob bounded down the front steps to the car.

He picked Frank up at his house and they rode downtown together in Bob's 1975 green Chevy Nova. It was after seven when they arrived in the TriBeCa area, getting dark, but it was daylight saving time. There was still an hour or more of sunlight before it would become too dark to continue their search. They circled the neighborhood several times unsuccessfully before stopping next to a pay telephone booth on the sidewalk.

"I want the number of the Ones Discotheque," Bob told the operator. "I think it's on Spring Street."

"I show a listing for a Ones Discotheque at 111 Hudson Street," she replied.

"Thanks, you just answered my question." Bob hung up and relayed the address to Frank.

They drove to the disco, parked nearby, and began walking in the direction of Greenwich Street. Frank Bose wore his 35mm camera hung around his neck like a pendant, but it was unlikely they would mistaken for tourists. Cops look like cops, smell like cops, they walk like cops and give off an unmistakable aura of legitimacy, especially in places where lawlessness is the norm. It was soon apparent to both of them that they had been identified as police officers by every street felon in the neighborhood.

Suddenly the warehouse was there in front of them—the concrete loading dock, the poised surveillance cameras, the outside lookouts; everything exactly as Anna Ruiz and Irma Garcia had described it. A lookout pretending to be blind approached them from the loading dock, squinting at them through half-inch thick eyeglass lenses, tapping a slender white cane before him on the sidewalk. "Did you see who that was?" Barchiesi gasped as they walked past him.

"Holy shit, yeah!" Bose replied, his voice cracking with excitement. Both of them had identified the man as Raul Garcia Feliciano, a fugitive wanted for questioning in connection with a murder. His thick lenses were a dead giveaway, along with a jagged scar that ran vertically from his left earlobe to his chin. Bose and Barchiesi had seen his want card and mug shot only a few days earlier. They continued down the street and ducked behind a building on the corner.

"How are we gonna take this guy?" Frank Bose eyed his partner quizzically.

"The guy's a suspect in a murder, we gotta take him in one way or another," Barchiesi replied. They were both painfully aware that they were off duty and an arrest was liable to result in gunfire. Off-duty cops who involved themselves in shootings were in for a lot of heartache and abuse from the department, whether their target was an identified murderer or not. The department was notoriously sensitive about shooting incidents involving policemen, even in uniform.

After a short discussion they made their way back to their car through a rear alleyway and began cruising the side streets looking for a pay phone, unaware that the First Precinct was less than three blocks away. Having identified a murder suspect, they realized the warehouse would have to be put on the back burner, at least for the time being. What they needed now was a uniform, better still, a lot of uniforms, if they were going to get Feliciano.

They drove past the warehouse again and spotted two recently arrived automobiles parked in front of the loading dock, one of them filled with plastic shopping bags bearing the printed legend I LOVE NEW YORK. Bose and Barchiesi pulled to the curb diagonally across the street and watched as the suspect Feliciano climbed into the second vehicle. They saw both cars execute a U-turn on Greenwich Street and head downtown. Bob Barchiesi eased his car into gear and followed them cautiously.

Sitting in the backseat of the second suspect vehicle, a twenty-two-year-old female Hispanic named Rose Castro nervously eyed the 1975 green Chevy Nova behind her. Like the others in her car she knew that the two men inside were policemen, and that they were intent on stopping their mini-convoy and at the very least inspecting its cargo. The first car was carrying Rock Solid cocaine from Tito Lopez, as well as an Uzi submachine gun for dealing with anyone who tried to interfere with its transport. It pulled into an alleyway ahead, where Rose knew it would peel off and wait in a parking lot for the police to pass. She looked again out the rear window as her driver followed the first car into the alley, beckoning the two policemen to follow with her eyes.

Frank Bose saw her clearly through the windshield of the Nova, and felt the hairs on the back of his neck stiffen. Her large, alluring brown eyes brought him back to another enticement, a time when another woman had beckoned him to follow and it almost cost him his life:

The year was 1969. The village was called Tan Loc, in a northern province of South Vietnam. He was a sergeant in the Marines taking part in a sweep of the village preparatory to establishing a perimeter. Ahead of them a peasant girl dressed in shapeless black pajamas paused and stared pointedly at Frank, daring him to follow her into one of the thatched huts with a toss of her head. Frank was uncertain about her motives, but the prospect of finding a weapons cache in the flimsy hut intrigued him enough to follow. Luckily he had been trained well. He felt the trip wire stretched across the red clay of the hut's entrance almost before his foot touched it, and hurled himself backward onto the hard-packed earth just as the grenade exploded inside, blasting the hut to smithereens.

It was the same girl, the same look etched indelibly in some corner of his mind. "I don't like it," he told Bob in a voice taut with tension as the car ahead turned into an alleyway and slowed perceptibly, goading them to catch up.

"It looks like an ambush to me," Barchiesi agreed, almost whispering. He had been on the streets long enough to recognize a trap when he saw one, but knowing it did little to ease the titanic knot that had developed in the pit of his stomach. Like Frank, he felt vulnerable and exposed in the ancient green Chevy. At that point, a siren and roof rack would have seemed like a godsend to both officers. At the very least they might have drawn the attention of other cops in the neighborhood to the fleeing suspects.

"We can't let these bastards get away," Bose rasped.

"At the speed they're going I think we can head them off at the other end." Barchiesi stepped on the gas and circled the block, approaching the alley from the opposite side, where a Transit Police Emergency Services truck was parked on Hudson Street. Frank held his shield and credentials out the car's window, signaling that they needed help, as the vehicle carrying Rose Castro appeared and Bob screeched the Nova to a halt in the mouth of the alley, blocking their path into the alley. The first car was nowhere to be seen.

What followed was a blur, the almost surreal drama of police officers acting on instinct alone when there was no time to make a measured judgment. Bose and Barchiesi were out of the Nova before anybody knew what was happening, leveling their weapons, shouting at the top of their lungs. "Police officers! Everybody out of the car!"

Further back, the driver of the other car observed the scene from his ambush location just off the alleyway and raced away in the opposite direction. Those inside gave no thought to a gunfight, even though they knew they held the advantage in firepower. They felt defenseless in the open. The sudden arrival of the Transit ESU truck gave the appearance of a growing police presence, and they had lost the anonymity of the unlit alleyway and their opportunity for an ambush. Seeing that their accomplices had escaped with their stash of cocaine, the occupants of the blocked vehicle, Raul Garcia Feliciano, Rose Castro, and another male named Tito Garcia climbed out of their car and surrendered meekly.

They were searched and read their rights, then taken to the First Police Precinct only a few blocks away. Since the arrest had been made out of uniform, it had to be verified by the Manhattan South Duty Captain, who was obliged to ascertain that the collar was legitimate and not a vindictive response stemming from some off-duty barroom or traffic dispute. Bob Barchiesi spoke to him from the desk phone and secured permission to have the homicide suspect, Feliciano, incarcerated in a cell, pending a report on his pedigree and outstanding warrants. The others were taken to a downstairs sitting room for interrogation.

Several detectives from the First Precinct were alerted and began questioning Bose and Barchiesi about the details surrounding the arrest of Raul Garcia Feliciano. How did they know they had the right man? the detectives wanted to know, reminding them that cases of mistaken identity were common. Bose and Barchiesi eyed each other in amazement. If there had ever been a homicide suspect who could be identified with one-hundred percent certainty it was Raul Garcia Feliciano. The eight-inch-long meandering scar on his left cheek was unmistakable. His Coke-bottle glasses had earned him the nickname "Goggles."

Feliciano was held, but lacking physical evidence that they were involved in criminal activity, Rose Castro and Tito Garcia had to be set free. Attempting to question them further before their release only convinced Bose and Barchiesi that they were wasting their time, at least for the present. Maybe the pair would be more cooperative when they were arrested later on, after the information about the warehouse in TriBeCa had been brought to the DA's office and the premises was raided.

"We'll be seeing you soon," Frank said as Rose Castro and Tito Garcia walked out of the First Precinct station house.

Garcia turned, his eyes narrowed. "You two better grow eyes in the back of your head," he snarled.

Chapter Seven

AUGUST 21, 1985

Bose and Barchiesi arrived at the district attorney's offices at 80 Center Street accompanied by Detectives Oleaga and Schwally from Manhattan South Narcotics and were admitted to a meeting room on the sixth floor. Inside, seated around a polished oak conference table, were Assistant DAs Roy Sweetgall, Lou Halpern, Pat Conlon, Rhonda Ferdinand, and Dora Irizarry. Irma Garcia and Raphael Martinez were ushered into the room, seated side by side at the oval table, and again read their Miranda rights. Both signed a form waiving their right to counsel, and Blondie began to speak, recounting virtually the same story she had told on the day of her arrest.

The district attorneys took detailed notes of her account while she spoke, nodding gravely to one another as she leveled more and more serious allegations against Alejandro Lopez and the Rock Solid organization. Both Frank and Bob felt their spirits rise when she answered their questions bluntly, without equivocation, leaving no doubt in the minds of both officers that the DAs would issue them a search warrant affidavit for the warehouse in Tri-BeCa.

DA Ferdinand broke the silence when Blondie ended her account. "It won't fly," she stated flatly. "Everything here is hearsay, not admissible in a state court." Without hesitation the rest of the DAs echoed agreement.

"The look is stale," Sweetgall chimed in. "How do we know anybody is still there? What happens if we get there and the place is empty?"

One by one the district attorneys voiced reluctance to issue an affidavit based on legal technicalities, and one by one Bose and Barchiesi attempted to counter their objections by citing what they felt were ironclad exceptions to the drug dealers' constitutional protections. Soon they both realized they were getting nowhere. For every point they made, the DAs countered with a multitude of procedural reasons to discontinue the investigation. By the time the meeting was ended, both officers found themselves buried beneath an avalanche of legal entanglements and bureaucratic timidity.

"I have to say something," Frank Bose declared when they rose to leave. "We've been sitting here for about two hours now, listening to you resident experts on narcotics tell us why we cannot get a search warrant to enter the warehouse on Greenwich Street. You've cited legal precedents chapter and verse, enumerated all the ways we can get in trouble if we proceed with this investigation, but not one of you has had the guts to stand up and say, 'Okay, we have a problem here. We have this enormous cocaine organization pushing hundreds of thousands of dollars' worth of illegal drugs onto the Lower East Side every week, but there are some legal and procedural difficulties we have to overcome before we can shut them down. Now let's put our heads together and figure out a way we can accomplish that.' "

"Not one of you has taken a positive attitude," Bob Barchiesi agreed. "It seems to me that the bunch of you want guarantees that the place is filled with dope before you go in there. Stop me if I'm wrong here, but the way I understand the law, all we need is 'probable cause.' If we have reason to believe there's contraband inside that building, the city of New York tells us we have the right to apply for a search warrant to investigate the premises."

"Let's take it to a judge," Frank Bose suggested. "Just give us an affidavit and let somebody on the bench work out the legal problems. That's what they get paid to do, right?"

The question was met with stony silence. Nobody in the room was about to stick their neck out. It was apparent that the officers and the district attorneys were operating under a vastly different set of priorities. For Bose and Barchiesi, the priority was arresting Alejandro Lopez and dismantling his cocaine empire by whatever means they could legally employ. For the assembled DAs, the priority was to obtain a quick, sure conviction without exposing themselves to censure or ridicule, or jeopardizing their careers by becoming overly aggressive.

"We left there angry and discouraged but we never for a minute considered giving this thing up," Bob Barchiesi remembered. "Somebody had to get this guy and at that point we were the only ones who were even trying."

Their next stop was Manhattan South Narcotics, where they

met with Sergeant John McCormack who was deputized to seek a warrant through the federal courts. McCormack ran the idea by Lieutenant William Allee, a sharp, knowledgeable Narcotics veteran, who authorized them to accompany a reconnaissance team to the warehouse while a warrant was being sought. It was like a shot in the arm for Bose and Barchiesi. Now they were dealing with cops. Something was finally being done.

It was early afternoon before they received word that a search warrant for the warehouse had been issued. A full assault team consisting of between forty and fifty helmeted Emergency Services officers armed with automatic weapons and pneumatic battering rams arrived at the scene and began their ascent to Lopez's fifth-floor loft. Frank and Bob accompanied them single file up the narrow, winding stairway, their hearts pounding with every cautious step. They could see surveillance cameras set into the wall of the staircase, and unconcealed microphones designed to record their conversation as they climbed. From a tactical standpoint, everyone in the assault team knew they could not have been more vulnerable. Even a lone gunman at the top could easily have raked the entire staircase with automatic weapons fire and effectively killed or disabled most of them before they had a chance to retaliate or find cover. Given what they knew about Lopez, they had no reason to suspect that he would meekly surrender without a fight.

Every cop understands that danger is an integral part of the job. Cops know that every time they enter an unknown building or alleyway, or enclosure of any sort, they are putting their lives on the line, so they train themselves to be alert for unexpected sounds and movements, to gauge the subtle aura of changing wind currents and the penetrating sounds of silence that accompany them through unfamiliar territory. In reality, there is no one waiting for them most of the time and that is a relief, but the uneventful times are times of learning, times of trying, and they are never afforded the luxury of letting down their guards if they want to stay alive for very long.

Arriving at the fifth-floor landing, the team was confronted with a door of solid steel, set in reinforced concrete. If the task force had planned a swift, surprising entry, the idea was soon abandoned. Even with the use of giant steel pincers known as "the jaws of life," ESU officers spelling each other in ten-minute shifts struggled for almost a half hour before they were able to pry the door open and enter Lopez's fifth-floor bastion. By that time they hardly expected anyone to be still inside, still they took no chances. One after another, steel-helmeted, flak-jacketed assault team members stormed into the loft with automatic rifles jutting into the leaden haze, clearing room after empty room, kicking down doors, screaming obscenities, releasing the tension they all felt.

Bose and Barchiesi observed the interior of the loft as the din subsided. It was exactly as Anna Ruiz and Irma Garcia had described it to them, from the large projection TV to the heavy punching bag hanging from the ceiling to the mirrored wall at the rear. Frank walked to the mirror and pressed the upper left-hand corner. Instantly the wall opened, just as Anna Ruiz and Blondie had told them it would, revealing a hidden compartment behind. An empty blue-steel safe stood against a wall in the room with its door open. Along the periphery wooden shelves were lined with scales, counterweights, and balances for measuring cocaine, chemicals for testing drugs, and thousands of dollars' worth of professional quality 35mm camera equipment. On one of the shelves they found a sophisticated Nagra playback unit, a five-thousand-dollar Swiss-made piece of electronics audio equipment used almost exclusively by undercover police wired for sound.

There was a heavy metal desk beneath a bulletin board on the wall. Bob rummaged through the drawers and uncovered a well-organized filing system that pinpointed various street locations used by the Lopez organization throughout Manhattan. Frank examined the various documents tacked to the bulletin board. Above a clutter of correspondence, receipts, and unidentifiable paperwork, the registrations to several expensive automobiles were prominently displayed, much as a physician or lawyer might display framed diplomas and credentials. Alongside the registrations, rows of vehicle and mailbox keys were hung and numbered.

A large decorative screen separated the office area from a make-shift bedroom in the back. Beneath the mattress of a canopied bed they found a fully loaded 380mm Beretta automatic pistol, and inside a closet they recovered a small drop safe, which was opened by Emergency Services and found to contain 702 glassines of Rock Solid cocaine along with several thousand dollars in US currency. It was far from the vast quantities of cocaine that had been described to them by Anna Ruiz and Irma Garcia but that was understandable. Too much time had elapsed between the raid on the warehouse and the release of Rose Castro and Tito Garcia, who had surely reported the incident back to a wary Alejandro

Lopez. He had probably taken advantage of that time to clear out most of his stock.

Still, it was a significant seizure from an informational standpoint. They had gained access to some of Alejandro Lopez's personal files and documents, and from them they could draw a clearer portrait of the druglord who up until now had only been a ghost. Now Lopez was more than a name uttered in whispers by the fear-stricken population of East Eleventh Street. Now they had documents, and documents gave him contours and substance. In stark black-and-white they delineated his flaws and preferences; what kinds of cars he liked to drive, what kind of clothes he wore. They could reveal the names of his creditors and whether or not he paid his bills. They could establish a pattern of living that up to now had remained a mystery to them. It wasn't everything but it was a start, and for that they were grateful.

"You know what I think?" Frank volunteered when they had left the loft and retreated to a nearby neighborhood saloon for what cops like to call "choir practice." "I think Lopez knew we were coming all along."

Barchiesi shrugged. "He had to know. What other reason would he have had to clear out all the coke?"

"But you gotta wonder. If he knew we were coming after him, why did he leave the packets and the money? What's this scumbag doing—sending us a message of some kind?"

"Maybe," Bob allowed. "He's a macho fuck, and he'd probably like nothing better than sticking it right up our asses where it would hurt the most."

". . . Like he's telling us, 'Okay you cocksuckers, here's Tito Lopez and here's Rock Solid. Now what the fuck are you gonna do about it?' " Frank concurred. "Can you imagine the arrogance of that son of a bitch?"

"You heard what Anna Ruiz and Blondie said about him. 'Nobody will ever catch Tito because he's too powerful. Tito's more powerful than the police, Tito's more powerful than anybody.' " Bob pointed out. "Maybe he's just handing us this shit to whet our appetites. Maybe he really does think he's invincible. Maybe he thinks this whole chase thing is one big fucking joke."

"Yeah, I'm getting a lot of laughs out of it," Frank noted wryly. "I wish I had the little prick here right now so I could tell him how much I appreciate his sense of humor. Maybe we'd find out how invincible he was then." He clenched his beefy fingers around an imaginary neck. "You know what he's gone and done? He's cranked this whole thing up a notch. Now it's really getting personal between him and us."

"And guess who's going to win?" Barchiesi toasted Frank with his glass, grinning.

"The good guys," Frank toasted back. "There's just one thing that bothers me about all this. If Lopez left that money and coke just to rub our noses in it, why did he leave all that other shit, the car registrations and files? That could be enough to hang him right there."

"The guy's got big balls," Bob replied. "That doesn't make him smart."

Chapter Eight

"Sometimes you come home from this place and you just want to hold your children and never let them go."

—Bob Barchiesi

In the summer of 1969, Tony Oliveri was a name to remember in the Great Kills section of Staten Island where Bob Barchiesi grew up. Barchiesi remembers Tony as being one of a handful of neighborhood athletes whose names were legend around the P. S. 8 playground courts or the football fields of Great Kills Park. They were guys like Ronny Cimonneti, who had almost single-handedly led St. Peter's to the quarterfinals of the all-city basketball championship in 1965, and Tommy Locheran, who'd played guard under Joe Paterno at Penn State and actually had a tryout with the Baltimore Colts. Everybody knew these guys, or said they did. Everybody had a favorite exploit to recount, or better still a personal recollection that had never been reported in the local newsmedia. To get up close and personal with guys like this was to grab a chunk of the reverence and esteem that surrounded them and to shove it in your pocket. To actually get to know them, or be allowed to play ball with them, was more than anyone had a right to expect.

Tony Oliveri was Rick Barry and Johnny Unitas all rolled up into one, a guy who could do it all better than anyone else on the basketball court and on the football field. Around town younger kids watched him with wide-eyed envy and spoke his name with passion and respect. They tried to imitate his moves, the way he dressed and talked, his style and swagger. And when they stepped onto the courts and playing fields they measured every shot, every acrobatic slam-dunk and pinpoint bullet spiral they attempted by the standards he had created.

Tony's girlfriend was Lucie Conigliaro, and there wasn't a male in Great Kills from junior high school on up who hadn't dreamed about having her. Lucie had dark almond eyes like Sophia Loren, soft, tanned skin that had never seen a blemish, a drop-dead body that could sustain an animated locker-room conversation for at least a half hour, and an insolent, Marilyn Monroe way of walking that caused grown men to freeze in their tracks. Teenage boys followed her from a distance like sniffing puppies, while mothers solemnly shook their heads and warned that anyone so gorgeous and provocative was bound to come to no good end. Lucie was that terrific.

But she was Tony Oliveri's girl and nobody seemed to resent it. It seemed natural that the two of them should be together, like twin stars shining in an undistinguished firmament. They were golden people and golden people got to take what they wanted out of life and leave the rest for everybody else. That was just the way it was. That was just the way it was always going to be for Tony Oliveri and Lucie Conigliaro.

Bob Barchiesi saw Lucie again after more than ten years. He was in a Manhattan courthouse, a member of the NYPD Street Crime Unit, waiting his turn to testify against a robbery suspect he had arrested.

"You're Bobby Barchiesi, I remember you from the neighborhood." The gaunt, frightened woman approached him in the crowded hallway.

He searched her face. "I'm sorry . . ."

"I'm Lucie, Lucie Conigliaro." Her voice was a rasp.

Bob tried not to react. The woman looked sixty, worn and wasted.

"You look like you've done pretty well for yourself, Bobby." Lucie's darting eyes rested momentarily on Bob's crisply pressed uniform, then drifted away in a mask of incomprehension. "I've been sick myself," she added almost as an afterthought.

Bob stepped back. The aromas of time and debilitation washed over her like a cloud; sweat and heroin and vomit coming from every pore, every patterned wrinkle in her unwashed clothing. She smiled wanly at him, exposing an uneven row of brown, rotting teeth. "Maybe you can do me a favor? My husband's up on charges here. Do you think you can do anything to get him out?"

His mind raced backward, to a day on the playgrounds of P. S. 8 in Great Kills when he had been allowed to play basketball with the legends for the very first time, when he stood in awe as Tony Oliveri effortlessly scored point after point, perimeter shots, hooks, driving lay-ups, to the delight of the adoring crowd who had gathered to watch him perform magic. Bob had wandered underneath the wooden bleachers that afternoon, flushed with pride and the heady feeling of acceptance. Tony was there, too, an elastic ligature wrapped tightly around his left bicep, the frayed ends secured in his teeth. He probed the flesh of his forearm tenderly, inserted the point of a hypodermic needle under the skin and set his jaw as he pumped the liquid into his veins. Then he sat back on the grass and let his shoulders slump, and he seemed to fall asleep.

"I'd really appreciate it." Lucie snapped him out of his reverie. "Maybe I could help you out someday . . ." Her sunken eyelids fluttered.

"I'm sorry," Bob managed to stammer before he walked off, leaving her standing alone in the hallway. He couldn't bring himself to ask if her husband was Tony Oliveri.

Barchiesi shook his head at the memory. "I wanted to cry. The hopelessness, the waste. That's the way it is with drugs, not just down here on the Lower East Side, but everywhere. Nobody's safe. Someday it could be one of my kids. I go home and I see them and I ask myself, 'Is some scumbag like Lopez going to be around to push poison at them when they're sixteen or seventeen?' I ask myself that all the time."

If the reality of drugs has left Bob Barchiesi filled with sadness and frustration, it has left Frank Bose consumed with skepticism and fear. "I don't know where this is all going," he confided, "but I don't see any hope at all unless society declares all-out war on scum like Alejandro Lopez. I don't mean limited war. I fought a limited war in Vietnam and you saw the results."

References to Vietnam peppered Frank's dialogue when he spoke about drugs. "Up until Vietnam I really didn't know what drugs were all about. I had sailed in the Merchant Marine and heard stories about drugs, but I'd really never had any personal experience. Then I got to Vietnam and everybody around me was doing them, Thai sticks, pills, you name it. It was cheap and easy to get, and I guess it made the duty easier for some of them, especially the guys who were really scared all the time.

"One night, about four or five weeks after going in-country in Vietnam, I found myself on guard duty at the base camp when we started taking incoming rocket rounds from the VC. They were firing a grid around us, walking their rounds in from the perimeter toward the base itself, and I gotta tell you I was scared shitless. Anyone in their right mind would have been.

"If you ever saw a rocket barrage like that, you'd have to admit it was a real spectacle, almost like a fireworks show if you could get over being frightened to death. The incoming rounds send up a shower of heated metal when they land, almost like hot magma spouting out of a volcano. If it wasn't such a terrifying experience I guess you could say it was a pretty beautiful thing.

"Anyway, there was this kid in the next bunker who all of a sudden hauled himself up on top of the sandbags, stoned out of his mind on pot. He just hung out there in the open, unprotected, leaning on his elbows and watching the rounds explode as they got closer and closer. Everybody was yelling like hell at him, trying to drag him back into the bunker, but the dumb bastard just perched up there on his elbows, grinning at the show like a fucking idiot."

Frank blinked, swallowed hard. "The kid took a direct hit. The last thing he said was, '*Shit, isn't that fucking beautiful?*' Then he was blown back into the bunker like he'd been shot from a catapult. His head was ripped right off. He just lay there without a head, thrashing around in the mud with blood pumping out of the empty neck cavity.

"I saw a lot of death during my tour and I guess I hardened myself to it like everybody else who was there. The guys used to say 'It don't mean nothing' when someone got blown away, as a kind of defense mechanism so they wouldn't go completely crazy. Well, everyone knew they all meant a lot, but none of them affected me any more than that kid in the bunker. I looked at him and I said to myself, 'If that's what this shit can do to your mind, I don't want any part of it.' I don't think it had anything to do with my becoming a drug enforcement officer but I gotta tell you, that image of him thrashing around without a head like that never really went away.

"Now I see young kids doing coke and reefer and I know they're in it for the fireworks. They see all the color and the spectacle and they say, 'Shit, isn't that fucking beautiful?' and all the while the rounds are exploding closer and closer to their heads." Frank shrugged, lowered his eyes. "It don't mean nothing, right?"

It is the children who affect Bose and Barchiesi most. "You come out here and you see the parents lined up outside buildings, waiting to cop drugs, and they have their kids with them," Bob related. "Three-, four-, five-year-olds playing on the sidewalks while their mothers and fathers are waiting to get fixed. Can you imagine? That's the earliest memory these kids are going to have, standing on a line with a bunch of junkies, buying dope."

"Nobody wins in this shithouse," Frank affirmed. "Only guys like Lopez. Everyone else goes right down the toilet sooner or later. Bobby and I have watched kids grow up in this neighborhood and get hooked by the time they're eight or nine. They never got a chance to know what being a kid is all about."

"The stuff you see down here will be with you for the rest of your life," Bob agreed. "You can't just go home and take a shower and wash it all off. Sometimes you come home from this place and you just want to hold your children and never let them go."

Chapter Nine

"Tell Little Tito that Bose and Barchiesi said hello."

IT was "bust balls" time at 507 East Eleventh Street. Encouraged by the operation at the TriBeCa warehouse and infuriated by Lopez's arrogance, Bose and Barchiesi stepped up their activities around the building, applying daily pressure on both the dealers and the purchasers of Rock Solid cocaine.

"Lopez sent us a message so we decided to send him a message," Frank Bose affirmed. "We were on him like white on rice. We knew it was unlikely we would ever bust him personally selling coke out on the street, or even that we would be able to shut his operation down completely, but we were at least going to put some hurt on him. He was going to know we were there."

By mid-September they had made more than forty arrests on the sidewalks and in the alleyways surrounding number 507: street lookouts, some only twelve or thirteen years old; steerers and expediters who directed and controlled the flow of traffic into and away from the building; dealers who handled the merchandise directly and sold it in small quantities on the sidewalks; even the unfortunate "mopes" who lined up in front of the building and exchanged their welfare checks for glassines of Rock Solid cocaine. Every arrest would have an impact, whether it was significant or inconsequential. Every piece of street scum that went down sent a message to Alejandro Lopez in clear, unequivocal terms. "We know who you are and we know what you are, and it will only be a matter of time before we know where you are," it emphasized. *Then you will be ours.*

To underscore the point, Bose and Barchiesi hit upon a unique message; a way of convincing Lopez that they would not go away, as well as an admonition to anyone in the Lopez organization who felt they might be intimidated by personal threats. Recalling the incident at the First Precinct a month earlier when Tito Garcia had warned them to grow eyes in the backs of their heads, they made a point of reminding each and every individual they busted that Little Tito Garcia was partially responsible. "Tell Little Tito that Bose and Barchiesi said hello," they reminded their prisoners after every arrest; or occasionally, "Tell Lopez this arrest is compliments of Little Tito." The message was not lost on those arrested or on the spectators along East Eleventh Street who relayed it to higher-ups in the organization. Alejandro Lopez knew they were there, and he was beginning to get the idea that they weren't going away. They were putting hurt on him.

"Mike Barron thought we were nuts," Bob Barchiesi reflected, alluding to Sergeant Mike Barron, head of the Seventh Precinct SNEU. "He knew what was going on, everybody knew about it and they thought what we were doing was great, but they still thought we were crazy for doing it. Guys like Mike who have been on this job a long time have a tendency to become cynical. 'Nobody really gives a shit,' he would tell us. 'As long as you're doing good they'll pat you on the back and tell you what a terrific job you're doing, but the first time you fuck up they'll hang you by the balls.'

"I don't blame Mike for having an attitude like that," Bob asserted. "Mike's a good guy and a good cop, but he knew what we were letting ourselves in for. He hated to see us setting ourselves up for a fall. This job does that to you, hardens you to the realities. There are so many layers of accountability and so many ways you can stick your head in the noose, guys just naturally become cautious. Most of the new people see it as an eight-hour-a-day job. They wouldn't think of making an off-duty arrest. They won't make decisions because they're afraid of being criticized. They see maniacs like Frank and me and they just shake their heads. They may admire what we're doing, but they think we're fucking crazy."

Crazy or not, Bose and Barchiesi persisted and soon they saw a pattern beginning to emerge on East Eleventh Street. They noticed that a number of their male prisoners had come originally from a small village in Puerto Rico named "Aguadilla," that they had settled in the Bronx, and that they all affected gaudy displays of silver chains and bracelets, an unusual departure from tradition in the Hispanic community, where gold jewelry was the favored symbol of machismo, wealth, and importance. Wearing the silver jewelry was apparently a sign of affiliation within the Rock Solid organization. To Bose and Barchiesi it was as if they had agreed to wear their rap sheets around their necks. It made identifying them just that much easier.

The building beckoned them, tantalized them; they began to resent the time they had to spend away from it. More and more they found themselves manipulating their schedules within the Street Narcotics Unit to include a dozen or more daily drive-bys of number 507, usually resulting in at least one arrest. It soon became a routine, and along with the arrests they developed a short-cut method of dealing with the interminable hours it took to process their prisoners. "I was inside wading through all the paperwork while Bobbie was out there on the street having all the fun, so I worked out a method of getting it done in a lot less time," Frank remembered, smiling. "I managed to write out my own case, get a DA to approve it, find a typewriter and type it up myself, then walk it through the system for arraignment, cutting the process down from six hours to about an hour and a half. It wasn't exactly what you'd call 'by the book,' but it worked. The prisoners got processed, and I got back out on the street, where I could help Bobby bust their balls some more."

Bob Barchiesi had moved upstate and he had an hour's drive into the city on the parkway every morning. "I did my best thinking of the day during that drive," he recalled. "Every morning I'd work out some new strategy for getting at Lopez, and I couldn't wait to get to work and tell Frank about it. The only problem was that he was doing the same thing on his drive in. It got to be a question of who could spit their ideas out first. When we weren't talking about it on the job, we were talking about it on the phone. My phone bill was getting into three digits."

There were lookouts on every streetcorner of East Eleventh Street and they were usually successful in warning the dealers and patrons at number 507 of Bose and Barchiesi's approach. The familiar cry of "*Feo bajando*" resonated through the hollow cavern of tenement buildings alerting and dispersing the long lines of customers waiting on the sidewalk. Mostly what was left by the time Frank and Bob arrived in their sector car or in one of the vintage taxicabs provided by Operation Pressure Point command, was a desultory clutch of laggards whose minds were too blown on dope to comprehend the danger.

On September 13, three weeks after the warehouse operation, the lookouts failed. Bose and Barchiesi, in plainclothes as usual, drove slowly down East Eleventh Street and were amazed to find a line of more than 150 men and women, waiting patiently on the sidewalk in front of number 507. The queue, which wound around the block onto Avenue A, was mostly white and judging from their dress, middle-class, some with small children in tow.

"Do you fucking believe this?" Bob gasped.

"This is just too fucking much," Frank agreed and pulled the car to the curb.

They double-parked and approached the queue on foot, not bothering to try to fit in and shield their identities from the waiting crowd of junkies, many of whom were so strung out with withdrawal that they couldn't have identified an approaching panzer division. Bob waited at the outskirts of the crowd while Frank took his place on the end of the line, still carrying his portable short-wave radio that crackled with police signals. At worst, they reasoned, the radio would chase everyone away. At best, the mob would be too dazed to even notice and Frank could work his way forward to an unseen Rock Solid operative who was dealing bags of cocaine through a barred window in the rear.

"Hey man, where's the place to get some Rock?" a heavy-lidded male Caucasian approached Bob Barchiesi as he stood near the crowd.

"See that guy over there with the radio . . . ?" Bob pointed to Frank. "He can tell you where to go."

The man sidled up to Frank. "Hey bro, this the line for Rock?"

Frank held the radio at eye-level. "Can you read what's written on this, you fucking imbecile?" he asked, astonished.

The junkie squinted at the printed inscription: "NYP, fuckin' D. *Oh shit . . .*" He backed away down the sidewalk, stumbling awkwardly over his feet and grinning idiotically.

A few others nearby shuffled uncomfortably, but nobody gave up their place in line. They stood impassively with their money clenched tightly in their fists, waiting to score their coke, too bombed or dazed with withdrawal to notice the squawk of police reports pouring out of Frank's radio. Frank removed a pair of handcuffs from the pocket of his Marine field jacket and held them unseen in his right palm. He gripped a folded ten-dollar bill in the other hand and waited his turn to buy cocaine as the line slowly shortened.

It was a plan he and Bob had devised weeks earlier, one they never believed they would get the chance to implement. Frank would wait his turn on line until he got to the window in the rear of number 507, exchange the folded ten-dollar bill for two glassines of cocaine, and slap the cuffs on the wrist of whoever handed them through the steel bars. The man in "the hole" would be their captive, cuffed to the bars that had afforded him protection. Up until now the scenario had been little more than a wistful fancy for both of them. They never really believed they would be allowed to get close enough to make it work. Fortunately for them, they had overestimated the intelligence of the drug community.

It was Frank's turn. Like a mongoose enticing a cobra closer and closer to its lethal jaws, he tantalized the dealer in the hole with the folded ten-dollar bill, offering it then pulling it back in an attempt to draw his hand through the bars where the wrist could be cuffed. The unseen dealer's fingers groped for the money, never quite reaching far enough through the bars for Frank to get a clear shot at handcuffing him. Finally in exasperation, Frank swiped at the fragment of wrist that presented itself and felt the hand withdraw behind the bars and the window slam shut in his face.

"I missed the fuck," he reported back to Bob Barchiesi as the crowd quickly dispersed around them. "He's locked up inside apartment two."

Bob called for a backup sector car and returned to the empty lot at the rear of the building. "I guess they figure we're not going to take the trouble to rout them out of there," Frank observed.

"Well, they got another think coming." Bob found a length of two-by-four lumber in the lot and lifted an end, motioning Frank to grab the other. "Where the fuck do they think they are, in a diplomatic mission?" They charged forward with the heavy plank, levering it between the bars and crashing through the opaque window glass. "*You cocksucker, we're coming in!*" It was a futile, frustrated response but it made them feel better for a few seconds.

An Emergency Services team arrived on the scene and determined that the solid-steel door leading into apartment 2 was practically impregnable, so they gained entry by pneumatically spreading and severing the window bars. Inside, the tiny apartment was empty. Frank and Bob looked helplessly at one another and at the incredulous members of the ESU team. "You see the place, one fucking door, one fucking window," Bob explained. "Nobody's come out of either since we've been here, so there's gotta be a body here someplace. The sonofabitch couldn't have vanished into thin air."

They searched the apartment inch by inch until they discovered a hole cut through the floor beneath a bed and a tunnel leading to the basement of the building. "How about it, feel up to a little cave exploring?" Bob asked Frank.

"Sure," Frank replied nervously. He had seen the "tunnel rats" in Vietnam, guys who burrowed beneath the earth to uncover hidden VC passageways and weapons caches. It took a special type of Marine to do that, and he wasn't sure he was that type of Marine. Now he wasn't entirely sure he was that type of cop. Cautiously he lowered himself into the tunnel.

The basement was semi-dark, reeking from rotting wood, slime-encrusted concrete, and piles of accumulated garbage. There was no sound as he made his way slowly forward, raking the blackness ahead with the point of his service revolver. An unearthly squeal froze him momentarily in his tracks as a dog-sized rat scampered from a pile of trash and almost tripped him, followed by another.

"Everything okay down there?" Bob yelled from above.

"Yeah, just great." Frank saw with relief that ESU had begun to illuminate the basement with floodlamps. He peered into the recesses of the small room, gauging the shadows cast by the overhead lamps until he saw a movement in one of the corners.

"Freeze, you little fuck," he growled through clenched teeth as he approached a cowering male Hispanic. "Who the hell else is down here?"

The Hispanic gestured helplessly. It was apparent to Frank that he was alone in the reeking cellar.

ESU officers pulled the prisoner upward through the narrow trapdoor into apartment 2, and Frank scampered after him, his flesh crawling as he brushed spiders and cockroaches from his clothing. "There's a grating that leads out onto the street down there but it's locked from the outside," he reported to Bob Barchiesi. "These guys are so fucking dumb they built themselves a tunnel leading to nowhere."

A gathering crowd watched as they led their prisoner out onto the sidewalk. Suddenly he lurched forward and pulled away momentarily before the officers were able to subdue him. Shouts from the crowd seemed to goad him on, driving him to new heights of frenzy as they encouraged him in Spanish and cursed the police who sought to restrain him on the sidewalk. A bottle was thrown, then another, and a heavy chunk of torn masonry. Soon the street in front of 507 East Eleventh Street was awash in a sea of flying debris and angry threats shouted in Spanish.

An attack dog was unleashed into the crowd and Bob Barchiesi found himself running full-force down the street after its fleeing owner. ESU police waded into the press of bodies with their nightsticks flailing, driving a swath through the infuriated mob which continued on toward the building from the flanks, hurling rocks and bottles at the arresting officers. Frank knelt on the concrete and sighted over the barrel of his revolver as the mob drew closer and more menacing. He felt the muscles in his jaw tighten reflexively as they bore down upon him, and the sudden inhalation of air that preceded his final warning before he cocked his weapon. *"Take one step closer and some of you motherfuckers are gonna end up dead!"*

The torrent of brick and glass subsided as the crowd began to sense that the police were gaining the upper hand. Resentfully they dispersed, the braver and more macho of the young males strutting defiantly in retreat, spitting disdainfully on the sidewalks and muttering obscenities about the police in Spanish. They called them *camarones,* meaning "little shrimp"—a disparaging reference to the stereotyped pale-pink faces of their antagonists. They felt the exhilaration of having achieved a standoff and for them a standoff was as good as a victory. Maybe now the *camarones* would see that they were men of serious intent and stop their daily harassment of East Eleventh Street. Maybe now they would be left alone to do business the way it had always been done.

A lazy orange sun dropped behind the file of tenement buildings and the lilt of salsa music bled slowly into the darkening sky. Warily the police secured their prisoner and departed the area while enough light remained to protect themselves. An uneasy calm returned to East Eleventh Street.

Chapter Ten

"L ITTLE Tito" Garcia slouched against the front of the Barcelonita Social Club and observed the dilapidated taxicab driving slowly up East Eleventh Street. As usual, the occupants of the cab parked across the street from number 507, exited the vehicle and began questioning everyone they encountered on the sidewalk. He thought briefly of leaving as they approached him but decided against it. Bose and Barchiesi would use it as an excuse to chase him down the street, push him up against a building and toss him.

Nervously he fingered the glassine of Rock Solid in his pants pocket. Another bust at this point could be a dangerous thing for him, especially since he was already in deep shit. Bose and Barchiesi's daily reminders to "tell Lopez this arrest is compliments of Little Tito" had not endeared him to the boss or enhanced his standing within the organization. Even though they knew the remark was nothing more than harassment, it subjected the organization to unwanted scrutiny and that was the last thing they needed. They had escorted Tito to a remote spot beneath the Brooklyn Bridge and told him of their displeasure. For emphasis they had held a loaded 9mm automatic to his head and suggested he was treading on thin ice; that he had better do something to redeem himself or he would end up as fish-food in the East River.

"Look who we got holding up the building here," Bose exclaimed as they approached. "It's that scumbag, Little Tito."

"What're you doing out here, Tito?" Barchiesi demanded.

"I came to see my friend," Tito muttered in response.

"What friend? Who the fuck are we talking about here?"

"Is he in the building?" Frank pressed. "What apartment?" The rapid-fire questioning was a familiar routine, one they used on almost everyone they stopped and questioned at 507.

Tito eyed them uncertainly. "I gotta tell you that the boss got a beef with you guys."

Frank and Bob exchanged fleeting glances. "What kind of beef?" Barchiesi asked.

"He don't like that you tore up his place downstairs," Tito responded.

"*His* place?" Frank Bose felt the hairs on the back of his neck stiffen. "The last time we checked, 507 was owned by the city of New York. When did Lopez inherit the fucking city, you wanta tell me that?"

"Where did you hear this shit?" Barchiesi demanded.

"I dunno, I just heard it . . ."

"That he's pissed off we wrecked his apartment?" Bob persisted.

"Yeah, something like that."

"Well, *tough shit!*" Barchiesi exploded. "What is this, all of a sudden he doesn't like the fucking rules? Now he's got cops who are willing to go the distance with him and he starts hollering 'no fair'? Well, you tell Mr. Lopez that we'll be back here every day and if he doesn't like it, he can move his action the fuck out of here!"

"Tell him we're doubling our efforts just because he's such an arrogant prick," Bose added. "Tell him we'll be back again tonight."

It was a significant encounter. For the first time an underling in the Rock Solid organization had actually referred to Alejandro Lopez as "the boss," and whether or not Little Tito had been sent by Lopez to deliver a message to the police, he had established a kind of communication between them. Now Bose and Barchiesi knew that their efforts had not gone unnoticed. Now it was becoming apparent that, if nothing else, Lopez was becoming angered by their daily harassment of his customers and street operatives. He was beginning to feel the hurt.

Little Tito was back on the street the following day when Bose and Barchiesi approached in the Pressure Point taxicab. He raised a shaking hand and signaled for them to pull up.

"You see that? The little fuck's scared shitless," Frank whispered hoarsely.

"Something's going down," Bob observed, removing his weapon from the shoulder holster and placing it handle-out on the seat between his legs.

Frank did the same with his revolver and maneuvered the cab to the curb near Little Tito. The tension was electric; both officers were keenly aware of the possibility they were being set up for an ambush. They kept their eyes riveted on Little Tito's hands, alert for sudden movements, waiting for the first available opportunity to exit the vulnerable confines of the cab. "Whatta you want, scumbag?" Bob demanded.

Tito hesitated. His eyes darted nervously up and down the street before he cautiously approached the taxicab. "How are you guys?" he asked tentatively. ". . . How are your families?"

Both Bose and Barchiesi stiffened at the mention of their families. Whatever he was up to, Little Tito had just taken it a step too far.

Tito sensed their anger and stepped back, away from the taxicab. "No, no, I mean is there anything I can do for them? Christmas is coming up. I thought maybe I could buy something for them; some gold chains maybe . . ."

"What the fuck is this?" Frank demanded.

"The heat's really on me. You guys are making it bad for me," Little Tito admitted. "Give me a private number where I can call you. Maybe we can do something about all this."

Barchiesi scribbled the number of his direct Pressure Point extension on a sheet of paper and handed it out the window to Little Tito. "We don't want to talk about this here," he whispered confidentially. "Call us back tonight between seven-thirty and eight and we'll set up a place where we can meet." He nodded curtly to Frank who pulled the cab away from the curb.

"That's *it!*" Barchiesi shouted triumphantly when they were out of sight of the building. "They're fucking finished now!"

"We're into the organization," Bose agreed, grinning broadly. "That little fuck's going to offer us a bribe to get off their backs."

Their elation was unbounded and like excited children they allowed themselves the luxury of indulging in wild, euphoric speculation. By the time they arrived back at the Seventh Precinct they had completely destroyed the Rock Solid organization and arrested Alejandro Lopez. Pressing unimpeded through the glow of absurdity, they pictured themselves in Colombia, single-handedly confronting the Medellín cocaine cartel and winning handily. There was no end to their jubilation. In a job where frustration is the norm, small victories can be a heady brew.

Convinced that they were going to be offered money by Rock Solid, Bose and Barchiesi began the tedious rounds of notifications required within the police department in the event of a bribe attempt. After informing their immediate supervisor, they notified the Internal Affairs action desk at their Poplar Street headquarters and submitted a written account to the IAD supervisor. The grind of paperwork and notifications soon took the edge off their elation and they were further disheartened when Little Tito failed to call at the appointed hour.

"We gotta talk," Bob told Frank that evening as they ate dinner at a local restaurant. The glow had evaporated for both of them and now they were faced with the reality. In this case, the reality was that if they were going to pursue the bribery attempt it would mean establishing what the police department called a "controlled pad." That entailed going undercover to accept payments, wearing hidden microphones, and recording the details of any conversations they would have with members of Rock Solid. It was dangerous from the standpoint of their personal safety, but that was never an issue they considered for a minute. What was far more dangerous, and ominous to both of them, was what it would mean to their careers and their reputations within the department.

It was a matter of agendas; Bose and Barchiesi's agenda and the agenda of the police department, specifically the Internal Affairs Division. For the officers, wearing a wire undercover afforded them the opportunity of learning more about the Rock Solid organization and further infiltrating its ranks until they had enough evidence to nail Alejandro Lopez and put him out of business. The department saw undercover controlled pads as a way to learn about corrupt police officers. The rationalization was this: criminals would talk to undercover police agents and during the course of their conversations they were liable to implicate other cops who might have been on the take.

As a result, cops who wore wires were viewed with suspicion by most policemen. As clean as they might have been in the past, there were no guarantees that they were immune from the scrutiny of IAD shooflies who were constantly on the lookout for bad cops. It made everybody nervous; it strained friendships. It was something to think about once the early glow of celebration wore away.

"If there's a problem, you're the one who's going to take the heat," Bob told Frank. "I'm a supervisor, they could expect me to be a prick. You're the one who'll be in the locker room with the guys. You're not going to make any friends doing this."

Frank eyed him evenly. "No matter what happens, we're both going to get a couple of chunks taken out of us. Let's just hope we don't find any dirty cops involved in this thing."

They returned to the street the following day and resumed activities against the occupants of the building at 507 with increased vigor and determination. By early afternoon they arrested a mid-level dealer named William Irizarry carrying ninety-three glassines of Rock Solid cocaine. It was a significant arrest, especially since it came on the heels of Little Tito's failure to contact them as promised. "Regards to Little Tito," they said pointedly to the crowd that had gathered in the hallway at 507 to watch the arrest. "Tell him Bose and Barchiesi said hello."

The message was not lost on the organization. That same day when they returned to the building they were approached on the sidewalk by a muscular young Hispanic who Barchiesi knew as Bobby Feliciano. He had picked up Feliciano on minor drug charges several years earlier and given him a break. Now Feliciano smiled ingratiatingly at him and offered his hand. "What's happening, man? Did you give Little Tito your telephone number to call?"

Barchiesi refused the handshake. "Why? What do you know about it?" he asked.

"Hey, stay away from that Little Tito," Bobby warned. "That fuck has a dangerous mouth, and it can get everybody into trouble. Whatever you want, you deal with me. I'm right next to The Man. Whatever Tito promised you, I can get you, and much, much more."

"Where is Tito?" Bose asked.

"We were going to whack him, but we knew you guys had dealings with him. We figured you'd hook us up with it if his body was found under a bridge somewhere."

"So what exactly is it you're offering us here?" Barchiesi asked him.

"Here, take this number . . ." Bobby wrote hastily on a small sheet of paper and gave it to Barchiesi. "You guys took a lot of papers when you went into the loft at Greenwich Street and the boss wants them back. He's willing to pay heavy to get them."

"What do you think we are—fucking idiots? You'll turn us over to the goddam rackets bureau as soon as we take your money!" Bob protested.

Feliciano looked wounded. "Hey, I don't do shit like that. I'm a man!" He pounded his chest. "Memorize that number and call me. I do square business. I'm right next to the boss, and the boss can make you rich."

The following day, September 23, Barchiesi and Bose met with Pressure Point coordinator Lieutenant John Sullivan, Pressure Point Commanding Officer Inspector Thomas Gallagher, and

Captain Donald Faherty of Manhattan South Narcotics to discuss the possibility of establishing a controlled pad. The meeting with Bobby Feliciano had strengthened their resolve to pursue the investigation no matter where it took them, and they were anxious to obtain departmental approval and get on with it before the trail grew cold. They recounted their story and the options were discussed. Finally Inspector Gallagher, a thirty-three-year veteran of the police department, commented:

"First of all I want to say that you guys have been doing a helluva job out there and you're to be commended," he began, eyeing them both benevolently. "That said, I have to give you both some advice. I don't want this to seem like I'm trying to rain on your parade, but I don't want to see either of you get hurt, so I feel I'd better tell you something about briberies." He paused, inhaled deeply. "The thing about briberies is nobody wins. You can do the best job in the world out there, and the only thing people will remember about you is that you took bribes. You'll never recover from it. You'll never get your reputations back."

Frank Bose felt a knot developing in the pit of his stomach. He glanced sideways at Bob and noticed that he was clenching and unclenching the muscles of his jaw. Deep down both of them knew that Gallagher was telling them the truth but neither of them wanted to hear it.

"Granted, everyone will know this is a controlled pad when you go out on the street, but how many will be around a month from now, or six months, or a year?" Gallagher asked them. He looked across the table paternally. "I know you're both committed to this and I can't tell you to pull out of it now, but I hope you'll take my advice and make your meets, do what you have to do, and turn it over to Manhattan South Narcotics as soon as possible. Get the hell out of it as fast as you can, before you're both ruined as policemen and as human beings."

Chapter Eleven

"The more we learned about this son of a bitch the
more we hated him."

—FRANK BOSE

A NY threat to their lives and careers Bose and Barchiesi may
have felt paled in comparison to their growing preoccupa-
tion with Alejandro Lopez. Up to now, information they had been
able to gather on the shadowy druglord offered little more than
basic statistics recorded in his arrest records, but beyond the
unemotional facts they became increasingly aware of the pattern
of cruelty and violence that characterized his remarkable rise to
power.

As more and more records on Lopez surfaced, the officers began to realize that the web of violence extended beyond his immediate associates and rivals in the drug world to the East Eleventh
Street community as a whole. An emerging body of police reports,
documents, and affidavits underscored the fact that in the three
years since Alejandro Lopez had obtained a lease on the city-
owned building at 507 East Eleventh Street, virtually the entire
downtown neighborhood had been held hostage by means of
threats, intimidation, and murder.

Murder, homicides; the deeper Bose and Barchiesi probed into
the grim history of East Eleventh Street, the more it began to
resemble a battle zone with a significant number of combatants
lost in action. The list of murdered on East Eleventh Street included competing drug merchants, members of the Lopez organization who had lost favor, residents of East Eleventh Street who
protested Rock Solid's takeover of the neighborhood, and innocent
bystanders who happened to be caught in the line of fire. Although there was no solid evidence linking Lopez with any of the
unsolved homicides, it was clear from his arrest reports, as well as
his army records, that he had long demonstrated a pattern of

personal violence, and that he had been considered a dangerous and sociopathic individual by law enforcement and military authorities.

Born in Manhattan's Bellevue Hospital on August 17, 1948, to Ernesto Lopez and Teresa Garcia, Lopez grew up in the barrios of the Lower East Side and quickly adapted himself to the outlaw metabolism of the streets. His arrest records showed a number of motor vehicle and insurance violations, several arrests for Assault, a charge of Criminal Impersonation, another of Weapons Possession, and one arrest for Grand Larceny. Most serious against him were the double charges of Criminal Possession of Narcotics and Criminal Possession of Dangerous Weapons, filed against him in the Nintieth Precinct in May of 1985. He had been questioned in connection with a brutal double homicide in Brooklyn that same month but, in the absence of evidence linking him with the murders, he had been arrested only for minor drug violations. There was no record of any disposition of the charges. There was no record that Alejandro Lopez had ever served a day in jail for any of the crimes he had committed.

It fit the pretense of invincibility he had established for himself on the Lower East Side. Lopez may not have been the untouchable icon depicted by fawning drug associates, but he was undeniably shrewd and street-savvy. He had operated outside of the law for years, practically daring the authorities to arrest him, and still he remained free; a larger-than-life legend whose name was whispered in solemn accolades and undertones of cold fear. Frank Bose and Bob Barchiesi understood the fear and awe he commanded, but they also understood that Lopez was far from the superhuman he was portrayed to be. He had made mistakes, lots of them, but in a city that led the nation in almost every category of major crime, he had managed to slide through the cracks in the system while other, more notorious criminals took the heat. In a business where false steps often meant death, he had managed to dance at the edge of the precipice for a very long time without falling off.

Bose and Barchiesi wanted nothing more than to push him over the edge of that precipice. Up to now every move they had made against him was calculated to increase the pressure coming at him from all sides until he finally made a fatal blunder. Lopez had responded typically, as they knew he would. His Hispanic sense of "machismo" had led him to threats and empty shows of bravado; and when he had become convinced those would not work, to bribery. Now it was simply a matter of recording the bribe attempts until they had given Tito Lopez enough rope to hang himself.

"We spent a lot of time weighing the pros and cons of this thing. We knew what could happen if we let down our guards for even a second," Bob Barchiesi remembered. "Forget about the personal danger; if criminals were the worst thing we had to deal with on this job, it'd be a snap. The real pressure was coming at us from the department itself."

"We were swimming in an eel-pot," Frank Bose elaborated. "Everywhere we looked there was another layer of command bearing down on us, another layer of accountability we had to deal with. Bob and I were in patrol, and the governing corruption body we were immediately accountable to was the Field Internal Affairs Unit, FIAU. We're accountable to Manhattan South Narco, which has its own governing body, the Field Control Division, equivalent to FIAU. Overall, the State Special Prosecutor's office is monitoring us, *and* the Internal Affairs Division, *and* Pressure Point supervisors, *and* Manhattan South supervisors . . ." He laughed, shook his head. "It was like being in the eye of a tornado. Everywhere we looked there was somebody else who wanted a piece of us."

It was one of the largest controlled pads of its kind the police department had ever dealt with and it was in danger of becoming a procedural and jurisdictional nightmare. The only way they could maneuver without becoming hopelessly bogged down in a bureaucratic quagmire was to establish a direct pipeline to Special Prosecutor Charles Hynes, who was the attorney in charge and had hands-on control of the operation. Everybody else would have their say, everybody would maintain the illusion of their own absolute control, no rules would be broken or circumvented, the chain of command would be preserved, and maybe, just maybe, they would be able to get on with the business of catching a major drug criminal.

On the evening of September 23 it finally happened. Sergeant Andy Brogan of the Narcotics Division's Field Control Unit arrived at the Manhattan South Narcotics district and wired Frank Bose with a hidden Nagra recording device. The recorder was strapped to the small of his back, its wire taped along his side, and a miniature microphone affixed to his solar plexus. Bob Barchiesi placed several telephone calls to the number Bobby Feliciano had given them and unable to reach him, he and Frank drove to East

Eleventh Street in an unmarked vehicle, followed at a distance by a surveillance van from Manhattan South Narcotics that maintained intermittent radio communication with them. They found Bobby Feliciano standing on the sidewalk in front of number 507.

"We want you guys off the spot," Bobby told them after he had led them several blocks away on Avenue A. "The boss told me I should offer you a thousand dollars a week to clear out."

"That's it? We just make believe you guys don't exist and you give us a thousand every week?" Bob clarified.

"That's what the boss said. You stay off the place and you get the money."

"We'll have to arrest somebody every now and then just to make it look legitimate," Frank told him.

"We can throw you somebody when you do that. Just give us your hit schedules in advance," Bobby said. "And there's one other thing. You took some important papers from The Man's loft at Greenwich Street and he wants them back. He's willing to pay you ten thousand dollars when you get them for him."

Bose and Barchiesi exchanged glances. Their hearts were racing with excitement. "Okay man, the paperwork will take some doing, but we're fine with the other. When do we see some money?" Bob asked.

"I don't got it here, but I want to give you something to show you I do square business. Enough so you can go out and have a nice dinner on me. Chump change, you know."

"How much?" Bose asked.

"A couple of hundred, just so you'll know where I'm coming from." Bobby glanced at his watch. "Can you come back in a couple of hours?"

They scheduled the next meet for 2230 hours that evening and returned to the Seventh Precinct with the recordings. Excitedly they wound the miniature sound tapes into the Nagra playback unit and activated the sound button. The tape was dead. The only sounds emanating from the room were the groans of the Narcotics officers present. "Seven thousand dollars worth of sophisticated Swiss recording equipment and it flat-out failed," Frank Bose recalled with amazement. "Nobody there actually said anything, but we knew what they were thinking. They were thinking we'd picked up something on the tape that implicated other cops, so we erased it ourselves."

They both knew what they had to do. Without informing anyone at the precinct, Frank Bose went to his locker, retrieved his own $190 Panasonic microcassette recorder and taped it under his clothing, routing the miniature power microphone up under the collar of his flannel shirt. Followed by the van, they returned to East Eleventh Street and met Bobby at the appointed hour.

"Hey man, is everything cool?" Bobby eyed Frank nervously as he approached stiffly on the sidewalk. Frank was carrying the Nagra in the pit of his back, his own microcassette recorder under his left armpit, and his service revolver in a shoulder holster. He was walking like a kid wearing a new snowsuit.

"It's cool, Bobby." Frank assured him. "I carry a lot of guns for protection. You can't blame me, can you?"

"Tell us again what Tito Lopez wants you to do," Bob urged.

Bobby eyed him queryingly. "You know, man . . ."

"Well, tell us again, just so we're sure we got it all straight here," Bob persisted.

Comically, Feliciano repeated the entire context of their previous meeting for the recorders. The hardest part for Bose and Barchiesi was keeping a straight face while he spoke. "I talked to the boss. Starting Monday you guys get a thousand a week," Bobby confirmed.

"This coming Monday?" Barchiesi pressed.

"Guaranteed. The boss also said that you get a big bonus on Christmas."

"How about the chump change you promised us tonight?" Bose asked. "We could use whatever you can spare."

"How about those papers I told you about? The boss will pay big money to get them back," Feliciano repeated.

"I told you that will take some work," Barchiesi said. "We'll probably have to bring somebody else in on it for that. In the meantime we need something to show good faith."

Bobby handed Frank an envelope. "How much is in there?" Frank asked, deliberately positioning himself so that Bobby's reply would be recorded by the microphone under his shirt collar.

Bobby eyed him suspiciously. "You sure everything is okay, man?"

"Seventy, eighty, ninety . . ." Frank counted the money audibly for the recorder. ". . . two hundred dollars in all, right?"

"It's chump change," Bobby said. "The real money starts next Monday."

"A thousand, right?"

"A thousand Monday, a thousand every week after that."

There was no turning back now. Standing in the gloom of East Eleventh Street, Frank Bose and Bob Barchiesi had committed themselves to becoming a part of Alejandro Lopez's Rock Solid cocaine empire. They were on the payroll.

Chapter Twelve

THE Seventh Police Precinct rises out of the parched pavement beneath the Williamsburg Bridge like a grime-encrusted artillery bunker, a solitary triumph of uninspiring architecture and irrational municipal planning. Inside, most of the rooms remain dark and steamy in the summer. The air-conditioning rarely works. Burnt-out fluorescent bulbs are not replaced. Most of the faucets run incessantly or not at all. There is no toilet paper in the bathroom stalls.

Most of the time the inadequacies are accepted with grace and resignation by the men of the Seventh Precinct. They understand that they are not unique. Most of the station houses in the city are old and falling apart, and the newer ones like the Seventh do not work at all. Cops tend to accept small indignities as the price they have to pay for doing what they like to do. Common inconveniences, like common experiences, seem to unite them. They become closer the more they have to bitch about to one another.

Upstairs in the sweaty, dimly lit locker room at the Seventh Precinct, Frank Bose felt the closeness of his fellow officers as they dressed and shaved and shot the shit. He joined the banter and laughed too loud the way cops did, and took pleasure in the special bond of brotherhood they experienced. There were cops there he could trust with confidences he could not even tell his wife; men he knew would go to the mat for him as he would for them in times of danger. Everyone in the locker room understood that special kind of relationship cops shared, even if they'd only known each other a short time. Once they had won each others' trust the barriers came down. There were few secrets between them.

That was upstairs. Frank descended the steps to the second-floor Narcotics office, entered, and closed the door behind him. Waiting for him inside were Bob Barchiesi and members of the team who were to take part in the controlled pad against Bobby Feliciano, Alejandro Lopez, and the Rock Solid cocaine organization. They studied the options and made their plans, and Frank was again fitted with a hidden recording device that everyone was sure would work. When the appointed hour had been reached and they were certain everything was ready, they descended the metal stairs to the first floor, where Frank passed friends he had left in the locker room just a short time ago. He nodded amiably. They did not know he was wearing a wire and if he could help it they never would. There were certain things that were just not meant to be shared.

On Wednesday, September 25, at 7:55 in the evening, Bose and Barchiesi met Bobby Feliciano on East Eleventh Street to discuss the details of their upcoming bribery payments. Feliciano suggested they meet regularly at a restaurant he knew in Little Italy, but the officers objected. "Little Italy's too hot," Frank Bose pointed out. "The Feds are down there, the State is down there. Everybody in the fucking world is down there." It was no lie. Bose and Barchiesi knew that in undertakings of this sort the chances of overlapping police operations could be great. The last thing in the world they needed was to cross swords with competing federal or state undercover investigations.

"I'll figure out a place over the weekend," Barchiesi assured him. "In the meantime you're working on getting us the money, right?"

"You got it Monday for sure. In hundreds, fifties, any way you want it."

"I spoke with the other guy about the papers," Bob told him. "He's a sergeant in Manhattan South, a good guy. We can trust him." He was referring to Sergeant John McCormack from the Narcotics Division, who was to be introduced into the controlled pad as the first step in turning the entire operation over to Narcotics. It was not a move Bose and Barchiesi desired but they grudgingly understood the realities. As much as they wanted Feliciano for themselves, they knew it was not an operation for patrol officers. They knew they would have to get out sooner or later and as Inspector Tom Gallagher had warned them, sooner was probably better.

Feliciano seemed nervous. "Do you think it's good, me talking to so many guys?"

"He's the only one who can get the paperwork for you, Bobby, but I gotta tell you he's going to want some heavy bread."

"How much?"

"He'll talk to you himself, but it'll be expensive," Bob assured him. "The guy's not stupid. He's been around a long time and he knows this is a one-shot deal."

"Whatever it is, Tito can pay it," Feliciano bragged. "Money don't mean nothing to him. Ten cents is like ten thousand dollars." He grinned proudly. "I can give him anything he asks. The boss trusts me to do the right thing."

Bose and Barchiesi used the opportunity to find out more about Blondie and Juahito. "They're *nothing*." Feliciano spit on the sidewalk. "That Juahito ain't worth shit. What he makes in a month, we make in a day. We don't fucking care about him."

"We can run him in for you if he's causing you trouble," Frank Bose offered.

"Don't worry, we'll take care of him," Feliciano asserted. "He's a big, fucking rat. The boss was talking about hitting him but we decided to leave him alone. He's out on parole for gun possession, and you don't get out unless you rat."

"Anybody else you want us to take care of for you?" Bose asked.

"Nah. There's a bullshit operation across the street, but they only deal a couple of grams a day. I can take care of them myself. I'm going to open up on Eighth Street and deal free-base coke; thirty to thirty-five thousand dollars an hour if they smoke it. They can smoke a thousand an hour. Thirty guys will smoke thirty thousand dollars in one hour. I'll need you to help me get that thing going. We'll all be fucking millionaires in six months."

"Six months; we all get out and nobody gets caught," Bose commented.

"We'll all fucking retire," Barchiesi added.

"I think we're all going to enjoy this," Frank affirmed. "I think this is going to be like a happy marriage. Just don't try to fuck me, Bobby."

"If it's a marriage, I can't go on calling you guys 'officer' and 'sergeant.' What do you want me to call you?"

"You can call me 'Pepe,' " Bob replied.

"I'm 'Junior,' " Frank said.

Feliciano grinned. "Pepe and Junior it is then. Call me with the location, and I'll be there on Monday with the thousand."

It was all so easy: a few meetings, some preliminary sparring, and finally agreement. They would turn their heads, drive a block or so out of their way to avoid seeing things they were not supposed to see, perform an occasional favor as long as it posed no great inconvenience, and they would be wealthy men; wealthier than a cop had the right to ever expect. And it was all on tape, the anomalous blending of drug criminal and police officers bonded and in harmony. They had become friends with Bobby Feliciano in the manner friendships are forged inside the Alphabet City underworld: friendships of expedience, friendships of necessity. And neither Bose nor Barchiesi doubted for a moment that Bobby Feliciano would put a gun to their heads and blow their brains out as soon as it became convenient for him to do so; as soon as they let their guards down.

Their next meeting was on September 30 at 2118 hours. The night air on East Eleventh Street was heavy with moisture and the mixed aromas of cooking grease and industrial smoke from the Con Edison plant a few blocks away. Bobby Feliciano climbed into the front seat of the unmarked car next to Frank Bose, who was driving. Sitting in the back, Bob Barchiesi and Sergeant John McCormack had unholstered their weapons and kept them resting on the vinyl seat between their legs. "This is the guy from Manhattan South I told you about. You can call him 'John,'" Frank introduced Feliciano to McCormack. "He's a good dude. You can say anything you want to around him."

"You gotta tell me exactly what kind of papers you're looking for, Bobby," McCormack said after they had driven to a pitch-black section of Fourteenth Street by the FDR Drive and parked near the Con Edison plant. "There's a lot of papers up there and it's going to take me time to get the right ones."

"The boss told me they were documents about property, something like that."

"You gotta do better than that," McCormack told him. "I can't just go in there and pull everything out. They can't just disappear like in the *French Connection*. Everything's vouchered; I take a paper out, I've gotta replace it with another paper, know what I mean?"

Feliciano thought about it. "I'll have to call the boss and find out which ones he wants."

"I don't want to take anything I don't have to take," McCormack clarified. "I need document numbers, dates, anything I can use to identify the right ones."

"I'll have to get back to you on that," Feliciano said.

"Well, don't take too long. We don't want this thing to go on forever," Bob Barchiesi told him.

"How about the money you promised us?" Frank asked.

Feliciano retrieved two packages from beneath his shirt and handed one each to Frank and Bob. "You won't be offended if I count it?" Bob asked, removing the wrapping from his package and leafing through a thick pile of ten- and twenty-dollar bills.

"Hey, I'm a man," Feliciano protested. "If I say it's all there, it's all there. Five hundred in each bundle. I ain't gonna fuck you guys over."

"Twenty, forty, sixty . . ." Barchiesi leafed through the stack of bills and counted out loud, clearly and distinctly for the hidden recorder. Painstakingly he announced the entire amount in twenty-dollar increments until the entire five hundred dollar total was reached. "It's all here," he announced to the others.

"Okay, Bobby, let's talk about our business," John McCormack said after Frank had counted the money in his package. "I don't want to stay here all night. Do you want to get the information about the papers and meet us back here in about an hour?"

Feliciano thought about it. "You know that telephone number I gave you guys last time? That's my aunt's place in the Baruch projects. You call her in an hour and she'll have all the information for you."

"We don't want to deal over the phone," Bob Barchiesi said. "It's not good business. When I call, just have her give us a location where we can meet again."

They were again sparring. In the world of undercover negotiations nothing is ever easy. Talk is clipped and labored, attempts at humor strained and inappropriate. Tapes of the encounters often run to lengths of agonizing silence and arduous breathing as the webwork of lies begins to wear them down. Simple things like meeting locations become questions of tactical advantage when they are viewed as possible ambush sites.

"You know the bus stop on Houston Street by the Baruch projects? Suppose I meet you there in about an hour?" Feliciano suggested.

It was a relatively well-lit area. "That's okay, Bob Barchiesi agreed. "You'll have talked to the boss by then, right?"

"Guaranteed."

"And you'll have a real offer for me," McCormack added. "No bullshit this time. I'm taking a real chance here so I want some real bread."

"You got it," Feliciano assured him.

"I want you guys to get to know each other, because John will be picking up our payments from now on," Barchiesi told Feliciano. "Junior and I can't afford to meet you like this every week. There's already talk about us out on the street."

"What kind of talk? Who's talking?" Feliciano challenged.

"People talk. Somebody opens his mouth and the first thing you know it's all over the street."

"I think your friend Little Tito might've started it," Frank Bose suggested.

"He's no friend of mine. He's a fucking fag, a little rat. The boss shoulda whacked him instead of sending him back to Puerto Rico to ride the horses," Feliciano asserted.

"Well, the point is, John here is the guy from now on," Barchiesi told him.

"You'll be back tonight though?"

"On Houston Street at ten-twenty, the bus stop in front of Baruch," Bose reaffirmed.

"I'll be wearing red and riding a bike," Feliciano said, exiting the car.

"I want a definite offer," McCormack reminded him.

"I'm taking care of business." Feliciano disappeared into the darkness.

Chapter Thirteen

"September thirtieth, 1985. The time is 2220 hours. I'm Police Officer Frank Bose, shield number 9260. This is being made on Panasonic recorder RG-427855. This is in preparation for a second meeting on this date with subject Robert Tito Feliciano. I'm secreting this recorder on my person of my own free will. This is now the end of the test."

T HE wail of an EMS siren knifed through the silence on Houston Street, followed by the roar of police and emergency traffic speeding past the undercover narcotics car parked in front of the Baruch housing projects. Inside the car, Frank Bose, Bob Barchiesi, and John McCormack kept a nervous lookout for Bobby Feliciano, already almost a half-hour late.

"What time have you got?" Barchiesi asked.

"Ten-forty," John McCormack replied.

"Where's the van? Do you think they can see us?" Frank Bose asked, alluding to the surveillance van that was one of several backup units accompanying them to the meeting.

"They're about a block behind us in the parking lot, it's okay." Bob Barchiesi tried to sound reassuring.

A long, nervous silence ensued, during which several vehicles cruised slowly by, the occupants scrutinizing them with the expertise of seasoned housewives eyeing a display of ripe fruit in a neighborhood bodega. They were open and vulnerable to every marauder who prowled the projects at that time of night, and the longer they waited the greater their apprehension grew. Bobby Feliciano was late and that was not a good sign. Every minute increased the possibility that they had been set up, that the next passing vehicle might blow them away with automatic weapons.

By the time Feliciano pulled up ahead of them and parked at the curb in a late model Chevrolet sedan, the tension was electric.

"What the fuck's going on? He was supposed to be riding a bike," Frank Bose rasped. Every inconsistency was a cause for alarm.

"The subject is here," McCormack reported aloud for the microphone. "He's getting out of the car."

"2256 hours." Frank Bose added crisply.

"*He's got something!* He zipped up his jacket," Bob Barchiesi said urgently. All three officers had spotted the brown wooden handle of an automatic pistol stuffed into Feliciano's waistband as he exited the Chevy.

Wordlessly Bob Barchiesi, sitting in the rear of the car, placed the barrel of his .38-caliber service revolver against the soft, upholstered back of the passenger's seat. Frank Bose then ran his left hand through his hair, an unspoken communication between them that both officers fully understood. If Frank were to make that same motion once Bobby Feliciano was seated in the front seat next to him, it would mean Feliciano had gone for his weapon. Bob would fire unquestioningly through the back of the seat and Feliciano would be dead before he could get the automatic halfway out of his belt. John McCormack gripped the handle of his own revolver resting on the seat between his legs and swallowed hard. Everyone expected the worst.

"Where've you been? We've been waiting for you," Frank asked as Bobby slid in next to him on the front seat.

Feliciano pointed to an all-night refreshment stand about a block away. "I was up there eating cuchifritos."

"You were eating *cuchifritos*? We had a meet scheduled, for chrissakes!" Frank moaned.

"I thought you were coming on a bike. We were looking for a bike," Barchiesi said. "Did you talk to the boss?"

"I couldn't find him," Bobby admitted. "But I came back here anyway. I want to be straight with you guys."

"So what are we dealing with here?" Frank demanded. "Does he want the papers or not?"

"He wants them, he wants them," Bobby assured him. "If you can get the papers, he's got the money. You just gotta take my word and deal with me. The boss don't want to be seen. He's a fucking ghost, whiter than milk."

"So how much money are we talking about here?" Frank persisted.

Feliciano refused to be pinned down. "The boss told me it don't matter what it costs. He needs the papers, he'll pay whatever you want."

Frank's eyes darted to Feliciano's waist and saw the bulge of the automatic beneath his hip-length jacket. "So what's our business here, Bobby? You mentioned some other locations you were interested in. Are we going to work with you on those, too?"

Feliciano grinned broadly. "Now we're talking. I'm taking over next month; Eleventh Street, Third Street, Henry Street. You guys get more for every new location."

"You're taking over *everything*?"

"You stick with me and we'll all be fucking rich."

"Just tell us what you want, Bobby," Frank said.

"There's a Dominican guy who's causing us some trouble. I don't think we're gonna pop him, though. We'll take him out with our product," Bobby asserted. "You know he could never stand next to my boss. My boss deals a million dollars' worth in one shot."

"You talking about Juahito?" Frank asked.

"He's no competition," Bobby asserted. "You know what I made myself on Saturday? I made thirty-five thousand from six A.M. to six P.M. I took it all myself. That fucking rat Juahito sells in one month what I sell in one day."

"We're going to have to drop by once in a while and take somebody off the street," John McCormack pointed out. "Just so it looks on the up-and-up."

Feliciano shrugged. "You can hit the street guy up for loitering and keep whatever drugs and money he's carrying. I'm not gonna lose much that way, know what I mean?"

"So you're cutting John in on the weekly payments no matter what happens to the paperwork?" Frank pressed.

"Yeah, John's in if he supports our operations, and don't hit where we're doing business."

"Just tell us where to stay away from," Frank assured him. "You're safe with us."

Feliciano was beginning to relax in the glow of his own self-importance. "You stick with me. Pretty soon everything down here is gonna be mine," he declared triumphantly.

"What about the big boss, is he splitting?" Barchiesi asked, still firmly pressing the point of his revolver at a point on the back of the seat that corresponded roughly with the center of Feliciano's shoulder blades.

"The guy's been in the fucking business for fifteen years," Bobby replied. "He's got all the money he ever needs. You should see the fucking mountain he owns in Puerto Rico, right on the fucking beach, man."

"No shit, the man owns a mountain? My mother-in-law's from down there in the mountains. She's in San German," Frank Bose lied, hoping to elicit more information from the unwary Feliciano.

"Yeah, I know that place. We're from San Antonio," Feliciano replied without thinking.

"It's a nice island. You oughta be thinking about going back to San Antonio someday yourself."

"After I make some big fucking money," Bobby asserted. "We're all going to make big money."

"John, too," Frank stated. "John gets the same as us from now on, right?"

"Sure. If the boss don't pay the extra for him, I'll pay it out of my own pocket," Feliciano bragged.

"Sounds all right," John McCormack asserted. "But remember you have to take a light fall every now and then."

"Sure," Bobby agreed. "A couple of smacks, a couple of punches, maybe a loitering bust. No big fucking deal."

"A *light* bust," Bob Barchiesi stressed.

"Hey, I been getting busted since 1966," Bobby told them. "It's what happens in this business. The Pressure Point guys busted me for numerous sales, and I'm still here."

Feliciano turned toward the car door and Frank almost came out of his skin. He was a millisecond away from passing the fatal signal back to Barchiesi. "Bobby, Bobby . . ." Frank said and shook his head to let Barchiesi know *not yet*.

"Hey, keep cool, man," Feliciano said. "We're all in this together."

"How about the paperwork?" McCormack asked again as Feliciano opened the car door. "We still on for that?"

"I'll talk to the boss tomorrow. That's my word to you," Bobby promised.

"And you'll have an answer when we call?"

"Call me tomorrow night at the number I gave you."

"Eight o'clock, okay?" Bose said.

"I'll be there." Feliciano climbed out onto the sidewalk and shut the door behind him.

There was an anxious moment when everyone held their breaths. Finally Bob Barchiesi sank back into the seat and exhaled a long, low breath of air. "Did you see the gun when he was sitting there?" he asked Frank.

"He kept going for his pants with his hand," Bose answered. "It's a goddam good thing I didn't have an itch on my head."

"It looked like a forty-five or a nine millimeter," McCormack observed, the relief reflected in his voice.

The relief was obvious for all of them. The tension inside the car eased almost immediately, like air being let out of a child's balloon. They were unhurt, they had managed to avoid a confrontation and the threat of violence, and they still had their reputations and careers intact as far as they knew. It was an important consideration. To all but a few insiders in the Narcotics Division, they were dirty cops, on the take from drug dealers. If there had been shooting, and injuries or deaths, they would have been found in the company of a known drug dealer for the purpose of taking bribes. It was a serious matter that would have been investigated by the Internal Affairs Division, whether or not they knew of the existence of the controlled pad. Their exoneration was far from certain. Even the allegation of corruption was enough to taint a cop for life, or follow him to his grave after he was dead.

For Frank Bose and Bob Barchiesi, the experience had elevated their relationship to a new level. If either of them had been uncertain about the degree of trust they had in one another, that uncertainty was forever vanquished in their shared response to the danger Bobby Feliciano posed. On the strength of a hand signal, Bob had been willing to shoot a man in the back and kill him. He had been willing to accept the fact that Frank's signal would completely justify the shooting, that it would stand up in any courtroom in the city if it came to that, and that his conscience would forever be clear based on his partner's judgment. Frank had never doubted he would do it for a minute. He never doubted that, no matter what might happen, his back would be covered. They were partners in the truest sense, and on that darkened street both of them knew they had arrived together at a place from which there was no returning.

Chapter Fourteen

Bose and Barchiesi continued to patrol East Eleventh Street as they had promised Bobby Feliciano they would, making only occasional arrests of the street people they encountered and maintaining a relatively low profile. Their routine was unvarying. Residents of the neighborhood could almost set their clocks by the officers' daily pass-bys. They could almost predict the exact spot where the patrol car would park, who the policemen were going to question, and what the results of that questioning would be. It was reassuring to those who knew what was going on as well as to those who didn't. Enough was happening to maintain the fiction that something was being done about cocaine trafficking in the area, not nearly enough was happening to make a difference, and that seemed okay with everyone on East Eleventh Street; everyone but Irma Garcia.

Blondie appeared to have her own agenda. Frank and Bob first became aware of it one late September afternoon when they saw her leaning out of her second-floor apartment at 507 East Eleventh Street. Knowing that she and Juahito had been released on bail, they were not surprised to see her there, but they were very surprised at her attitude. She waved delightedly at them and hailed them over to a spot on the sidewalk beneath her window. "Nice day," she said and grinned, releasing a small, folded piece of paper from her hand then disappearing back inside her apartment.

They watched the paper as it fluttered downward and retrieved it when it landed on the sidewalk. *Apartment 7*, her cryptic note read. . . . *Rock and money*. The officers shot quizzical glances at one another, then entered number 507. It was too intriguing a prospect to pass up. Upstairs they found the apartment open and unoccupied, and a cache of Rock Solid cocaine inside, as well as $2,500 in small denominations and an unloaded .357 stainless steel Ruger. Mystified, they seized the contraband and returned to headquarters, where they vouchered it.

Bose and Barchiesi were puzzled by the events, unable to agree on a plausible explanation for Blondie's actions. She might have been working for Lopez, they speculated, providing them with a kind of bonus payoff from the boss for staying in line. Or she might have simply been protecting her own interests, using them to harass her competition in the building while she awaited disposition of the upcoming criminal charges against her and Juahito. Whatever her reasons she was certainly not to be trusted. Still the seizures were a welcome relief for Bose and Barchiesi. Undercover work is by nature reactionary, and they were both tired of taking their cues from scumbags like Bobby Feliciano. They were glad to be back in The Rock; glad to be on the offensive again.

On October 1, at 7:30 in the evening, thirty-two-year-old Nelson Alphonso arrived at 507 East Eleventh Street and went immediately upstairs to apartment number 7 on the third floor. Using a passkey, he entered the apartment and went to the kitchen, where a row of wooden cabinets was set high on the wall above the sink and stove. He felt along the thin wooden molding at the top until he located a hidden latch and released it, allowing the entire bank of cabinets to swing outward into the room on unseen metal hinges. He reached behind the cabinets into the cutaway recess in the wall and removed a compact Interdynamic Tech 9mm machine gun that had been secreted on one of the shelves. He lifted the weapon by its trigger assembly, released the magazine, and pulled back on the bolt, ejecting the bullet already in the chamber.

Alphonso walked to the room's only window, where a dusty shaft of sunlight penetrated the slats of a venetian blind. Carefully he raised the machine gun to the light and sighted down its compact barrel until he was satisfied it was clean and in working order. He peered through the blinds onto the street below and noted with satisfaction that the earlier gathering of neighborhood residents had already begun to diminish. Despite the cool relief of an early October breeze, they knew that the street was not a smart place to be that evening. Inside the building, their small apartments were choking with hot, stale air and the penetrating smells of a thousand meals, but they would be safe there. On the streets of Alphabet City, word of danger spreads like a prairie fire.

There was a fresh magazine in the recess behind the cabinets. Alphonso clipped it into the machine gun, cranked a round into the chamber, and went outside into the hallway. From his vantage point on the third-floor landing, he surveyed the stairwell leading to the lobby below, and sighted along the barrel at his field of fire.

Two flights of stairs, the lobby, and the first-floor landing were well within his sights. Anyone entering the building would be an easy target even before they got to the stairwell. They would have no chance whatsoever of retreating once they began to climb the narrow steps. The Interdynamic Tech was capable of firing 850 rounds a minute. That gave him a little more than three seconds of firing time to do the job he had been assigned to do and it was more than enough. Casually he sat at the head of the stairs, lit a cigarette, and waited.

2022 hours: An undercover Narcotics vehicle made a slow westbound turn from Avenue B and headed down East Eleventh Street. Inside the car, Frank Bose, Bob Barchiesi, and John Mc-Cormack kept a careful lookout for Bobby Feliciano, who they felt was somewhere on the block. They had been unable to reach Feliciano at the telephone number he had given them and they had decided that another face-to-face meeting was necessary to emphasize the point that McCormack was to be the sole contact between them and the Lopez organization from here on in. Now, driving down the silent street, they realized something was terribly wrong.

"I don't like this," McCormack rasped from the rear seat. "The fucking street's practically empty."

"It doesn't smell right," Frank Bose agreed. Like John McCormack, he and Bob knew that the sidewalks should have been alive with people this early in the evening. They understood enough about the residents of East Eleventh Street to know that they would normally be out in force on a cool October evening like this; bopping and jiving, moving rhythmically to the ear-splitting sounds of salsa music blasting from their hand-held consoles.

"Don't stop . . ." Bob Barchiesi communicated urgently from the backseat. "Keep on going and circle the block again."

Instinctively, all three officers clipped their shields to their chests and drew their weapons. Frank drove on past number 507 and turned onto Avenue A heading southbound. "I can feel the adrenaline pumping," he told the others.

Nelson Alphonso took a final drag on his cigarette and ground the butt into the cement floor of the landing at number 507. Downstairs the front door opened and a young lookout named Jesus Colon stepped inside. He squinted in the semi-dark lobby and searched the stairwell until he caught sight of Alphonso on the third-floor landing, then pointed backward over his shoulder with the thumb of his right hand. Upstairs Alphonso saw the signal. He crouched on one knee and pressed the metal stock of the machine gun into his right shoulder, training the point of the barrel on the fifteen-year-old lookout as he turned and went back outside.

"Who the fuck is this coming?" Barchiesi rasped as they again drove onto East Eleventh Street and spotted Colon walking uncertainly toward them.

"*Look at him, look at him!*" McCormack's voice was hoarse with urgency. "He's scared or something. There's something not right about this kid."

"This fucking stinks!" Barchiesi said nervously. "It's all wrong out here."

It was a feeling none of them could deny, a feeling each of them had experienced before even though none of them would ever be able to adequately explain it. "It would be like trying to explain a headache," Frank Bose asserted. "It's just there, and you know you've gotta do something about it. Anything can trigger the feeling; a smell, a blade of grass out of place, maybe a silence where there ought to be noise. You feel the hairs coming up on the back of your neck. You're clenching your jaw, your muscles are like rock. Nobody knows what the fuck to expect, you just know something bad is going down."

"Watch this fucking kid," McCormack warned as they neared the solitary figure on the sidewalk. "He's heading toward the building."

Frank observed the youth pause in front of number 507 as they approached, then dart inside when they drove by, almost daring them to follow. He could feel the tightness in his throat, and a fluttering like bird's wings in the pit of his stomach. When he spoke his voice shook. "I don't like this at all. I think we're being set up here, John."

"Just head on down the street," McCormack instructed. "We'll circle around again and see if we can spot Bobby on the next pass."

Almost on cue, Feliciano had appeared on the corner of Avenue A and East Eleventh Street when they returned. "We've spotted the subject," McCormack reported for the hidden microphone. "He gave us the high sign and he's leading us away from the area. We're going to try and pick him up on Avenue B."

Bobby was casual when they pulled up beside him. He slid into the front seat next to Frank Bose, hardly bothering to notice that Barchiesi and McCormack had climbed out of the backseat onto the sidewalk. They did not want to be caught inside the car in the event of an ambush. Their instincts and their training told them they could provide better cover from the street.

"What's up?" Frank asked Feliciano, trying to disguise the tension in his voice.

"The boss told me he don't want the papers anymore. He says fuck the papers," Bobby replied nonchalantly.

"*Fuck the papers*? You know how much shit we had to go through to bring John in on this?" Frank fumed.

"It's okay," Feliciano assured him. "I told the boss he had to pay John anyway, same as you guys. He told me to do whatever I thought was right."

"The money's got to go to John," Frank asserted.

"Fifteen hundred, every Monday for sure," Feliciano promised. "I'm a fucking man. You can count on me."

"That's good, because the word is out on the street about these two guys," John McCormack clarified from outside the car window. "We're afraid they're going to get popped if they keep on meeting you this way."

Feliciano shrugged. "So you're my man from now on," he told McCormack. "Every week I meet you and give you fifteen hundred, okay?"

"Every two weeks," McCormack demurred. "That way we cut our chances of getting nailed in half."

"And Pepe and me will be on the block in uniform, doing our regular thing," Frank added. "Don't acknowledge us if you see us coming down the block. Don't even try to contact us. You got anything to tell us, wait until you meet with John and tell him about it."

"Maybe you should toss me every now and then just to make it look real," Feliciano suggested. "You know, put me up against a building and push me around a little bit."

"Sure, we'll make it look real," Barchiesi grinned.

"Fucking beautiful . . ." Bobby nodded solemnly.

"The point is, we trust you to do the right thing," Frank said.

"Everybody trusts everybody, fucking beautiful," Bobby reaffirmed. "I'm going to talk to the guys over on Third Street and see if I can get you hooked up there, too."

"Are you telling us your boss is operating over on Third Street, too?" Bob Barchiesi pressed.

"Third Street, Henry Street; we're all over, man. Every location you back us up on, you get another five hundred apiece."

"Next Monday, right?"

"You call me and we'll set up a meet," Bobby assured them.

"You'll give John fifteen hundred in three packages, okay?" Bob Barchiesi insisted.

"Fifties and hundreds, no more bullshit tens and twenties," Bobby promised, laughing.

"I'll drive by and you just throw the packages in the car," McCormack told him. "That way we won't have to take the chance of meeting and being seen."

"We could really be fucked if this all got out," Bose added.

"Fucking beautiful, we don't have to talk or meet no more," Feliciano observed.

"You just drop the money in the car, like you're making a night deposit in a bank."

There was laughter all around. "Okay, we're out of here," Bob Barchiesi said, climbing into the car with John McCormack. "We'll see you Monday."

"Monday," Bobby grinned.

"Safe home."

Back at 507, Nelson Alphonso smoked his last cigarette and stood resignedly on the third-floor landing. He carried the 9mm machine gun back to apartment 7 and again secreted it in the wall behind the kitchen cabinets, fully loaded, with a live round still in the chamber. It would be ready when he needed it again, he reasoned, and that would likely be soon. His targets were not going away. They would keep on coming at the organization until their eagerness got in the way of their intelligence and they blundered into his gunsights. There was no need for concern. He had plenty of time.

Chapter Fifteen

S OMETHING was definitely wrong. Bobby Feliciano had failed to make any of his appointed meets in more than a week. He had made no attempt to contact John McCormack as he had promised, and he had made himself conspicuously scarce in the East Eleventh Street neighborhood. It was not a good sign. Everybody involved was getting the impression that the operation was falling apart, and the reason, they all agreed, was Feliciano's reluctance to deal exclusively with John McCormack. Bose and Barchiesi had gained his trust and his grudging respect, everyone now realized. If the operation was to go forward, they would both have to go back undercover.

On the morning of October 10, Special Prosecutor Ed Boyar contacted both officers and told them that their return to undercover operations had been cleared through Pressure Point headquarters and the Narcotics Division. A meeting of all police personnel concerned were held in the offices of Manhattan South Narcotics, where it was decided that the premises at 507 East Eleventh Street were to be rousted that day. John McCormack was to initiate a typical buy-and-bust operation in the building during which Bose and Barchiesi were to confront Bobby Feliciano if they found him.

Bobby was there, inside the Barcelonita Social Club on the first floor of the building. "Hey man . . ." Bobby grinned uncertainly at the sight of John McCormack coming through the door followed by his Narcotics team.

"What the fuck's going on, Bobby?" McCormack demanded when he'd shoved Bobby out of earshot. "We set up a meet and you never show. You give me a number to call and you're never there. Do we have a deal or no?"

"Hey, relax man," Feliciano shrugged. "You want the money now? I got plenty stashed upstairs. You wait here and I'll get it."

"I don't want it now," McCormack objected. "What is this bullshit anyway? What do I gotta do, hunt you the fuck down every time I'm supposed to get what's coming to me?"

Bose and Barchiesi entered the club before Feliciano could answer. "I don't know what's with this fucking guy," McCormack reported to them in a whisper Feliciano could hear. "He tells me he'll meet me Friday and he's not there. I can't reach him on the goddam phone. I think this scumbag is really jerking us off here."

"Is that right, scumbag? Are you jerking us off?" Bob Barchiesi growled as he pushed Feliciano against a wall. "We had a fucking agreement that you were going to pay John our money. You never showed up for the meet you guys had scheduled, and we never saw any payments!" He tightened his grip on Feliciano's shirt collar, causing Bobby's eyes to bulge grotesquely. "We want what's coming to us, scumbag. Where's the fucking money?"

Feliciano gestured helplessly. "I wanted to be there but I had to fly to Puerto Rico. There was a big fucking earthquake down there, man. I got family there that needed help."

Bose and Barchiesi knew about the earthquake. They also knew it had taken place in Guatemala, more than eight hundred miles away. "That really breaks me up, but I gotta tell you we're not putting up with any more of this bullshit!" Barchiesi told him through clenched teeth. "We want our fucking money!"

"I told John I got it upstairs," Feliciano whined.

"We don't want it now," McCormack said, indicating the other Narcotics officers present with a jerk of his head. "These guys are not with us. We can't let them see us taking the money from you, know what I mean?"

"Next Friday, then. We'll set up another meet for next Friday. I'll be there, on my mother's grave," Feliciano solemnly asserted.

Bob Barchiesi cast a sidelong glance at Frank Bose, who had detained another male suspect he recognized as Nelson Alphonso. "Keep an eye on Bobby," he told Frank. "I want to talk to John for a minute."

Frank watched him lead John away from the others and understood what was happening. McCormack was reluctant to accept the bribe money today because it wasn't a part of the prearranged plan. John also knew that Inspector Gallagher's previous warning about bribes was as valid for him as it was for Frank and Bob. Controlled pad or not, police officers who accepted bribes were letting themselves in for a lot of grief. He had agreed to be a part of the operation only under the condition that he be allowed to pick up the payments with an absolute minimum of contact between

Bobby and himself; better still none at all. Feliciano's offer of immediate payment was a curveball he was not prepared to deal with at this time. Frank and Bob both knew he had a lot to lose, as they did. The only difference between them was that he still cared and they didn't. They were going to catch Alejandro Lopez no matter what price it extracted from their careers and their lives. McCormack couldn't go that far. Most cops couldn't.

"I think we should take the money," Barchiesi told him confidentially. "If we don't take it we might as well arrest him right now and collapse the whole operation."

McCormack hesitated. "I don't like the way this thing is going down," he muttered.

"It's okay, everything's on the tape," Bob reassured him. He knew what John was thinking. The Nagra had failed before. If it happened again they could voucher the fifteen hundred Feliciano gave them, only to have him come back at a later time and swear he had given them five thousand.

"We can pick it up on Friday, when we have a backup truck," McCormack argued.

"Look, what kind of fucking idiots is he gonna think we are if we come in here busting his balls about not getting paid, then we refuse to take the money? The guy's a scumbag but he's not completely stupid," Bob pointed out. "If I was him and I saw that, I'd be on the next fucking plane to Aguadilla."

McCormack nodded with resignation. "Okay, it's yours. You take the payment from him and leave me out of it."

They returned to the others. "I'll take fifteen hundred now," Barchiesi told Feliciano in a low voice.

"It's upstairs . . ." Bobby turned to go. "I'll be back in a few minutes."

"Whatta you think, I'm fucking *stupid?*" Barchiesi scowled. "Send one of your shitkickers up to get it."

Feliciano directed a man he called "Macho" to get the money from his upstairs apartment, then entered into a general discussion with the officers about which member of his Rock Solid sales force should be arrested as a token gesture to make the visit look legitimate. It was decided they would bust a female dealer named "Norma" on their way out. "We gotta do this, Bobby. You know how it is," Frank told him apologetically.

"Hey man, I been around. I know how it works," Feliciano asserted. "You do what you got to do."

Frank had an idea. "You want me to score some coke from this guy while we're here?" he whispered to John McCormack.

McCormack groaned. These were guys who never stopped coming at you. "This is not a good idea," he pointed out.

"It'll open up the door for you to move your undercover people in here and bust them for sale," Frank persisted.

John thought about it and finally relented. Delighted, Frank turned to Bobby Feliciano. "I'm going to a party later on, Bobby. Can you do me a little blow?"

Feliciano smiled broadly and signaled Nelson Alphonso nearby. "Do my man a gram here," he ordered. Obligingly, Nelson reached into the front pouch on his sweatshirt, removed a half-gram vial of Rock Solid and gave it to Frank.

The man named Macho returned and handed a package to Feliciano. "Sorry, but it's all tens and twenties," Bobby apologized, passing the package along to Frank Bose. "I didn't know you guys were coming or I woulda got you hundreds."

"It's okay . . ." Bose methodically counted the entire fifteen hundred dollars aloud for the tape and separated it into bundles of five hundred each. "Okay, it's all here," he reported to McCormack and Bob Barchiesi.

"Then we're out of here," McCormack breathed a sigh of relief.

"I gotta talk to you before you go," Bobby confided to Bose and Barchiesi. "I got a problem with that guy I told you about before."

"What guy?" Barchiesi asked.

"The Dominican, the one I told you was doing grams across the street."

"What about him? I thought you said he was a nickel-and-dime operation, that you weren't worried about him."

"The boss wants to take him out. He'd like you to close the block off so he can bring the Uzis down and whack this little rat motherfucker," Bobby reported. "There'll be a lot more money in it for you."

"Whatta you mean 'close off the block'?" Barchiesi questioned him.

"You know, one guy at one end, the other guy at the other end. You just make sure nobody comes in and gets in our way," Feliciano replied matter-of-factly. He was talking to cops who were on the payroll now. He had a right to expect small favors in return.

"When is this going down?" Frank Bose asked.

"I dunno, a couple of days. I'll let you know."

Bose and Barchiesi returned to the Seventh Precinct, vouchered the bribery payments, and placed a call to the Special Prosecutor's office, reporting Feliciano's request that they close off East Eleventh Street between Avenues A and B. The following morning a meeting was held on the seventeenth floor at Two Rector Street, the offices of Special Prosecutor Charles Hynes. They were admitted to a large meeting room where the entire Prosecutor's staff listened to their account of the previous day's meeting.

"We have a real problem here," Frank pointed out to the assemblage. "Either we close down the block, which would effectively make us accomplices to a homicide, or we arrest Feliciano now and collapse the controlled pad."

"What do you want to do?" Hynes asked them.

"We want to take him down," they both agreed.

"Then do it."

No further authorization was needed. All proper police personnel were notified and that afternoon they met with Pressure Point Commander Colin McCabe to map a strategy for Feliciano's arrest. "We're going to make an example of this son of a bitch," McCabe asserted. "We're going in there with Emergency Services, helmets and vests, shotguns, the whole nine yards. We're gonna light up the whole goddam street and let them know what happens when they try to bribe policemen, you folla?"

Bob looked at Frank, whose face was turning a deep shade of red. "Maybe we could try it another way," he suggested diplomatically. They both knew that McCabe was an okay administrator but was way out of his depth when it came to planning street operations. "I think it'd go down better if Frank and I went in there alone, in uniform, and pretended we were doing business as usual. We could tell him that we need a phony bust to take the heat off back at headquarters. We'll cuff him and tell him it's all bullshit, that we're gonna release him as soon as we get out of sight of the building. That way we all get out nice and easy. We make our collar and nobody gets hurt."

McCabe pondered the proposal. What he wanted more than anything was a piece of the action, but Barchiesi's plan didn't appear to have any flaws. "Okay," he finally relented. "I'll be following you in a backup vehicle and I want you in constant radio contact. Your code name will be 'Phoenix.' When you've made your arrest, inform me by relaying the code 'Phoenix has landed,' you folla?"

Frank almost choked before Bob was able to whisk him out of

McCabe's office. By the time they were in the patrol car on their way to East Eleventh Street, both of them were convulsed with laughter. "*Pressure Point Phoenix to Pressure Point Commander . . .*" Frank radioed back to McCabe in a following vehicle. "Do not, repeat, *do not* acknowledge my transmissions, and I will not acknowledge yours! We are making a turn onto East Eleventh Street. We have reached the point of no return. *Do not acknowledge . . .*" There were tears streaming out of Bob Barchiesi's eyes.

They found Bobby at the bar of the Barcelonita Social Club. Frank approached him conspiratorially. "I gotta make it look like I'm taking you in, Bobby. People on the street are starting to talk about us, and it's getting back to my bosses."

Feliciano seemed surprised for a moment, then readily allowed himself to be handcuffed. "*Phoenix has landed,*" Frank reported straight-faced into his radio, and instantly the street outside came alive with the wail of police sirens. "Oh shit . . ." Bobby Feliciano's shoulders slumped. "I had a feeling."

The door to the social club came crashing inward and a dozen blue-helmeted ESU troops charged inside. They secured the room in seconds without a shot being fired, then stood back in amazement as Lieutenant Colin McCabe dressed in full battle regalia hurled himself into their midst, waving his revolver before him like an Olympic saber. "Everybody up against the wall!" he screamed frantically. "I'm gonna fucking kill anyone who moves!"

Bob felt his eyes misting. He didn't dare to look at Frank for fear his partner might say something that would push him over the edge into hysterical laughter. Frank did not let him down. "Phoenix is now releasing the prisoner to Pressure Point Commander," he reported solemnly into his dead radio. "That is the end of this transmission. Over and out."

Chapter Sixteen

"WE were off the controlled pad and I guess in a way we were relieved, but in another way we were sorry we had to let it go," Frank Bose recalled shortly after the arrest of Bobby Feliciano. "Bobby and I had taken it as far as we could, so we had to figure out another way of keeping the thing going. There was no way we were just going to let it drop. Lopez was still out there and we knew we had to get the son of a bitch, by whatever means necessary.

"The thing of it is, none of this stuff just happened. We knew how Lopez operated and we knew all we had to do was keep applying the pressure on him until it was coming at him from all sides. Then the snake would start to devour his tail and all we would have to do was keep up the pressure until he eventually swallowed his own head.

"It wasn't just mindless stuff, dumb cop routines like in *Hill Street Blues*. Bobby and I knew what we were up against. We knew the job would blow us away if we fucked up even once, so we calculated every move we made, like a chess match, or a high-stakes poker game. Lopez would up the ante and we'd see him every time. We had to be thinking about our next moves every minute. We figured every move from every angle imaginable, and finally decided on whatever course would get us where we wanted to go without laying us wide open to anyone, the job or the Lopez organization. Sometimes it was hard to tell which was worse.

"Cops say things like that, but I guess we never really doubted whose side we were on. We were the good guys and they were the bad guys, and everything that went down only convinced us of that more and more. You remember Blondie? Bobby Feliciano wasn't behind bars for more than a couple of days before she was trying to take over his business, and fuck us in the bargain. Her lawyer called Captain Donald Faherty of Manhattan South Narcotics and asked for a meeting to discuss two corrupt cops. Blondie had told him all about us, about our meetings with Bobby, the payments, everything. As an ex-DA, he had to know the department wanted nothing more than to nail dirty cops. The only thing he didn't know was that it was a controlled pad, so there was nothing he could milk out of it for his clients.

"The prosecutors all had different reasons for wanting a piece of this thing. Mostly it was procedural or jurisdictional. The prosecutor's office is like a beehive, only instead of working together, they're all buzzing around in different directions, looking to get an edge on each other and advance their careers. They know one of the easiest ways of scoring points in the promotions race is to get the inside track on corrupt cops."

Frank paused reflectively. "It's funny how things happen. Bobby and I probably would have gone through this whole thing not really knowing what was going on with Blondie if I hadn't happened to be in DA Ed Boyar's office one afternoon on an entirely different matter. The telephone rang, and after he'd listened for a few seconds he motioned for me to pick up the other extension on his desk. It was Blondie, telling him all about meets Bobby and I'd made on the controlled pad. She had exact dates, times, amounts paid. She could almost recount conversations we'd had word for word. I just listened, stunned, I never said anything. I wasn't so much surprised at how much information she had; Bobby and I both figured that she was probably Lopez's partner and had picked most of it up from him. What really got to me was how tight she was with Ed Boyar.

"When he hung up, Boyar just gave me this kind of funny look, like I was supposed to know what it was all about. Later on, when Bobby and I talked about it we both realized it was all part of a fucking field test they had given us. Somewhere in one of those apartment seizures Blondie had been feeding us, a pin-lens was hidden in a wall or a piece of furniture, televising everything we did when we were in there. It recorded every seizure, every glassine, every weapon, every dollar we took out of the place; and later on they checked those totals against everything we vouchered back at the station house. If we'd been one glassine or one dollar off they would have hung us by the balls."

He took a deep breath. "I guess we must have passed."

Epilogue to Part One

O N January 25, 1986, a low-level street operative for the Rock Solid organization named Ralph Rodriguez warned Frank Bose and Bob Barchiesi of threats Alejandro Lopez had made against their lives and the lives of their children. One week later his bullet-ridden body was found on an icy Brooklyn street.

PART TWO

"Take calculated risks. That is quite different from being rash."

—GENERAL GEORGE S. PATTON

Chapter Seventeen

"Today's the day."

—MEL FISCHER

B Y the end of 1985 Bose and Barchiesi felt they were spinning their wheels in the Lopez investigation. Despite the pressure they had applied for almost six months, despite the arrests of scores of drug dealers directly and indirectly associated with the Rock Solid and Pony-Pak organizations, and despite the obvious impression they had made on Alejandro Lopez himself, the drug trade on East Eleventh Street seemed to be flourishing. As fast as Pressure Point officers were able to pull dealers off the street they were replaced by eager new recruits, and the steady traffic of cocaine in and out of the building known as "The Rock" seemed as undiminished as the ragged lines of junkies who waited each day to buy it.

Their discontent mounted with each new arrest, knowing that as uniformed officers they were powerless to do much more than nibble away at the periphery of the organization while the drug-lords at the center remained beyond their reach. They could temporarily interrupt the cycle of cocaine transactions on East Eleventh Street, but they knew they would forever remain incapable of stemming it completely if they remained where they were. Something had to be done. Neither Bose nor Barchiesi was willing to accept the idea of "business as usual" on East Eleventh Street.

Both agreed that the only legitimate shot they had at getting to Alejandro Lopez was in the Narcotics Division. They reasoned that, as Narcotics officers, they would have the backup and authorization they would need to pursue their investigation with authority. They would have the power to obtain subpoenas, they could utilize undercover operatives for "buy-and-bust" operations, they would be able to initiate surveillances. As members of Narcotics, they knew they could finally put some teeth into their pursuit of Lopez and Rock Solid, but they also knew that their being reassigned and ending up as a team in the Narcotics Unit was a near impossibility. Things like that just didn't happen in the NYPD.

At least not for everyone else. For Bob and Frank it was a foregone conclusion that they had to be partners in Narcotics. They knew their chances of teaming up with someone else who shared their determination to get Lopez were next to none, and Lopez was the only reason they had for transferring to Narcotics in the first place. Both of them agreed that unless they were free to pursue him with additional clout and resources, they would abandon the investigation altogether, apply to Street Crime or some other division where their work might produce results instead of stagnation, and leave the drug business to police officers with less aggressiveness and a higher threshold of frustration.

Fortunately, Captain Donald Faherty of Manhattan South Narcotics had been highly impressed by their work in the controlled pad. Even more than by their spirit and initiative, he was impressed by their thoughtfulness, by the fact that they were more than a couple of gun-slinging yahoos with an axe to grind. He saw that their methods were sound, that their arrests stuck, and that they were willing to go the distance to get the job done right. Faherty knew a good thing when he saw it. In a police department made tentative by lawsuits and civilian complaints, smart cops were as important as tough cops—maybe more. In Bose and Barchiesi he had both.

Faherty was an important ally in a police department where a strategically placed telephone call from one commander to another could make or break a career. Anyone who knows anything about the way it works, knows that all the ability in the world isn't worth much without "juice" higher up. An influential mentor is worth his weight in commendations. Don Faherty wanted Bose and Barchiesi on his team, and they did nothing to discourage him from thinking that was the place they wanted to be. In fact, their plan was for Bob to interview for Narcotics first, since experienced sergeants were needed in the division, and when he was accepted he would bring Frank in. Then they would dance with whomever it took to get back on the street together; back where they would again be a haunting presence for Alejandro Lopez, a bugbear with longer claws and sharper fangs.

Bob interviewed for Narcotics on December 7 and was accepted into the division in two days; an unheard-of circumstance in the police department, where six to nine months is the normal wait for transfers when they are granted at all. Frank applied for transfer a day or two later and, with a well-placed word from Don Faherty, followed Bob into the Narcotics Division in three weeks. "We waltzed in," Frank remembered. "As far as I know, nothing like it had ever happened up there before. We were just happy to be in the same division, but neither of us dreamed we'd ever end up on the same squad. That was just too much to hope for."

Fate was with them. Lieutenant Freddie Solomon from the Narcotics Street Enforcement Unit wanted Frank in his squad. He made the mistake of going to Narcotics Supervisor Captain Bob Kerner and making the request. Kerner knew Bob Barchiesi from when they had both served in the Street Crime Unit, and knew that Bob wanted Frank in his squad. Frank and Bob were well aware that Kerner hated Solomon's guts and delighted in busting the lieutenant's balls every chance he could. The next day Frank found himself in Bob's squad in Spanish Harlem. It could only happen in a movie, or in the NYPD, where old scores never go unsettled.

There were new procedures to be learned, new paperwork to become accustomed to. Bose and Barchiesi never lost sight of the fact that Lopez and Rock Solid were their main targets, but, for the time being, the investigation had to be put on hold while they familiarized themselves with their new duties. As a supervisor, Bob set about building a Narcotics team with Frank as the cornerstone, and by late January 1986, they were ready to resume operations at 507 East Eleventh Street.

Despite the appearance of "business as usual" at 507 East Eleventh Street, Lopez and his associates knew that the pressure posed by police, and in particular Bose and Barchiesi, had greatly affected their ability to move cocaine in and out of the building. Sales were down, and unless the pressure could be reduced their Manhattan enterprise was in danger of collapse. Knowing that, the organization had already begun to move large portions of their cutting-and-bagging operation outside of New York State entirely.

The threats against their children, and the subsequent murder of Ralph Rodriguez, crystallized Bose and Barchiesi's determination to get Lopez. Now it had become personal. Both officers knew that the threat on their own lives was only an outgrowth of the business they were in and the way they conducted it. Lopez's threat to cut their children into pieces and mail them back in shoeboxes was something else altogether. It transcended the ill-defined rules of pursuit and flight, and turned the confrontation into a one-on-one vendetta. Now they knew that it was no longer a matter of whether they would arrest him, but when—and whether they would be able to bring him in without beating him to death first.

Sergeant John McCormack had obtained an old police photo of Alejandro Lopez and given it to Bose and Barchiesi shortly before their transfer to Narcotics. Now they had a face to accompany the reputation. Now they could identify particular features; dark, deep-set eyes, an aquiline nose, a full moustache, a curious grin, as if he was mocking the police who had arrested him. They had enlarged the photo and hung it on the bulletin board at the Twenty-third Precinct. For them it became a distorted shrine, drawing them to it each morning they arrived at work, compelling them to stand before it and search for new significance in his enigmatic half-smile. They adopted a slogan borrowed from Mel Fischer, whose intrepid search—carried on despite twelve years of failure and the personal loss of his son and daughter-in-law—resulted in the location of the Spanish galleon *Atocha* and its millions of dollars in unclaimed treasure. "Today's the day," they would tell each other, and throw a dart or push-pin at the portrait, trying to obliterate the derisive sneer.

Beneath Lopez, the portraits of Irma Garcia and Raphael Martinez were only slightly less prominent on the bulletin board. If Alejandro Lopez was an enigma to Bose and Barchiesi, Blondie and Juahito were as transparent as glass. Where Lopez had shielded himself behind layers of subordinates, they had operated out in the open, almost oblivious to the danger they faced from the police. They were either incredibly arrogant or incredibly stupid, Bob and Frank had decided; and knowing the caliber of drug merchants they encountered on the Lower East Side, it was probably a combination of the two. Blondie was arrogant and Juahito was stupid, and sometimes the distinctions became blurred.

Whatever their motivation, time was running out for Blondie and Juahito. On April 7, a hearing was held in New York State Supreme Court to determine whether or not the evidence gathered against the two had been illegally obtained, and if so found, could be legally suppressed. Representing Raphael Martinez was a somber, deliberate middle-aged attorney named Jeffrey Ressler, a former Queens, NY, District Attorney. Representing Irma Garcia was Valerie Vanleer-Greenberg, a feisty and argumentative young lawyer whose courtroom demeanor resembled that of a football linebacker preparing to charge. Representing the People, Assistant District Attorney Patrick Conlon faced a highly respected Judge Leslie Crocker Snyder.

A law-school graduate from the University of Virginia and a member of the District Attorney's staff since August of 1983, Conlon was keenly aware of the thorny legal issues involved in the case. Five district attorneys before him had refused to write up the complaint against Blondie and Juahito based on their fear of constitutional questions, but Conlon was tough, and more importantly he had integrity. Like Frank Bose and Bob Barchiesi, he was willing to leave constitutional interpretation up to the judge.

"It was an interesting time," Conlon remembered. "And certainly one of the most intriguing cases I'd gotten to work on at that point. From a strictly legal standpoint, the case itself had a lot of problems, but it presented a terrific challenge and the more I became involved with it, the more I could see that here were two cops who had really done their homework and were walking into the courtroom prepared for whatever was going to happen. They knew the law cold: admissible evidence, exceptions; it was pretty clear to me from the start that they'd been willing to go the extra mile to make their arrest stick.

"All in all, I'd have to say that Frank and Bob's attitude played a large part in my taking on this case. Nobody likes to lose, especially district attorneys, and this was a tough case from the start. But it's hard to turn your back on the kind of professionalism and dedication these guys showed. They were exceptional officers. I think we made a damn good team up there."

After a series of preliminary motions, an in-camera hearing was conducted in the private chambers of Judge Snyder to determine whether Anna Ruiz would be admitted as a reliable informant. The arrest of Martinez and Garcia in August 1985 had resulted largely from the statements Anna Ruiz had given Bose and Barchiesi during her interrogation at the Seventh Precinct. If that testimony was deemed credible, it could be used against the defendants in their upcoming trial. If not, it would be excised and considered inadmissible, severely restricting the prosecution's case.

Ressler and Vanleer-Greenberg argued that Ruiz was unreliable since she was attempting to strike a bargain with police to save her own skin, but after reviewing her statements, Judge Snyder ruled in favor of the prosecution. Anna Ruiz's testimony was credible, she maintained, based on the fact that she had readily implicated herself in crimes greater than those with which she was being charged. Judge Snyder also ruled that, since it was obvious Ruiz would be killed by her former associates if her identity became known, she should be referred to as "Madame X" in the hearing and the upcoming trial.

Frank Bose was the only witness for the People, and for six days he sat from ten A.M. to five P.M. and testified to the events surrounding the arrest of Blondie and Juahito, enduring blistering cross-examinations by defense attorneys that seemed to Frank to verge on personal attacks. Their aim was to hammer at him with the same questions over and over again until he eventually became tripped up in an inconsistency they could use to discredit his entire body of testimony. Valerie Vanleer-Greenberg in particular showed unusual animosity toward Bose and the police department. Her questions came at Frank like mortar volleys; cynical harangues that dripped with antagonism toward cops and outrage over their unjust treatment of her client.

Irma Garcia was a poor, harassed mother of two small children—Greenberg told Judge Snyder—forced to live among drug dealers by a brutal, uncaring, racist society. She was the unfortunate target of a vendetta by Officers Bose and Barchiesi, who had harassed her at every opportunity, violated her constitutional safeguards, and stolen her property. Most importantly, Vanleer-Greenberg hammered away at the point that the original stoppage of Blondie and Juahito's van had been unconstitutional. Both she and Jeffrey Ressler argued strenuously that the officers had no legal reason for stopping the van in the first place, and that the traffic violation they observed was no more than a ruse to conduct an illegal search of the vehicle. There is a doctrine in law called "The Fruit of the Poisonous Tree" stipulating that any evidence gathered as a result of an unjustified premise will be held as inadmissible. Both attorneys knew that if the stoppage was ruled illegal, their clients were as good as free.

Under redirect examination by Patrick Conlon and questioning from Judge Snyder, Frank Bose admitted that it was possible he might not have halted another vehicle for the same traffic violation. Certainly he and Bob Barchiesi had used the stoppage as a pretext for conducting a legitimate search of the suspect vehicle, but ticketing drivers is a legitimate police function, he pointed out. He had issued traffic summonses before; he would again.

A number of character witnesses were introduced by the defense, all of them found to be unreliable and perjurious. One of them, Edgar Perez, testified that he had witnessed the policemen perform in an illegal manner in two different locations at the same time. Like the other character witnesses produced, he denied using drugs himself and disavowed any knowledge of drug sales on East Eleventh Street, swearing that he had no criminal record when in fact ADA Conlon had evidence that showed he had recently pleaded guilty to a multi-count drug indictment.

In her own behalf, Irma Garcia claimed that she had been forced to store the cocaine found in her apartment by members of The Rock. She also swore that they had violated no traffic rules on the day their van had been stopped by Bose and Barchiesi. Enlarging on her attorney's extraordinary characterization of her, she portrayed herself as a victim of racism and police brutality, and called on the compassion of the court for her small children.

The court remained unmoved. In an unusually hard-hitting written decision, Judge Leslie Crocker Snyder characterized Bose and Barchiesi's performance as correct and clearly within the law. By contrast the defendants, Martinez and Garcia, were found to be completely unreliable and self-serving witnesses. Their contention that they had been denied due process of law was largely disallowed, Judge Snyder finding that in all cases but one, the defendants had clearly been informed of their Miranda rights and had testified freely. The prosecution could use their own testimony against them without suppression, as well as the testimony of Anna Ruiz, now called Madame X.

The decision was a complete victory for the district attorney, as well as Bose and Barchiesi. Referring to Frank Bose's testimony, Attorney Jeffrey Ressler told his client at the end of the hearing that "this guy is the best I've seen yet. I couldn't shake him, I couldn't rattle him. Everything he said was consistent from beginning to end." Faced with an unwinnable trial and the prospect of additional testimony from Bob Barchiesi, which they knew could only prove more damaging, both defendants agreed to plea-bargain to lesser charges—each pleading guilty to an A-2 felony, possession of more than two ounces of narcotics—charges that carried from three to six years in prison at the court's discretion. Bail was continued and they were given thirty days to clear up their personal affairs before sentencing.

Exhausted from his six-day ordeal, Frank Bose took a break to be with his family, but the lure of Alejandro Lopez and Rock Solid soon drew him back. One evening a few days later, he found himself in an unmarked patrol car with Bob Barchiesi at the wheel, cruising slowly down East Eleventh Street. "Get a load of that!" he gasped as they drove past number 507.

Bob Barchiesi slowed the car in front of the building and observed Blondie and Juahito sitting contentedly on the sidewalk beside an open-pit barbecue grill while a whole pig turned slowly on a rotating spit, a wrinkled apple set inside its mouth, its charred flesh emitting clouds of greasy smoke into the chasm of the street. "They must be celebrating their last few days of freedom," he observed wryly.

Frank couldn't resist it. He rolled down the window on the passenger's side and caught Blondie's eye. "Bye-bye," he waved playfully.

She was on her feet in an instant. Like a lunatic Don Quixote, armed only with a metal fork dripping with pig fat, she hurled her considerable girth into the street after them, screaming vile curses in Spanish at the top of her lungs. Bob pulled slowly forward and kept the car a few feet ahead of her stabbing thrusts with the fork, while Frank continued waving out the open window. Behind them, Juahito squinted uncomprehendingly up the street at the burlesque, then took another swig from his can of beer. Finally Blondie ran out of steam and stood in the middle of East Eleventh Street, waving the impotent fork after them. Their eyes were filled with tears from laughter and the acrid smoke from the roasting pig. It was the most fun they'd had in months.

Chapter Eighteen

"When I first came on the job there was a lot of camaraderie among individual officers and throughout the department in general. I believe today's bureaucracy discourages that and tries to eliminate it because they feel it breeds abuse and corruption."

—Bob Barchiesi

T HE downpour continued, cold and hard and wind-driven, drumming an almost horizontal tattoo against the rusted fire escape outside the second-floor training room of the Twenty-third Precinct. Inside, the room was thick with the smells of cigarette smoke and wet wool, and the din of nervous voices colliding in the steamy air. Deputy Chief Francis Hall paused briefly in the outside hallway, straightened his tie, smiled wanly at his executive officer, Inspector Thomas Foley, and opened the door.

The noise subsided as Chief Hall strode briskly from the doorway to the front of the room and stood before an empty blackboard, streaked pale gray from thousands of washings and erasures. "Good afternoon . . ." He cleared his throat and scrutinized the assembled police officers, most of them seated at wooden classroom desks with the overflow backed against the sills, radiators, and layered green wainscoting that lined the room beneath the blackboards.

". . . First of all, I want to congratulate all of you for having been assigned to this special detail. As you know, it's not by accident that you're here. You are the elite of the Narcotics Enforcement officers in the city of New York. Each and every one of you has distinguished him or herself in the field of Narcotics Enforcement during your careers. Your records bear that out, and personally, I feel fortunate to have officers of your caliber working under my command."

He stared out over the sea of faces to the rain-swept window beyond. "I'm sorry you all had to trek up here on such a terrible day, but the weather is unfortunately one of those things over which we have little control. The police department proposes and God disposes, I'm afraid."

He paused for a smattering of polite laughter. "At any rate, I'm certain that there is not a man or woman among you who isn't willing to put up with a little foul weather to be here. And I'm equally sure that there are thousands of police officers in the city of New York today who would put up with a lot worse to be sitting in those seats you're sitting in today. This is a prestigious assignment, one that can only lead to more prestigious career assignments in your futures, and the almost-certain promise of a gold shield for you if you keep your noses clean and stay out of trouble."

Somewhere near the center of the room, Bob Barchiesi shifted his weight uncomfortably and winced at the remark. He glanced across the room at Frank Bose, who had suddenly found something interesting on the sleeve of his jacket to pick at. It looked like it was going to be a long afternoon.

"I don't have to tell you that this Special Anti-Crack Unit is the first of its kind in the history of the New York City Police Department," Hall went on. "It is the first time a unit has been established specifically for the purpose of dealing with a single drug, in this case, crack cocaine. That should surprise nobody in this room. You have all had ample opportunity to see what crack is doing to our city. As members of the various Narcotics units throughout the five boroughs, you have witnessed the devastating effects of this drug firsthand, and you have seen the ferocity and determination of the vermin who sell it." He hesitated for a moment, allowing it to sink in. "We intend to be just as determined as they are. As members of this elite one-of a-kind unit we intend to serve notice to the crack merchants of this city that the police will not sit idly by while they peddle death on its streetcorners."

Frank Bose leaned against the windowsill, listened to the tattoo of rain beating against the glass and the sound of an unhinged metal grating on the outside fire escape shuddering against the side of the building. His eyes met Bob Barchiesi's in an instant of shared insight, then drifted off to the various notices and postings hung about the training room before returning to the rainsplattered window and the hypnotic beat of the loose metal grating, *thwack, thwack* . . . The rhythm submerged the chief's droning address and kept him at least partially alert.

"I want you all to know that I expect nothing but your best, but I also want you to understand what we're up against here . . ." Hall's tone had become fatherly. "As Narcotics Enforcement officers, we have to be honest about the problem of drugs, otherwise we're simply a gung-ho mob without a realistic strategy. Realistically, drugs were here long before any of us were around, and they'll be here long after we're all gone. We're not going to eliminate drugs from our city; not this Special Anti-Crack Unit, not any Narcotics unit."

He scanned the group. "That may not be the way we like it but it happens to be the cold, hard truth of the matter, and if any of you want to take it personally I can tell you right now that you're in the wrong business, and probably in for a lot of trouble. This is not a personal crusade. This is not a job for police officers who feel they're above departmental rules and regulations when it comes to the apprehension of drug criminals. It is a job for professional law enforcement personnel who understand the problem and are willing to fit into the team concept as we have defined it. And make no mistake, we are a team . . ."

Frank shot a glance across the room at Bob, who was curled like a pretzel in the tiny classroom desk. *Don't take it personally!* How often had he heard that said over the past four years? . . . *It's a job, just like any other job.* Ever since he'd entered the department, Frank had held what he now suspected had been a naive belief: that if he could only get to the next level of police work, things would be better. He had convinced himself that somewhere just beyond his reach there was a place where the bureaucracy wouldn't get in the way of law enforcement, where he would be free to make collars that needed to be made, and feel good about being a cop again. Now he knew better. Every level brought its own bureaucrats from the levels below, and procedures and prohibitions remained as stifling as ever. It left no room for initiative or for dreams. It was a job, just another job.

He knew that most of the officers assembled in the room felt that way about their work; most policemen felt that way. It was a job, plain and simple, and anyone who let their personal feelings interfere was letting themselves in for a lot of heartache and abuse from the bosses. It wasn't that they didn't want to do a good job out there. They simply learned the bitter truth early on; that cops who tried too hard, who made off-duty collars or arrested criminals who were not their responsibility by job definition, ended up on the short end of the stick.

Frank knew that everyone in the department was suspicious of go-getters, especially chiefs who saw them as threats to the stability of their commands. Go-getters rocked the boat and shook up the citizenry. They were so intent on arresting criminals that they left themselves and the department wide open for civilian complaints and lawsuits. He had no way of proving it, but he firmly believed that most bosses, from precinct COs to chiefs, would rather have cops who did nothing in their commands than cops who put them in the spotlight. Doing nothing can't get you in trouble. It can't screw up a safe, predictable career track.

Chief Hall's spiritless presentation muscled in under Frank's thoughts. "Teamwork is what wins ball games, not hotdoggers who are only interested in goosing their personal statistics. If we think like a team, and we act like a team, there's every likelihood that there will be men on base when it's our turn to come up to bat. That means when we score, we score big, and that's good for everybody's stats, not just our own." He smiled at the relevance of his own metaphor. "Not to mention that as a member of a team, individual officers will be less likely to fall victim to corruptive practices . . ."

Bob Barchiesi tried to stretch in the cramped seat. He'd heard this speech before, in at least a dozen of its not-so-subtle variations. This time it was crack, a new way street people had figured out to kill themselves. Any asshole with a couple of glassines of coke, some baking soda, water, and a frying pan, could cook up a batch for himself and stick it in a pipe or sell it to his neighbor for next to nothing. Bob had no reason to suspect that it was any more or less a threat than ordinary cocaine or any other drug, but he knew it had captured the public's fancy. He knew the newsmedia wanted to tell the public there were cops out there who were concerned, who were doing something to stop it once and for all.

But what they were hearing was that it was just more of the same thing. The public wanted to believe something was being done about crack, and the NYPD was taking steps to make them believe that. The fact that it was largely smoke and mirrors didn't make much difference. People wanted to think their police departments were protecting them from drug criminals. They just didn't want policemen muscling in on criminals' constitutional guarantees. Most times, that boiled down to drug dealers who went scot-free on legal technicalities or who never got arrested in the first place because the cops were handcuffed by rules and prohibitions, or just plain scared of the repercussions.

". . . Make no mistake, nobody wants to be corrupted," Chief Hall continued in a dry monotone. "Nobody starts off being a corrupt cop, but the amounts of money out there are staggering, and the lure of easy, untraceable cash can be almost irresistible to the best of cops, to the best of partners. So don't any of you take it personally when we tell you that the team strategy is designed to keep everybody honest. That's just the way it has to be. The citizens of this city want to know that this so-called 'War on Drugs' is being fought by honest cops . . ."

Bob eyed the gaunt, angular chief standing at the head of the classroom. Hall was a good cop, a cop who had spent most of his life on the job. He must have known a time when things were a lot different on the police department, a time when they were a lot better for cops. Bob had only been on the force since 1979 and he remembered how different things were then. Cops got paid to catch criminals and that was pretty much what they did, without having to keep one eye on their asses every time they had to make a move. That was the way it must have been when Hall came up back in the late fifties or early sixties, he thought. There must have been a lot of spirit among policemen, a lot of pride. Nobody had to walk around all day with an iceberg in their chest, waiting for the axe to fall.

Now it was different. Now everyone was afraid that Commissioner Ben Ward would wake up one morning with a bug up his ass, read in the morning papers that some mugger or drug dealer had charged policemen with violating his constitutional rights by arresting him, and tell somebody within earshot that it pissed him off. Nobody would ask a critical question. Nobody would try to find out whether the initial charges had merit, or whether Ward was pissed off at the cops involved or simply the circumstance. They would just panic. Phones would start ringing off the hook and a snowball would begin plummeting downhill through the bureaucracy until Internal Affairs Field Service units were prowling the precinct hallways looking for bad cops. That was just the way it was in the police department in 1986. There wasn't a whole hell of a lot any of them could do about it.

A quiet murmur of agreement filled the Twenty-third Precinct training room as Chief Hall reminded the police officers that their personal safety was paramount. "I can't stress this strongly enough. We are dealing with extremely dangerous individuals here and the risk to the safety of Narcotics officers is high. We are not looking for heroes. We do not want funerals. What we want out there is a safe, competent, uncorrupted force of policemen and women who are willing to put in the time, keep their noses clean, and be team players."

He relaxed behind the wooden lectern and eyed them all benevolently, like a schoolmaster who had just graded an assignment that nobody failed. "Whatever happens, I want you all to know that I am proud of you and I know you will comport yourselves in the best tradition of the police department. Again, nobody is expecting miracles. Drugs have been around since before any of us were here. Drugs will be around long after all of us are gone. We may not be able to win this thing outright but if we play like a team, maybe, just maybe, we can take it into extra innings. Let's be honest and alert out there. Don't embarrass yourselves or the police department, and welcome aboard."

The rain had stopped. A warm spear of dusty sunlight penetrated the yellowing blinds in the Twenty-third Precinct training room, casting shadows on the faces of the assembled police officers. Frank Bose felt the warm sun on his back, massaging the soreness that inevitably came when he stood too long. Across the room, Bob Barchiesi uncoiled his six-foot three-inch frame from the classroom desk and stretched, stifling a yawn. He stood while Frank Bose pushed through the crush of bodies to his side, and returned his silent grin. There was no need for words between them. They knew that, no matter how many rambling speeches they were forced to endure, no matter how many rules and prohibitions they had to face, they would do the job the way they knew it was meant to be done. It *was* personal, for both of them. Lopez was still out there.

Chapter Nineteen

DESPITE their cynicism, Bose and Barchiesi knew that their assignment to the Special Anti-Crack Unit provided them with additional leverage in their pursuit of Rock Solid. Not only were they seen as members of an elite and highly regarded force with increased resources and prestige, but their schedules were more flexible and they were now able to travel freely as a team throughout the city, wherever they believed the interests of the unit would be served. East Eleventh Street was one of their earliest calls. There was no reason to suspect that, as canny businessmen, the organization would not involve itself in this new drug phenomenon. And if not, what the hell. Junk was junk, slime was slime. The further up the Narcotics ladder they were able to climb, the better chance they had of nailing Lopez.

In late May 1986, an incident occurred that cemented their reputations with their new commander in Anti-Crack, Deputy Inspector Martin O'Boyle. The newly formed unit was under the microscope of voracious press coverage, scrutinized by a wary police bureaucracy and eagerly watched by a beleaguered citizenry hungry for news of some small victory in the war against drugs. They needed something significant to appease the media and soothe the anxious politicians.

It came unexpectedly, by way of a late-thirties Hispanic female named Lily Santana. She showed up at the Twenty-third Precinct on 102nd Street between Third and Lexington avenues one afternoon looking puffy and wasted. Her long black hair was matted; her dark brown eyes partially hidden behind chalky layers of inexpertly applied pancake makeup designed to hide her bruises. There were deep purple welts on her upper arms and that portion of her chest that could be seen. She had been crying.

Lily wanted to report her old man for selling dope, she told them. She related that her common-law husband, Eduardo Santana, dealt crack cocaine out of an apartment in Spanish Harlem with a Dominican woman named Amanda Savinon. Without actually coming right out and saying it, she implied that her old man and Amanda were more than just drug partners. Lily could take getting the shit beaten out of her every now and then, but she drew the line at infidelity. She wanted that motherfucker behind bars where he belonged.

Bose and Barchiesi listened to her account with mounting interest. Particularly intriguing was her assertion that the operation distributed thousands of pre-packaged vials of crack at a time, that every vial and every rock was uniform in size and shape, and that they were capable of filling an order for thousands of vials in a matter of days. If that was true, it was something never before seen in the city of New York. Up to now, crack production had been strictly a small-time enterprise. Local dealers would cook up a batch until it became hard, then break it up into smaller chunks, or "rocks," which they painstakingly measured into vials as evenly as possible. There was no such thing as uniformity. Certainly nobody had the wherewithal to turn out more than a few hundred vials a week. What Lily was describing was an organization capable of mass production, and there was no question in their minds that Lily was telling them the truth. She knew too many facts, was willing to name names and implicate too many people for her story to be a fabrication.

Using Lily as a contact, Bob sent Undercover Officer Elsa Gonzales to an apartment at 172nd Street and Amsterdam Avenue, where she purchased five hundred vials of crack. The price was right; five dollars a vial, half of what they had been paying on the street. More importantly, Lily Santana's information was right on the money. Every cube of crack in every vial was uniform, there was no doubt each had been stamped out by a press. They were mechanized and they dealt in quantities that allowed them to sell in volume discounts. This was no mom-and-pop operation.

Several days later Elsa made a second buy of twelve hundred vials at the same location, at which time she informed the dealer Guzman that she would need another five thousand. It was an enormous amount, vastly beyond any purchase of its kind that had ever been made by New York police, but Guzman calmly assured them it could be handled. The merchandise would be ready in two days, he told them. His people would meet them at a place of their choice to complete the transaction. What he did not know was that a special task force of Narcotics agents would be waiting there to arrest them.

Barchiesi settled on a location at 166th Street and Broadway, across the street from Columbia-Presbyterian Hospital, for the meet and the arrest. It was an ideal site, hemmed in on both sides by tall apartment buildings and easily accessed from either end by police vehicles. The hospital parking lot was rimmed with a high barbed-wire fence, inside of which they could place a surveillance van and be right on top of things. There was good visibility from almost anywhere on the sidewalk, and an ornate subway entrance across the street from the hospital afforded concealment for plain-clothes officers.

The Drug Enforcement Agency (DEA) offered to provide the twenty-five thousand dollars needed to conduct the buy but, as supervisor in charge, Bob Barchiesi refused, preferring to keep it an NYPD operation from start to finish with the DEA acting in a backup capacity. Frank Bose constructed a flash bankroll out of stacked newspapers and glued it inside an old attaché case with real hundred-dollar bills pasted on top. It looked real as hell.

The plan was set. Vans, radio cars, and backup units would converge on the area from opposite ends and close off the block as soon as the signal was given that the buy had gone down. Special officers dressed as doctors, orderlies, and vagrants would spring into action and surround the suspects' vehicle before they could drive it away. A backup team of DEA agents waited below on the subway steps, ready to move out onto the sidewalk at Bob's order. Everybody was ready, everybody was anxious. If Guzman and his people were dumb enough to show up with five thousand vials of crack that day, they were as good as busted. It was practically foolproof.

The suspect car arrived on schedule and Undercover Officer Elsa Gonzales approached the vehicle on foot. She paused for a moment in conversation, and exchanged the attaché case for a small bundle. Casually, she removed her eyeglasses to signal the nearest surveillance van that the buy was going down. The van was then supposed to radio Bob Barchiesi that the signal had been received, alerting him to instruct all backup units to close both ends of the street. Before he had a chance, DEA agents, misinterpreting her signal, charged out of the subway onto the sidewalk.

"*Oh fuck!*" Bob watched disbelievingly as the suspect car screeched away from the curb and sped up Broadway. Frank slammed the Chevy into gear and took up pursuit, narrowly avoiding the DEA agents who stood in the street, watching the crack dealers depart through the crush of traffic. With one hand on the steering wheel and the other on the horn, Frank muscled the Chevy between tightly packed lanes of sluggish vehicles while Bob screamed out the side window, warning anyone within earshot to get the fuck out of the way. Vials of crack spewed from the window of the escaping automobile and scattered on the pavement below.

The suspect vehicle careened in and out of view, gone for moments in the scramble of rush-hour trucks and autos, reappearing for tantalizing seconds in the spaces between bumpers and fenders only to be lost again behind a wall of traffic. They came to a congested intersection and Frank drove through the signal light with his horn blaring. Up ahead Lieutenant John Fahey's vehicle had taken up the chase and almost caught up with the fleeing drug dealers. Bob was leaning halfway out the window on the passenger's side, screaming at the top of his lungs. The Chevy rattled and wheezed like an old asthmatic amid the chorus of screeching brakes and squealing tires.

Suddenly the crush of vehicles parted and they were on top of the drug dealers, who had become trapped behind a wall of stalled vehicles. Bob and Frank were out on the street instantly, guns drawn, shouting at the suspects inside to get out with their hands up. Frank leaped onto the trunk of their car and trained his revolver on the street behind while Bob and other converging officers yanked Guzman, Savinon, and a second female out onto the pavement. They surrendered meekly.

It was one of the biggest crack busts ever; everybody was happy. Crack was now big business, and the Special Anti-Crack Unit had proved itself to be an effective arm of drug enforcement. The press and politicians were satisfied for the time being, and Deputy Inspector Martin O'Boyle was firmly in Bose and Barchiesi's corner. It was the juice they needed to continue their quest of Alejandro Lopez.

As for Lily Santana, she showed up from time to time at the Twenty-third Precinct after that, usually with her three small children and a hard luck story. She had no work and no means of support, she told them. They had no place to live, there was no food for the children, her mother was heavy into booze and drugs. Bob and Frank helped her out with a few bucks of their own whenever they could, but the most they could get the department to spring for was a couple of nights' shelter in a seedy welfare hotel.

There was a drug rehabilitation center downtown run by a

woman Bob had gotten to know back in Pressure Point. He and Frank pursuaded her to take the whole family in and try to get Lily and her mother back into shape. The kids would be taken care of, she reassured them. They would have a chance to get their lives back together if they kept their noses clean and showed a willing attitude. It didn't last long.

They received a telephone call from the rehab telling them that the grandmother was drunk and causing trouble, so they had to drive downtown in the middle of the night, remove the entire family, and take them to the homeless shelter at Broadway and Church Street. It hurt. Bob and Frank knew that the shelter was a garbage dump where the refuse of humanity huddled in dormitories waiting to die. They watched Lily's sobbing children at the windows of the shelter as they drove away, and knew that they could do no more. The family was in the system, being disposed of. Maybe some of them would survive.

"I wanted to cry," Frank remembered, "and I know Bobby did, too. It felt like we were betraying those children. I had a daughter practically the same age as that little girl with her face pressed against the window and the tears streaming down her cheeks. God, it really ripped us up inside."

Their car was crawling with lice from the children's hair and clothes. They drove to Beekman Downtown Hospital, got themselves scrubbed with medicinal soap and had the car de-loused, then returned to the precinct and spent the rest of the night drinking strong, black coffee. Neither of them felt much like talking.

Chapter Twenty

"All of a sudden things started falling into place, one thing after another like a road map telling us where to go. There's no way it could have been just coincidence. As crazy as it sounds, we have to believe it was some sort of divine intervention."

—FRANK BOSE

ON October 23, 1986, Blondie and Juahito failed to appear in court for sentencing. An outraged Judge Leslie Crocker Snyder ordered the district attorney to initiate a check for their whereabouts, and unable to locate them, reinstated the original charges against both. If and when they were captured they would automatically be convicted of Criminal Possession of Narcotics in the First Degree and face fifteen years to life in prison.

Judge Snyder commented that the disappearance of Blondie and Juahito, while it posed an unhappy legal circumstance, had a bright side for the people of New York. Pony-Pak had disappeared from 507 East Eleventh Street with them, she noted from the bench with some satisfaction. It was a long way from ridding the area of drugs altogether, but it was one less brand of poison to contaminate the streets of Alphabet City.

Despite the apparent setback, Bose and Barchiesi stepped up operations against the drug merchants in The Rock with the increased clout that membership in the elite Anti-Crack unit afforded them. As a supervisor, Bob Barchiesi could now send undercovers into the area to make cocaine buys and extract information. Now the odds were even. Spanish undercovers, black undercovers, undercovers with purple hair and earrings converged on 507 and scooped up unwary drug dealers. The department's most up-to-date surveillance equipment was employed to monitor criminal activities in and around the building and, for the first time, it began to look like a noose was being drawn around Alejandro Lopez's Eleventh Street fortress. Then Pony-Pak reared its head once again.

Undercover operatives began to return with packets bearing the all-too-familiar black stallion imprint, but as well as being wrapped in pyramid papers, Pony-Pak cocaine was being heat-sealed in colored plastic bags. Not only had Blondie and Juahito found a way to ship their product back to the same old stand, but they had upgraded their packaging. Bob and Frank were pissed off, at the runaway pair and at the system that released them in the first place.

"There are two kinds of people in this world," Frank Bose reflected. "People who are basically decent and the ones who set out to take advantage of them. Judge Snyder is a tough, smart jurist but she's basically decent. Blondie and Juahito asked her for compassion, and when she showed it, they kicked her in the teeth. That's the way scumbags like them beat the system all the time. They know that good people can't find it in their hearts to believe how rotten they really are."

Bose and Barchiesi discussed countless strategies for apprehending Blondie and Juahito. Most of their off-duty deliberations took place in a Manhattan restaurant called The Wicked Wolf, which they found by accident one evening after work and returned to on a regular basis, despite the fact that they could never agree on its precise location and bickered like an old married couple over the best way of getting there. "We could track Lopez all over the country but we couldn't find The Wicked Wolf half the time," Bob Barchiesi laughed. "After a while it got to be kind of a challenge."

One of the strategies that seemed to make the most sense was called "buying up": purchasing greater and greater quantities of Pony-Pak from higher and higher level dealers, until Blondie and Juahito could no longer trust their underlings to handle the transactions. Up to now, undercover police had asked only for cocaine and settled for what they got. From here on in they would ask specifically for Pony-Pak, and increase the amounts they bought from day to day until the fugitives were lured out of hiding by the promise of greater and greater profits.

The plan was intended to capitalize on Blondie and Juahito's greed, as well as the hatred most street dealers felt for Blondie, and using that to extract information about her. It was unlike anything Bose and Barchiesi had ever experienced before. Even among rival drug dealers there is an unwritten code stipulating that disputes and age-old animosities are to be settled among themselves, however bloodily, and the surest way to commit suicide on the streets is to become known as an informer. Still they turned over on Blondie, and nobody seemed concerned that they would be held accountable by someone higher up. Blondie had screwed them all at one time or another and it was payback time.

There were problems, and most of them had to do with the structure of The Rock itself. Both the Rock Solid and Pony-Pak organizations had insulated themselves behind its grimy walls. Intently handling all transactions from inside, they exchanged cocaine for money through barred openings in the walls or dropped quantities from upper story windows while the purchasers waited on the sidewalk below. The plan took into account the unwillingness of law enforcement agencies to enter buildings, and their obsessive fear of violating citizens' rights. "We will sell you any quantity you want, but on our terms," the drug merchants would tell prospective customers. "If you want our product, you will wait outside on the street."

"That was what separated these people from your normal drug dealers," Frank Bose related. "Normally, the drug dealer is the easiest criminal in the world to catch because he has to deal out in the open where his customers can see him. No matter how smart or sophisticated drug dealers may be, they have to do two basic things in order to succeed. First they have to handle the drugs, and second they have to handle the money. Catching them is simply a matter of executing what we call 'Hansel and Gretel' police work: following the money and drug trail backward until we can occupy the exact moment in time and space when they're handling one or the other."

By December of 1986 they had significantly reduced the drug traffic at 507 East Eleventh Street and obtained a lot of information about both the Rock Solid and Pony-Pak operations, but Blondie and Juahito remained at large, and Alejandro Lopez was as mysterious and elusive a figure as ever. By now both Bose and Barchiesi had reached the conclusion that since street sources were willing to furnish them with an abundance of evidence against Blondie, they would follow the Pony-Pak trail in the hope that Lopez might surface somewhere along the way with his hands on the drugs or in the till. The strategy was sound, but neither of them had dared hope for what was to come next.

On December 22, Bose and Barchiesi drove home from a

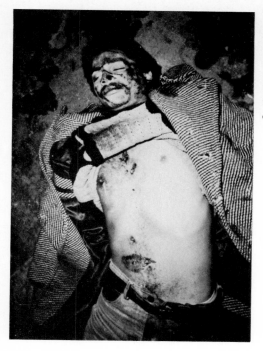

Body of Ralph Rodriguez, found on Halsey Street in Brooklyn. Rodriguez first warned Bose and Barchiesi that Tito had threatened to kill their children. (*Frank Bose*)

Members of Operation Pressure Point team: (left to right) Dorian Irizarry, Frank Bose, Bob Barchiesi, Billy Fitzpatrick, and Mike Rodriguez. (*New York Daily News*)

Mug shot of Alejandro Lopez taken after a 1983 arrest. (*Frank Bose*)

Lopez's fifth-floor loft in TriBeCa, where the cocaine was cut and bagged. (*Frank Bose*)

The Rock—Alejandro Lopez's cocaine citadel at 507 East Eleventh Street in Alphabet City. (*Frank Bose*)

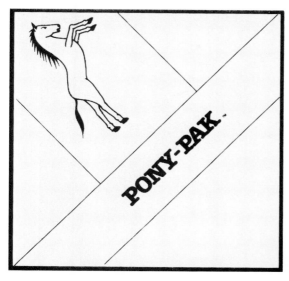

Pyramid paper wrapping for "Pony-Pak" brand cocaine.

Sergeant Bob Barchiesi and Police Officer Frank Bose in front of apartment #6 on 507 East Eleventh Street. (*New York Newsday*)

Raphael Martinez (Juahito) and Irma Garcia (Blondie) after their arrest in the Fort Lee Holiday Inn. (*The Bergen Record*)

The seizure made in Blondie's and Juahito's Fort Lee Holiday Inn bust included $424,000, one machine gun, three handguns, and approximately five pounds of cocaine. From left: Jerry Speziale, Frank Bose, Fort Lee PD Lieutenant James Matt, Bob Barchiesi, NYPD Deputy Inspector Martin O'Boyle, and Bergen County Prosecutor John McClure. (*The Bergen Record*)

Bose and Barchiesi posted Lopez's mug shot on the bulletin board at the Anti-Crack office, and used it as a dart board. (*Frank Bose*)

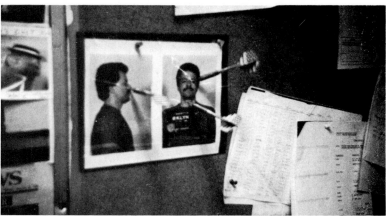

Lopez kept detailed daily transaction records for his Rock empire, which averaged $12 million a year. This record, taken in the Edgewater raid, and which Frank and Bob referred to as the Piano Roll, showed a gross take of about $1.5 million over two months. When they went back and compared their activities and reports to the dates on the roll, they found Lopez's take was down almost 50 percent from normal. This was the period directly following his threats against their children, when they had stepped up all their efforts against The Rock. Lopez, who normally ran three shifts a day of street dealers, had been forced to reduce to two. (*Terry McCabe*)

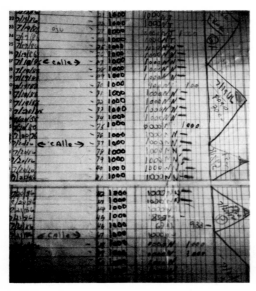

The Piano Roll is almost twenty feet long. (*Terry McCabe*)

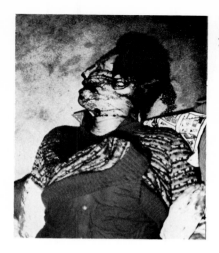

The beaten, mutilated body of John Lunievicz, murdered at The Rock. (*Frank Bose*)

A section of Alejandro Lopez's fortress in Aguadilla, Puerto Rico. Note pit bull enclosures in foreground. (*Frank Bose*)

Alejandro Lopez at the time of his extradition from Puerto Rico. (*Frank Bose*)

Judge Leslie Crocker Snyder (*Alex Calabrese*)

Assistant District Attorney Patrick Conlon (*Jan Press / Photo Media*)

Christmas party at The Castle Harbor, a watering hole in the East Bronx that boasts a downstairs rathskeller large enough to hold most Metropolitan Police functions, from graduation celebrations to award ceremonies to retirement dinners. Shortly before midnight they were headed eastbound on the Cross-Bronx Expressway in Bob's new Yugo sedan when Bob looked out the window on the driver's side and saw something that shot him bolt upright in his seat.

"Holy shit, do you see what I see?" he gasped at Frank.

Bose turned and immediately spotted a rental Chevrolet in the far left-hand lane with a man they both recognized as Juahito's nephew, Willie Gonzales, in the passenger's seat. Sitting beside him on the driver's side, Juahito gripped the steering wheel and squinted through the Chevy's windshield.

"Try to imagine what we felt at that moment," Frank reflected. "I mean, what do you think the chances of something like that happening are, one in eleven million? Of all the places in this world that asshole might have been, he ends up right next to us on the Cross-Bronx Expressway. I don't think either of us had ever been on that road more than a half dozen times before in our lives, and there he is—so close we can practically reach out and touch him. Don't try to tell me that's just a coincidence."

Willie leaned halfway out of the Chevy and signaled with his arm as Juahito veered in front of the Yugo and sped on ahead of them toward the George Washington Bridge. *"Catch that motherfucker!"* Frank screamed at Bob as the Chevy pulled away.

"What the fuck do you think I'm *trying* to do?" Bob howled back, pressing the Yugo's accelerator all the way to the floor as the distance between vehicles slowly widened. The Yugo was a cheap, serviceable car but it wasn't built for high-speed pursuit, especially with more than five hundred pounds sitting in the front seat. Frank and Bob shouted impotently at the departing Chevy, rocking back and forth in the seat, trying to impart some forward thrust to the sputtering Yugo. Their spirits rose as they picked up speed downhill, then sank as they slowed again to a crawl at every uphill incline. The Chevy drew farther and farther ahead.

"I gotta tell you that the car would've done fifty without Frank in the front seat," Bob joked. "With him there, I was lucky to squeeze thirty out of that piece of shit."

Frank nodded, suppressing a grin. He was the one who had talked Bob into buying the Yugo in the first place. They had both attended the New York Automobile Show a few months earlier, and Frank had expressed a real interest in the car. "I was thinking of buying it, but Bobby showed up a couple of days later with a brand new one, so I figured I'd wait and see how he did with his," he admits, laughing. "Needless to say, I didn't buy a Yugo."

The plan was to follow the Chevy until it led them to Blondie, but their pursuit of Willie and Juahito was a foregone mismatch. Despite their straining, body English, and shouted curses, they could not squeeze an extra mile per hour out of the underpowered Yugo. Yard by painful yard, they watched Willie and Juahito pull further away until they disappeared into the blackness ahead. The best they could do was manage to record the Chevy's license-plate number for later investigation.

In the following days, Bob ordered Jerry Speziale to run the license-plate number through the computer at the Anti-Crack Unit. Jerry hadn't been trained to operate the computer, but Frank had gotten him interested a couple of months earlier and Jerry had taken to it like a duck to water. Whenever he had any spare time you could find him at the computer working out programs of his own, and he soon became the unit's resident expert. He had a real knack for it, and the tenacity to track any item through to its conclusion no matter how long it took. He took the information on the Chevy that Frank and Bob had given him as a personal challenge and programmed it every way the machine was designed to operate, plus a few he had thought up by himself.

It paid off. Jerry came up with information that the white Cheverolet Caprice, New York plate number 504 ZTT, was registered to Avis car rental and had been leased by Willie Gonzales with his own credit card from their Kennedy Airport office a few days earlier. Jerry ran the credit-card number in the computer. Then, carefully cross-checking computer records, he found out that both Blondie and Juahito were credit-card holders as well. Finally, Jerry's dogged research provided them with locations in Manhattan, the Bronx, and Queens where the fugitives or their associates might be found.

The Queens address, 133-59 244th Street, Rosedale, was verified by another mystifying coincidence. A Manhattan District Attorney who had heard about their inquiries telephoned to inform them that he knew of an Emergency Services sergeant who had owned a home in Rosedale but was forced to sell it a few months earlier. The sergeant's neighbors raised all kinds of hell day and night, engaging in noisy rituals and screaming confrontations. He had gone so far as to call the police on several occasions, but their behavior had only become worse as time went by. Finally he felt he had no choice but to move away and leave the neighborhood to the not-so-tender mercies of the raucous neighbors, Irma Garcia and Raphael Martinez.

On January 3, Frank, Bob, Louie Torrellas, Jerry Speziale, Hector Ocasio, and Lieutenant John Fahey drove out to Queens in three separate vehicles to investigate the location. They arrived at the Rosedale house in the early afternoon and observed several expensive cars parked in the driveway, including a Rolls-Royce Silver Cloud III sedan and a Corvette sportscar. One of the cars, a white Cheverolet almost identical to the one Frank and Bob had encountered on the Cross-Bronx Expressway, had been rented from the same Avis office at Kennedy Airport.

A drive-by of the premises left no doubt in their minds that they had the right place. The lawn was a jumble of scattered junk and oddly matched artifacts, most of which they recognized as having come from Blondie and Juahito's Eleventh Street apartment: furniture, rugs, and broken pieces of pottery; gaudily painted religious statuary propped incongruously next to a plaster likeness of Elvis Presley. They could clearly see the pinpoint red light of a television surveillance camera pointing back at them in the center of the convex-glass front window.

The police vehicles were parked out of sight and after a walk-by surveillance of the house by Louie Torrellas and Hector Ocasio, Frank and Bob questioned a neighbor and verified that Blondie and Juahito were indeed the current occupants of 133-59 244th Street. Now they had sufficient corroboration to seek a search warrant for the location, and a special procedure for obtaining warrants by telephone had been recently initiated. Bob persuaded Lieutenant Fahey that unless they were able to enter the house that day they would lose the element of surprise, and Frank placed several calls to New York, eventually obtaining authorization from Assistant District Attorney David Molton for the officers to enter the house without announcing themselves and search the entire premises for drugs, weapons, and contraband. Molton, along with ADA Patrick Conlon, was one of the few people Frank and Bob had encountered in the DA's department who would take the bull by the horns and attempt to solve problems rather than ignore them or simply explain them away. He was one of the most aggressive, positive-thinking members of the District Attorney's staff, a go-getter in the courtroom who was respected by cops as a prosecutor with intelligence, integrity, and guts.

Hector Ocasio and Louie Torrellas were sent to cover the back while the remainder of the team hit the house from the front. Jerry Speziale forced the front door open with a pinch bar while Frank held his hand over the eye of the surveillance camera and everyone spilled inside with their weapons drawn, screaming at the tops of their lungs.

Bob and Lieutenant Fahey broke left off the main foyer, and Frank broke right with Jerry Speziale. There was activity in the rear, noise and movement coming from the kitchen in the back. Instinctively Frank came in low with his service revolver riveted before him, his heart pounding louder with every tentative step. Suddenly the sensors in his brain came alive with terrifying movement and a swell of inhuman caterwauling. He froze in his tracks and felt his finger tighten on the trigger as the image before him lashed out in his direction; then he slowly decompressed as the sensors placed the movement and sound in context. Before him, surrounded by a confusion of loose feathers and droppings, an angry, squawking chicken struggled to free itself from the leg of the kitchen table where it was bound.

At the same time, Bob was proceeding cautiously toward the stairwell of the house when a hulking apparition dropped in front of him and brushed his face. He recoiled, an involuntary shout came hoarsely from the depths of his tightening chest as he focused his eyes across his trembling gunsights at the specter dangling before him: a moth-eaten, life-size gorilla costume hung from the ceiling at the stairway entrance.

The tension was broken. "I got a gorilla suit here," Bob chuckled to Frank. "How about you?"

"A fucking chicken with a hole almost in it," Frank shot back, and they both doubled up laughing.

When their hearts began beating normally again, they completed the sweep of the house and found it uninhabited. Behind the house, near an above-ground swimming pool, Frank found a pole imbedded in the ground that was capped with a sloping wooden roof to form a kind of shrine. Inside was a conglomeration of severed chicken's feet, feathers, loose tobacco, coins, and shreds of torn paper covered with scrawls and dried blood. "What the hell do you make of all this?" he asked Bob.

"Looks like chicken shit to me," Barchiesi answered.

Chapter Twenty-one

JOSE Cuadrato was happy to see Jerry Bartone on East Eleventh Street. Jerry bought Pony-Pak in large quantities—fifty to one hundred glassines a buy—and he didn't ask a lot of questions. Jose, who was known as "Joey," managed Pony-Pak operations out of Blondie and Juahito's old apartment at 507 East Eleventh, supplying street dealers from his stash inside, and dropping larger amounts from the window to customers who waited below on the sidewalk. If the buy was for more product than he could handle, he would share some or all of the action with Carlos Zapata, called "Pito," who operated out of number 519 next door. Together they could supply any quantity Jerry wanted, and Jerry wanted more and more as time went on. The transactions got far too large for the street dealers to handle, so Joey and Pito stepped right in and took over. Neither of them had any idea that Jerry Bartone was really Jerry Speziale, an undercover cop.

As part of a multipronged attack strategy, Speziale and other undercovers "bought up" Pony-Pak from Joey and Pito inside, while Bose and Barchiesi and the Rock Solid team continued to arrest and "turn" street dealers outside in an effort to obtain more information about Blondie and Juahito. During the summer of 1986, they learned that the fugitive pair visited the area often, mostly in disguise, and that they had walked East Eleventh Street openly the previous Halloween dressed in gorilla suits.

The final prong of the attack strategy came on January 27, when teams of Narcotics officers swooped down on at 507 and 519 East Eleventh Street, executing simultaneous warrants on Joey's and Pito's apartments. A team headed by Bob Barchiesi entered 507 and took down the door to apartment 6 with a battering ram, only to be confronted by a snarling pit bull that had to be subdued by Emergency Services. Joey Cuadrato was arrested and a small quantity of Pony-Pak cocaine was confiscated, along with a handgun and silencer. At the same time Frank Bose's team entered apartment 2-S at number 519 and arrested Pito Zapata, who supplied them with information that Blondie and Juahito were staying somewhere in the Bronx with Willie Gonzales.

The teams then jointly executed a third warrant at Holland Avenue in the Bronx, the address Jerry Speziale had provided through his credit-card checks on the computer. Willie Gonzales was out, but his wife allowed the officers to enter the apartment and search the premises while they waited for him to return. They found Blondie and Juahito's clothing and effects in a rear bedroom, as well as two cartons containing several hundred thousand recently printed Pony-Pak wrappers. There was no doubt they were in right place.

Willie returned an hour later and was met inside the front door by the officers. Frank Bose ushered him into an adjoining room and began to question him in the presence of Lieutenants John Fahey and Jerry Robbins. "Okay scumbag, you're going to jail for harboring a couple of fugitives. Tell us where they are and maybe I won't haul your ass in," Frank told him. "I don't really care about you, Willie. You've got a wife and family, even a job, and I really don't want to have to lock you up, but if you don't give me what I want, I'll put you in jail for anything I can, and see to it that you stay there for as long as the law allows."

"I wanta help you guys out but I can't be a rat, you know that," Willie protested. "What if she finds out it was me who told you?"

"I don't know what you owe these people," Frank said. "But whatever it is, I hope it's worth your freedom, because you're going away, sure as shit."

Willie gulped hard and stared straight ahead.

Outside the room, Bob Barchiesi continued searching the small apartment. He spotted a telephone number with a 201 area code written on the kitchen wall and dialed it on a hunch. "*Fort Lee Car Service,*" the reply crackled over the receiver. Bob hung up and went into the next room, where Frank was taking a break from Willie's interrogation. "How's it going?" he asked.

Frank shrugged. "I dunno, I don't think we're going to flip this guy. I think he's scared shitless of what Blondie might do to him if he opens his mouth."

"Let me try something . . ." Bob entered the room where Lieutenants Fahey and Robbins unsuccessfully continued to question Willie. "How's it going, Willie?" he asked.

Gonzales eyed him suspiciously.

"Lemme tell you something," Bob went on. "We already know a lot more than you think we know. All we want from you is corroborating information, and if we catch you in a lie we're going to nail your ass to the fucking wall."

Willie's Adam's apple trembled.

". . . Now I'm gonna tell you this once and you're gonna tell me what I want to hear or you're history, Willie. We already know Blondie and Juahito are in Fort Lee, all we want from you is the address."

The bluff worked. Willie's shoulders slumped and he let out a low moan. "They're in the Fort Lee Holiday Inn, man," he blurted. "They rented a couple of rooms there." The revelation seemed to embolden him, and he asked if he might be permitted to keep the property that Juahito had left in his apartment. Blondie owed him money and had run up enormous charges on his credit cards, he asserted. Even the rooms in the Fort Lee Holiday Inn had been charged to him. It did not seem to occur to him that, though he stood little chance of recovering his money before, he stood none at all if Blondie and Juahito were captured. Like Frank Bose says, you don't have to be an Einstein to be a drug dealer.

"Try and figure it," Bob Barchiesi reflected. "I don't know what made me pick up the telephone and call that number written on the wall, I just did it. It was the way things were starting to happen for us now. You can call it dumb luck, or coincidence, or whatever the hell you want to call it. We have to think it was a lot more than that."

John Fahey had been in Narcotics long enough to know that going to Fort Lee in pursuit of the fugitives was bound to cause jurisdictional problems, and the last thing the NYPD wanted was problems. Jerry Robbins was more enthusiastic about the idea but was having trouble convincing his fellow lieutenant. Finally Bob interrupted their deliberations:

"So we can't go?" he asked, checking his watch. "Okay then, we're off duty here, right?"

Fahey and Robbins eyed him quizzically.

"I mean, if we can't go out there on the job, we're going out there off duty," Bob elaborated. "No big deal. We're not going out there kicking down any doors or anything like that. We'll just notify the New Jersey State Troopers and let them take the collar, but we're taking these fucks one way or the other." He cast a sidelong glance at Frank, who was nodding enthusiastically.

Lieutenant Fahey blanched. "Any way you can get ahold of

Judge Snyder and ascertain their status as fugitives?" he asked tentatively.

"I can give it a try." Frank shrugged. After several attempts, he was able to reach Judge Snyder, and her reaffirmation that the fugitives were being sought by the court seemed to satisfy the lieutenant. Fahey knew a cop named Jimmy Flynn in Bergen County Narcotics whom he wanted in on the operation, so they called and set up a meeting at the Port Authority Police building on the Jersey side of the George Washington Bridge.

Later that evening Detective Supervisor Jimmy Flynn arrived at the meeting point accompanied by a half dozen members of the Bergen County Narcotics Task Force; guys who looked like junior high school students to Frank and Bob, and who they later learned had little or no police experience. The Fort Lee Police Department would have to be included in the operation, Flynn told them. It was a tricky jurisdictional issue, and they didn't want to step on anyone's toes.

Bose and Barchiesi, along with lieutenants Fahey and Robbins, Officers Jerry Speziale and Joe Alvarez, and the Bergen County Narcotics Task Force, drove to the Fort Lee Police headquarters and were met there by Lieutenant James Matt, head of Fort Lee Narcotics, a sharp, knowledgeable, veteran police officer who took over the operation and politely relegated the Bergen County Narcotics whiz kids to backup duties. By ten P.M. the entire assault team was assembled, everyone had been given their assignments, and they were ready to move in on Blondie and Juahito.

Frank and Bob had advised Lieutenant Matt that he would probably recover upwards of two kilos of cocaine in the raid, and that they could expect to find automatic weapons on the premises. When they related that, one of the Fort Lee detectives went to a metal cabinet, unlatched a two-dollar padlock and retrieved a fully automatic 9mm machine gun. "He didn't even have to sign for it," Frank Bose related, shaking his head in amazement. "If that had been the NYPD, we'd need ten Emergency Services officers, a captain, a DI, and a chief to get the cabinet open. It'd take an act of Congress to get the weapon out of the building."

It was almost midnight on January 27, 1987 when they arrived at the Holiday Inn, and, snowing heavily. Icy pellets driven by the wind obscured their vision and stuck tenaciously to the frigid macadam surface of the parking lot as they waited for Lieutenant Matt to return from inside, where he had gone to inform the management of the impending raid. Bob had suggested using pneumatic battering rams but Matt objected. He returned shortly with several pass cards and the news that there were three rooms registered under the name Gonzales. Three teams would be organized, one team for each room, and they would let themselves in quietly and with a minimum of fanfare.

Frank was part of a three-man team that included one uniformed officer and a Narcotics officer, both armed with shotguns. They arrived at their designated room on the second floor, and Frank drew his service revolver while one of the officers inserted the pass card and the door sprung open. *"Police, freeze!"* Frank shouted as they scrambled into the darkened bedroom and leveled their weapons at the faint outlines of a man and woman cowering against the wooden headboard of the bed. Beyond the pair's muffled whimpers, the only sounds in the room were the crack of shotgun rounds being racked into their chambers.

"Oh, shit . . ." Frank backed toward the door when he realized that the naked couple they had caught in the middle of their lovemaking was clearly not Blondie and Juahito. He signaled for the others to depart and nodded embarrassedly. "Sorry about that," he muttered. "Just pretend we weren't here."

"I'm gonna sue you!" the naked man howled.

"I don't blame you," Frank said, backing out the door.

Upstairs they joined the other team as they prepared to enter a suite of side-by-side rooms on the twelfth floor. Lieutenant Matt tried the pass card in the door but it remained firmly shut. Suddenly in a flash of misplaced inspiration, one of the Bergen County Narcotics officers took it on himself to knock on one of the doors and announce himself as room service. "This was not what you'd call a real smart move," Bob Barchiesi remembered wryly. "Inside we could hear showers going on, toilets flushing, windows being opened. These people were real scumbags but they weren't completely stupid. They knew they didn't order anything from room service and they were getting rid of everything they could before we got inside."

Bob banged on the door to the adjacent room. "Police!" he screamed. "Open up before we break it down." To everyone's surprise, Irma Garcia's son hesitantly opened the door, allowing them to stream inside, where Bob discovered a door to the adjoining room and kicked it open. Next door Blondie sat on the side of the bed in a wrinkled nightgown, strangely shrunken, her ashen face etched with fear. She rolled forward onto the floor, groaning, certain that in the next moment police bullets would rip through her body.

Blondie was cuffed as she lay on the floor, and lifted to a standing position. Her puffed, chalky face was drained of color and her shoulders shook involuntarily. She registered shock when she saw Frank Bose and Bob Barchiesi standing among the arresting officers. "I know you hate me, but what I did, I did for my kids," she muttered to them.

Frank glanced around the small room, cluttered with weapons and drug paraphernalia. "So this is all in the name of motherhood, huh?" He turned his back on her disgustedly.

Juahito squatted on a sofa with his back to the open window. His face remained fixed in an imbecilic grin as he casually tossed handfuls of empty glassines over his shoulder, out into the swirl of wind and snow. "If he'd had a brain in his head, he would have been tossing the white powder out instead of the glassines," Bob remembered. "There's no way we would have been able to recover any of it in all that snow outside. But like I said, these people are not rocket scientists."

Both suspects were quickly cuffed and an initial search of the room uncovered an Interdynamic Tech 9mm machine gun, a .38 caliber revolver, a .357 magnum and thirty rounds of live ammunition, as well as a then undetermined quantity of bagged and unbagged cocaine. A plastic shopping bag on the floor near the bed was searched and found to contain almost ten thousand dollars. Satisfied that everything had been done, Frank and Bob decided to leave. They had gotten what they wanted and from there on in it would be New Jersey's show. They told Lieutenant Matt they would meet him back at Fort Lee headquarters. Before they left, Frank went to the room next door, called New York, and informed Judge Leslie Snyder of the arrests as she sat in night court session.

The prisoners were brought to Fort Lee headquarters where Frank and Bob were allowed to interrogate them. In characteristic fashion, Blondie immediately sought to place the blame on others, specifically Alejandro Lopez. "I don't know why you arrest me, a hardworking mother who's got nothing, when Tito Lopez has homes in Puerto Rico, airplanes to take him where he wants . . . The Man lives in luxury while you persecute me and my family."

"We'll be glad to take Tito," Bob volunteered. "Just tell us where we can find him."

Real fear crept into Blondie's eyes. She knew that a prison term was preferable to the fate that awaited her if she informed on Lopez.

A stunned Lieutenant Matt called Fort Lee headquarters from the Holiday Inn with the startling disclosure that they had recovered a total of $424,000 in cash hidden in garbage bags. The amount, far and away the largest money seizure ever made by the Fort Lee Police, had everyone gasping for breath. Not only did it propel the arrest of Blondie and Juahito into another realm of importance for them, but it destroyed forever Blondie's assertion that she was simply a poor, hardworking mother. Blondie was quick on her feet, if not credible. She told them the money belonged to Tito Lopez from sales of his Rock Solid cocaine and that she and Juahito had stolen it from his Ninth Street apartment.

Blondie's face remained a mask of hate and defiance as she and Juahito were led out of the interrogation room in handcuffs. Juahito seemed numb, not really comprehending what was happening, but he recognized Frank and Bob as he passed them and grinned broadly, waving his manacled wrists like a deranged butterfly to offer them a handshake. "Can you imagine that dumb fuck?" Frank wondered. "I mean, we just sent him away for what will probably be the rest of his life and he wants to make friends."

Despite the late hour, a press conference was scheduled for nine A.M. to include Bergen County Prosecutor John McClure, the Fort Lee Chief of Police, and the head of Bergen County Narcotics. As the ranking NYPD officer, Bob Barchiesi was asked to participate but knowing a little bit about New York Police politics, he phoned Deputy Inspector Martin O'Boyle in New York. "If I'd showed up on the morning news with my face plastered on the screen next to all that Jersey brass, they would've had my balls," Bob laughed.

O'Boyle put on his best suit and made it to Fort Lee in time for the televised press conference. Later that morning, news viewers throughout the metropolitan area watched as he and other law enforcement officials posed somber and dignified beside more than five pounds of high-grade cocaine, an impressive array of cocaine paraphernalia and weapons, and a display of currency totaling $424,000, while network voice-over announcers recounted details of the carefully planned raid on the Fort Lee Holiday Inn and the subsequent arrest of Irma Garcia and Raphael Martinez. Frank and Bob stood unobtrusively in the background, almost lost behind the file of ranking dignitaries.

Chapter Twenty-two

THE morning after the arrests of Blondie and Juahito, a resolute Tim Fleischer of Channel Seven Eyewitness News stood unflinchingly in the freezing winds that gusted through the parking lot of the Fort Lee Holiday Inn and began his televised report:

"The trail police officers had been following led here . . ." he pointed to the cream-colored structure looming behind him, ". . . where last night they burst into a room at the Holiday Inn. Inside they found Irma Garcia and Raphael Martinez, and all the appearances of a full-fledged drug operation." Recounting the amounts of drugs, weapons, and currency seized in the raid, Fleischer went on to credit Bose and Barchiesi for their role in the investigation and capture:

"Irma Garcia and Raphael Martinez had both been convicted on drug charges but fled before sentencing. For Sergeant Barchiesi and Officer Bose, that meant starting their investigation all over again to try to find the fugitives, who were bold enough to allegedly continue their drug operation after their flight from justice . . ."

Interviewed by Chris Borgen from CBS News, Frank and Bob briefly described their investigation and the scope of the cocaine organization still operating out of The Rock. "The cocaine, complete with its own brand name, is being sold in I LOVE NEW YORK shopping bags from a location on the Lower East Side," Borgen reported. "But the man reputed to be the ringleader of the operation is still at large."

The raid and the arrests of Blondie and Juahito were news. One by one, TV news crews lined up in the windswept parking lot to relate the details of the operation, and metropolitan newspapers gave it banner coverage. In the January 30 issue of *New York Newsday,* columnist Bob Drury reported the details leading up to Blondie and Juahito's arrest, including the account of Bob and Frank's incredible sighting of Martinez on the Cross-Bronx Expressway. "We've been trying to get these guys for over two years," Drury reported Frank Bose as saying. "Now, Operation Pony-Pak has ceased to exist."

"It was the first real publicity this case had received, and I'm not sure whether it helped us or hurt us," Bob related. "If it did anything at that point, I have to think it opened the eyes of a lot of people in the NYPD. I don't think they had any idea of the magnitude of the Rock Solid operation or the amount of drugs being sold out of 507 East Eleventh Street. I think the broadcasts might have served to get the information out to all five NYPD bureaus at once, and if that's true, then they accomplished a lot. Normally you can't get the Narcotics Division, Detective Division, and Patrol to share information or even talk to each other."

Frank Bose agreed, with qualifications. "Sure these people were making a fortune. They were millionaires but they thought like street urchins. I can't tell you how many times we were helped along during this investigation because they'd do something stupid like shoplift a two-dollar item from a store when they had thousands of dollars in their pockets, or drive an unregistered vehicle because they were too lazy or just too far removed from mainstream society to pay the ten bucks it would take to make it legal. Sitting in a cockroach-infested tenement or a luxury hotel, deep-down they're still street scum. Their money could buy them a lot of things but it couldn't buy them respectability. That comes from inside."

With Blondie and Juahito safely in custody, Bose and Barchiesi were free to concentrate almost exclusively on Alejandro Lopez. Seeking to duplicate their previous success with the computer, Jerry Speziale programmed Lopez's name into the memories of police computers throughout the tri-state area. New York and Connecticut returned negative results but, despite repeated efforts using a variety of codes, Jerry found the name blocked on New Jersey computers. Curious, he drove down to Trenton on his own time, hand-searched the Motor Vehicle records, and came up with a 1983 silver BMW registered to an Alejandro Lopez at 63 Edgewater Place, Edgewater, New Jersey.

It had to be the same Alejandro Lopez, especially since Frank Bose remembered seeing an insurance card for a silver BMW tacked to the bulletin board in the TriBeCa loft they had raided eighteen months earlier. "I know it sounds crazy, but this card stuck in my mind because the insurance agent who had written the policy on the car lived in the house directly across the street from me. Call it another coincidence . . ." Frank shrugged and smiled.

Frank, Bob, and Jerry Speziale drove out to Edgewater and spotted the silver BMW parked in the driveway of number 63, a gray, three-story clapboard house surrounded by a white picket fence in an unassuming middle-class neighborhood that overlooked the New Jersey Palisades and the Hudson River. If Lopez was there, and they could only assume he was, Frank and Bob would have to set up a surveillance operation and they knew it wouldn't be easy. Unlike the noisy, congested streets of lower Manhattan, the Edgewater neighborhood was quiet and free of traffic. Any permanent vehicle parked along the almost-empty curbs would be easily identified by street-knowledgeable drug dealers. Strangers would arouse immediate suspicion.

Bose and Barchiesi had been given unusual latitude to investigate Narcotics cases. As a result, a lot of the newer Narcotics officers were anxious to get on their team. George Sikoryak was one of them and he cornered Jerry Speziale shortly after their return from Edgewater.

"You're shitting me," he exclaimed when Jerry told him where they had been. "I got a friend who lives in Edgewater."

"Well, we're looking at number sixty-three," Jerry told him.

Sikoryak's jaw dropped. "My good friend lives across the street!"

Jerry was on the phone before George Sikoryak recovered from the shock, and within a few hours Bose and Barchiesi had secured the friend's permission to use her house as a surveillance location. "She was all for it," Frank remembered. "She was a college girl with a couple of roommates, and they were intrigued by the excitement of the thing. We went in there that night before they could change their minds, pulled into her garage, and I set up a complete electronics surveillance system; 35mm cameras and tripods, a portable videocassette player, monitors, the works. There was a bay window on the second floor that looked straight down on Lopez's front door, so we set everything up there and waited."

"The arrest of Blondie and Juahito really eased the way for us," Bob Barchiesi recollected. "The inspectors don't particularly want their guys nosing around over in Jersey, but the Pony-Pak bust had given us some credibility. They were more inclined to listen to us now, and to give us what we needed when we requested it. They even gave us a private cubicle of our own upstairs at the

Two-Three, so I guess you could say we were becoming the fair-haired boys of the unit."

On February 24, at 8:24 P.M., the surveillance cameras were running when three male Hispanics identified as Harry Banchs, Ricky Moreno, and Alejandro Lopez's brother, Eduardo, exited the house across the street and pulled out of the driveway in the silver BMW. Driving a private automobile, Bob Barchiesi took up mobile surveillance of the BMW, accompanied by Detectives Louis Torrellas and Hector Ocasio in a separate vehicle. Together they tracked the BMW across the George Washington Bridge to New York, where the subjects parked in front of a building at 3929 Carpenter Avenue in the Bronx. Two of the subjects entered the building, returned shortly carrying a white plastic shopping bag bearing the now familiar I LOVE NEW YORK logo, and got back into the BMW. They drove to the vicinity of Avenue A and St. Mark's Place, where Ricky Moreno, aka Javier Padillo-Sosa, left the car and continued on toward 507 East Eleventh Street.

"By now there was no doubt in our minds that they were transporting Rock Solid cocaine from the cutting-and-bagging location to the intermediate drops and then on to 507, but we weren't ready to make any arrests right then. The plan was to shadow these people and gather evidence against them while we were waiting for Lopez to show himself," Bob explained. "You have to understand how we felt at that point. Here we'd spent better than a year and a half tracking a guy we'd never even set eyes on, a guy we'd grown to hate, and all of a sudden it was starting to look like we were dead on track. We'd sit there and watch that house for hours on end, and every time a light would go on or off inside, our hearts would start beating faster."

"We were logging a lot of off-duty hours," Frank recalled. "Bob, Jerry, and I would hit the location on our way into work. I was driving a beat-up 1973 Volkswagen blue Bug, and Jerry had an orange one; of course Bob had the infamous Yugo. We'd just drive by, circle the block a few times to make sure nothing unusual was going down, then head on in to work through the tunnel. After work, Bob and I would be back there, every night, night after night. There was never any discussion about whether or not we'd go, whether or not there was anything else to do that night. Bob and I would just show up every night and wait for something to happen. Sometimes Jerry would be with us, but mostly it was just the two of us out there. Some nights we wouldn't even go home."

At 8:30 P.M. on February 26, while Bose and Barchiesi waited diagonally across the street in an unmarked police vehicle, a male Hispanic identified as J. D. Gordo, aka Aaron Davila, left the house at 63 Edgewater Place, carrying a full I LOVE NEW YORK shopping bag, got into a brown Cadillac with an expired registration sticker, and headed for the Lincoln Tunnel. Bob pulled the unmarked car carefully from the curb and followed at a close distance until Gordo arrived at East Ninth Street in Manhattan, where he circled the block several times, double-parked in front of a fire hydrant, and crossed the street on foot.

They were out of their own car in an instant, sprinting up five flights of stairs to the roof of the building across the street. Winded, they crouched in the darkness at the roof's edge while Frank focused the telephoto lens of his 35mm reflex camera on J. D. Gordo, whom he photographed exchanging the contents of the I LOVE NEW YORK shopping bag with another male Hispanic inside a basement apartment at 328½ East Ninth. Through the long lens, Frank clearly saw him remove two transparent plastic bags filled with smaller glassines of cocaine and place them beneath his tan field jacket before handing the remainder to the second man and leaving the building.

They descended the staircase to the street and followed him as he walked up Ninth Street. He turned northbound on First Avenue and continued two blocks uptown to Eleventh Street, where he entered Alejandro Lopez's citadel at number 507, carrying his cargo of Rock Solid cocaine.

"I've gotta tell you that we gave some serious thought to taking him right there," Frank related. "We had him cold with the drugs in his possession and based on our observations the conviction would've held up in court, but it probably would have collapsed the intermediate drop at 328½ East Ninth and spooked them all back into hiding. That wasn't what we were after. The last thing we wanted was to scare them into folding up their New Jersey operations and disappearing for good."

Bob Barchiesi shrugged. "Busting Gordo would have been the safe thing to do, but we weren't thinking about safety at that point. We were tossing the dice, hoping the numbers would come up Lopez."

Chapter Twenty-three

"For me it was like being strapped down while somebody mainlined a gallon of adrenaline into my bloodstream. It was instant excitement, better than sex."

—FRANK BOSE

BESIDES Frank and Bob, the surveillance team at 63 Edgewater place consisted of five members, all experienced Narcotics officers from the NYPD Anti-Crack Unit: Jerry Speziale, Elsa Gonzales, John Verwoert, Louie Torrellas, and Hector Ocasio.

Jerry Speziale was something of a nut. He relished undercover work. Frank characterized him as looking like "your typical white mope from New Jersey with an earring," and laughed heartily as Bob recounted story after story about Jerry's undercover escapades. "Jerry kept you laughing all day. He's a funny, personable guy, a good-looking guy with this crazy streak in him," Bob said. "He really got into the undercover. He'd come into the house with ripped-up clothes, coal and tar rubbed all over. He'd go down to a theatrical supply store and buy fake scars to put on his face. He was the kind of guy who would make a drug buy and start wrestling with the perp in the middle of his radio transmission, laughing like hell. I'd be sitting in the car and hear this grunting and banging around, and Jerry's crazy cackle: 'I got him, Sarge' . . ." Bob shook his head. "They don't make undercovers like Jerry anymore."

"These were all first-class people we had out there," Frank agreed. "Elsa Gonzales hated undercover work but she did it anyway, that takes real courage. She called herself 'Coco' on the street and no matter how much she dreaded making buys, she'd go right back in every time. She wore dark glasses and a babushka wrapped around her head on the street and her hair was always combed way down on her forehead. All you could see of Elsa's face was about a half-inch of skin."

Bob smiled at the characterization. "If the dealers couldn't see her, she couldn't see them either. She'd walk up to them and mutter, '*Yo quiero fosforo?*' She always opened up by asking them for a match. Her eyes would be glued to the sidewalk, and if you asked her what they were wearing, there was no way she could get it right. But she went in there where there was a lot of danger, and that's more than a lot of guys I know would have done. Elsa had plenty of guts.

"Louie Torrellas was the kind of guy who loved the street," Bob remembered. "He'd go out there with a cane and a bottle of Heineken and sit on a bench or just hang around in the background in filthy old clothes and 'ghost' the undercover. That means he acted as backup and made the transmissions while the buy was going down. He was a perfect ghost, and unlike a lot of the undercovers today, he had the balls to carry his radio in a bag and report into the bag while he was drinking his Heineken. He didn't give a shit who saw him do it either. He knew they were all too juiced or too dumb to know what was going down."

"Hector Ocasio was really smart and capable," Frank asserted. "He was well-spoken and he knew more about the regulations and the paperwork than most cops ever will. He was the only cop I ever met who could tell you to the penny what his paycheck was going to be any given week, including overtime and night differential, but he earned every nickel. Out there on the street he was as good or better than anybody; he just didn't give the job one minute more of his time than they were willing to pay him for, and I can't really fault him for that. You have to be nuts like Bob and me to work for nothing."

"John Voerwort was a super-nice guy," Bob related. "He was fairly new on the job and I guess he was afraid of making mistakes, so he was more deliberate than most of the others on the team. But he was eager as hell to learn, and once he got going, there wasn't a better investigator out there."

In addition, other Narcotics officers worked tirelessly in the operation against the Rock Solid organization:

"Joe Alvarez was a hard worker," Frank and Bob agree. "The kind of guy who would give you the shirt off his back. He was a veteran with ten or twelve years on the job at that point and a background in the Street Crime Unit. A real standup kind of guy, someone you could count on if the going got rough.

"We called Bobby Geis 'The Goose.' Goose was really into the technical aspects of investigation. He was fascinated by electronics and couldn't learn enough about it. He loved the street and hated drug dealers, so there was nothing he liked better than going out there with electronic scanners and beating the scumbags at their own game.

"Gabe Galiano looked like Edward James Olmos from *Miami Vice*. He had a gritty street appearance that made him a great undercover. Nobody would hesitate to sell this guy drugs, and when he teamed up with Jerry Speziale, the drug dealers didn't stand a chance.

"Ray Davis was called 'Baba.' He was soft-spoken and intelligent and very street-wise. Ray could talk his way into any location to make buys and blend right in with the street population. You could count on him to do anything that was needed. He had a lot of guts.

"Lieutenant Jerry Robbins had a great technical background. He loved gadgets, loved to scrounge up things to work on. Robbins liked doing the work, liked being out there on the street doing buy-and-bust, doing cases. He gave us as much latitude and support as he possibly could, and that meant a lot.

"John Fahey was a tough, veteran lieutenant. He'd been on the job for twenty-five years and had been in Narcotics since 1972. He knew how the Narcotics Division worked, so he tended to be a bit cautious in his approach. Looking back, we can hardly blame him."

Everyone involved in the case felt they were on the verge of finding Alejandro Lopez and the excitement was infectious. As the days passed and more and more evidence linking Lopez and Rock Solid with the Edgewater operation surfaced, it became not so much a matter of whether they would nail Lopez as when it would happen. It was now a matter of waiting him out, and waiting was the hardest part. Surveillance is tough, grinding work, always demanding alertness from minds and bodies that can become desensitized from boredom and lack of sleep. Crouched in the cold and discomfort of their surveillance vehicles, the crunching discipline was made easier for Frank and Bob by the fact that they knew their enemy was close at hand. They could feel his nearness overlaying their thoughts, their conversations, their languor; hear the rasp of his labored breathing and smell his nervous sweat in every frigid gust of air.

On February 28 their patience was rewarded. At 8:30 P.M., driving a department rental vehicle, Bob, Frank, and Jerry Speziale arrived at 63 Edgewater Place and parked abruptly when they spotted a flurry of unusual activity in front of the location. From their vantage point, fifty yards across the street on a diagonal, they identified four male Hispanics, Eduardo Lopez, Nelson Alphonso, Ricky Moreno, and J. D. Gordo, aka Aaron Davila, loading a rented U-Haul van and a black International Scout with contents from the house. A slow-moving Cadillac approached them and pulled up directly in front of the U-Haul. In the front seat, a man and a woman spoke briefly before the man exited the driver's side of the Cadillac and headed toward the van.

"It was like a jolt of electroshock shot through me," Bob recalled. "There he was, Alejandro Lopez, not fifty yards away from us. There was no mistaking him, I would have known that face anywhere. Frank and I had been throwing darts at it for months."

Frank agreed. "For me it was like being strapped down while somebody mainlined a gallon of adrenaline into my bloodstream. It was instant excitement, better than sex. I could feel my body surging forward in the car and I had to consciously pull back, otherwise I might have run him over. This was the guy who had threatened to cut my little girl into pieces, standing right there in front of us where Bobby and I could get at him and grind him into the pavement. The only thing stopping us from doing that was us. That took a helluva lot of self-control."

The man they saw and identified as Alejandro Lopez was tall, well-built, and undeniably handsome, with an abundant shock of ebony black hair combed straight back on his forehead. Beneath his full moustache, the sneer that they had come to intimately know seemed permanently fixed, reflecting the air of power and arrogance mirrored in his walk, the haughty, defiant toss of his shoulders.

"There's no way you could ever understand what that was like," Bob elaborated. "Granted, this was the guy who had threatened our families' lives, and we had every reason in the world to hate him for that, but for me there was another dimension to it. This was what we were paid to do as policemen. This is the reason we became cops in the first place, this is what it's really all about. Lopez was our enemy, and everything we'd done for two years was calculated to bring us to this very spot, up close and face-to-face with him. You've gotta believe that's a great feeling. There's a lot of professional pride involved . . ." He paused, smiled. "And I have to admit it's a lot of fun."

Observing the pair through high-powered binoculars, Frank watched the female occupant of the Cadillac, Lopez's girlfriend,

Lisette Mazzola, known as "Vivian," exit the car on the passenger's side carrying an I LOVE NEW YORK shopping bag, join Lopez on the sidewalk, and accompany him inside the house while the others continued loading the van with household items and I LOVE NEW YORK shopping bags that appeared to contain drug paraphernalia.

There was no realistic way they could make an arrest at that time. They were out of their jurisdiction and were authorized only to observe and report. The last thing they needed was to give away their position and be identified by Nelson Alphonso, who they knew could recognize them, or any of the others including Lopez, who they suspected had at the very least been given their descriptions. A gunfight would be likely to erupt and win or lose, they knew that when it was over they would be in an untenable position as far as the job was concerned. Still, their eagerness and curiosity were hard to keep under control. Everybody wanted a closer look and finally, since Jerry Speziale was the only one of them who could not be immediately recognized, Bob gave him permission to make a walk-by surveillance.

"Jerry just sauntered down the sidewalk and barged right into the middle of them," Frank related. "He deliberately bumped into Nelson Alphonso as he walked by and got a good look at what was going down."

It was not a ploy designed to produce a lot of results but it made them all feel better and confirmed their earlier identifications. Now all they could do was wait, hunkered down in the cramped confines of the surveillance car, until the International Scout was completely loaded and Alejandro Lopez, Nelson Alphonso, and Ricky Moreno drove it away from 63 Edgewater Place. They followed the Scout at a safe distance until it arrived at a quiet suburban street in exclusive Englewood Cliffs, New Jersey, and pulled into the driveway of an expensive one-family frame house at number 17 Ridge Road.

Bose, Barchiesi, and Speziale circled the block several times in an effort to avoid detection in the residential area, stopping near 17 Ridge Road on every pass long enough to ascertain that the subjects had begun to unload the contents of I LOVE NEW YORK shopping bags and transfer them to the garage of the house. When they were satisfied that the unloading process would take several hours, they drove back to the Anti-Crack Unit in Manhattan, where they signed out and returned to the Edgewater surveillance site in their own cars.

Bob was driving his Yugo and as he approached the location it began to overheat, sending billows of white steam mushrooming into the icy night air like a smoke signal. Angrily he drove to an out-of-the-way spot nearby, abandoned the Yugo, and joined Frank in the front seat of his undersized blue Volkswagen. Jerry was in his own orange Bug, and together the cars made an unlikely undercover duet as they resumed their frigid night watch at 63 Edgewater Place.

"It was freezing," Bob recalled, "and we were huddled up like pretzels in the car, but the only choice we had was to wait them out. It was almost five in the morning before the U-Haul finally moved out of there and we were able to follow them back to Englewood and confirm that the furniture was being loaded in the same location as the drugs. The sun was starting to come up, our teeth were chattering and we were operating on pure adrenaline, but we never let them get out of our sights. We'd come too far to lose them at that point."

"In a way, it had to happen the way it did," Frank suggested. "Lopez was just running true to form. He had millions of dollars in cash, homes, horses, airplanes, and half the population of the Lower East Side so terrified of him they wouldn't even say his name, but he couldn't be more than the street urchin he was. With all that, he was being evicted from the Edgewater house for non-payment of rent. Go figure it."

Chapter Twenty-four

IN police work, as in the rest of life, the rush of events sometimes outstrips the ability of mere mortals to manage them,
and as things begin to spin out of control, the efforts of honest
men and women deteriorate into a parody of good intentions and
misplaced fervor. Such was the case with what Bose and Barchiesi
have come to label "The Great Bergen County SWAT Team Assault."

FRANK and Bob knew they would have to move fast. Having
tracked Alejandro Lopez for more than two years, they knew that
he would not stay put at the Englewood Cliffs address for very
long. His entire Rock Solid cocaine empire had been built upon
layers of subordinates who shielded him from exposure and provided an effective buffer between him, his customers, and the
police. He could control his multimillion dollar drug empire from
behind the scenes while his underlings took the heat, and use his
seeming ability to elude capture as proof of his invincibility. Out in
the open for the moment, Lopez was uncharacteristically vulnerable, but it would be only a matter of time before he again returned
to the safety of hiding and the opportunity to capture him might
be lost forever.

A strategy was devised: a series of lightning strikes against all
three known Rock Solid locations, designed to cripple the organization and hopefully arrest Lopez and his chief subordinates.
Warrants were issued for the premises at 328½ East Ninth Street,
three apartments in The Rock at 507 East Eleventh, and the
house at 17 Ridge Road, Englewood Cliffs, to be executed simultaneously on the afternoon of March 12, 1987. Bob Barchiesi was
to coordinate the entire operation by radio from New York with
Lieutenants Becker and Robbins, while Frank Bose was to over-
see operations in New Jersey along with Jerry Speziale, Elsa
Gonzales, and Louis Torrellas. Because of the jurisdictional priori-

ties involved, New Jersey Police authorities had to be apprised of the situation at 17 Ridge Road, and overall responsibility for the Englewood Cliffs strike was turned over to the Bergen County Narcotics Task Force.

On the afternoon of March 12, Frank and the others arrived at task force headquarters in the Englewood Cliffs Volunteer Fire House, where they were met by Bergen County Narcotics Supervisor, Lieutenant Jack Quigley, and the Team Commander of the Bergen County Hostage Negotiating Unit, which in reality was nothing more than a thinly disguised SWAT force, along with representatives of the Englewood Cliffs Police Department and Bergen County Sheriff's Office. Jerry Speziale gave everyone an overall background briefing on the Rock Solid organization, as well as warning them what they might expect when they got to 17 Ridge Road.

"Let's secure the location," the SWAT commander said, nodding thoughtfully as he listened to Jerry's presentation. His face hardened as Jerry recounted the organization's violent history. "Better get the ram in there and hit it hard," he added as Jerry stressed the likelihood of violence. "And let's get some tear gas cannisters out there." Finally Frank recounted the threats that he and Bob had received from Lopez. "*That's it,*" the commander uttered resolutely. "Get out the stun grenades!"

Back in New York, Bob Barchiesi set up a mobile command post on the southwest corner of First Avenue and East Ninth Street, and deployed undercover operatives throughout the area who would remain in radio contact before and during the raids on 328½ East Ninth and 507 East Eleventh streets. Anyone observed on the street prior to the operation and recognized as a major player in the Rock Solid organization would be arrested. Everyone inside the subject premises at the time they were entered by police would be picked up. All money, drugs, weaponry, and contraband found at the locations would be seized. As soon as the Ninth Street warrant had been executed, Bob would give the signal to begin the Englewood operation.

Frank Bose and Jerry Speziale arrived at the Englewood Cliffs location at approximately six P.M., where they set up an observation position in a surveillance van parked on John Street overlooking number 17 Ridge Road. Louie Torrellas and Elsa Gonzales were parked further down the hill in Louie's private car, ready to follow anyone who left the house to their eventual destination if Frank gave the order. From his vantage point on the hill, Frank had a clear view of the house below, nestled in a shimmering mantle of newly fallen snow, surrounded by other neat, picture-perfect homes that dotted the gently rolling hills like a miniature village in a child's electric train set. He gulped the clean, frosty air, felt it tighten in his nostrils and energize his senses with icy fingers of exptectancy as members of the advance task force cautiously took up their positions and waited.

At 6:30 P.M. Alejandro Lopez's henchman, Ricky Moreno, driving in a 1983 BMW sedan, left the driveway at 17 Ridge Road and headed for Manhattan. Frank radioed Louie Torrellas and Elsa Gonzales to follow him, then notified Bob in New York of his approach. Based on past surveillances, he knew that Moreno was likely headed for one of the downtown locations controlled by Lopez and that he would be arrested there.

The mobile surveillance of the BMW sedan was terminated at 6:57 when Louie Torrellas radioed that they had lost the car in heavy traffic. Now all they could do was wait, and after almost two hours it appeared as if Frank had been wrong and Moreno might elude capture altogether. Bob could not afford to wait any longer. Every passing hour increased the possibility that they might be detected, and the onset of darkness made the task ahead just that much harder. He was about to give the signal to move in when the glare of a headlight in his rearview mirror reflected the image of the BMW slowly cruising by. As it passed, Bob saw that Moreno had picked up a passenger whom he recognized as Eduardo Lopez, Alejandro's brother. "There are two of them," he whispered into his radio as Moreno and Eduardo Lopez parked the BMW in front of number 328½ East Ninth Street and walked toward the building. "Take them now before they can get inside."

Undercover Detectives Hector Ocasio and Mike Treglio emerged from the shadows, weapons drawn, and confronted the two as they stood on the entrance stairwell to the building. Lopez and Moreno were taken completely by surprise and surrendered without a struggle. They were handcuffed and read their rights while the rest of the police team swarmed past them down the stairs and smashed in the front door to the basement apartment with a steel battering ram. Inside, a male Hispanic bolted and attempted to escape through a small window in the rear of the apartment, but Bob was able to grab him by his ankles and pull him back. He was searched and identified as David Lopez, another brother of Alejandro who had until then been unknown to the police.

Eduardo Lopez and Ricky Moreno were searched on the out-side steps of the building and relieved of approximately four thou-sand dollars in cash, most of it carefully separated with stenciled and numbered index cards listing quantities of Rock Solid cocaine sold, corresponding dollar amounts paid, and the names of dealers responsible for sales. Bob Barchiesi recognized the cards as being identical to drug records they had seized earlier at the TriBeCa loft and The Rock at 507 East Eleventh Street, and which they had identified as the primary system of bookkeeping for the Rock Solid cocaine organization. By modern business standards it might not have been considered sophisticated, but it was the most effective narcotics record-keeping police had seen up to that point. Every bag, every payment, and every cash shortfall was accounted for. If nothing else, Alejandro Lopez ran a tight ship.

A shotgun and a .38 caliber pistol were found inside the Ninth Street apartment along with additional records of drug transac-tions, but little else. Two more individuals were arrested when warrants were executed at 507 East Eleventh Street, apartments 10 and 12: a mid-level manager named Harry Banchs and a street dealer named Mary Luiz Martinez. No evidence or contraband were found in either apartment and Bob radioed Frank to begin the operation in Englewood Cliffs.

From his position in the van overlooking 17 Ridge Road, Frank radioed the New Jersey supervisors, who were parked in a second vehicle across the road, to begin the operation. He received a return transmission from Lieutenant Jack Quigley requesting that he wait until the Bergen County SWAT Team had arrived and secured the area. That was okay, strictly normal procedure. What followed was anything but:

Frank heard them first; the hoarse, rhythmic chanting of rap-idly moving men he had first heard in Marine boot camp at Parris Island: "*I don't know, but I've been told Eskimo pussy's mighty cold! Sound off, hut-toop . . .*" The chant swelled above the sound of booted feet beating against the pavement in precision, piercing the quiet night like an oncoming locomotive. "*Count cadence, count! Hut, toop, treep, whore . . .*"

Four abreast, moving in quick-time to the metronome of pound-ing feet, the Bergen County SWAT team jogged down the street with their M-16 automatic rifles carried at high-port, each clad in identical Ninja black jungle fatigues, vests, and field caps, filling the frosty air with billows of condensation from their measured chanting like the snorts of charging stallions. *"Hands on the trigger, safeties off! Sound off, hut toop . . ."*

Jerry Speziale's jaw dropped. He had never been in the military and he'd never witnessed a spectacle like this before. "This I gotta see," he gasped.

Frank accompanied him outside the van and they watched with wonderment as the team jogged down the hill to the house and deployed around it. They communicated by grunts and hand signals, leveling their weapons as they inched forward, leapfrogging from tree to tree in the yard, crawling on their bellies to the safety of rocky outcrops on the snowy front lawn. By prearranged signal, one of the troopers emerged from hiding, charged the front door of the house, and crashed it inward with a battering ram. At almost the same instant, a second trooper lobbed a stun grenade through the open doorway and the house blew up in front of them.

"From where we were standing up above, it was like somebody flipped a switch in this little electric-train house and the whole place lit up red," Frank recalled. "There was this muffled *thud*. Windows and doors blew out, along with the windows in the neighbors' houses. Jerry and I were on our knees in the snow with tears streaming down our cheeks. There was no way we could have helped anybody down there if trouble had broken out. We were just too cracked up laughing."

Before they could regain their composure, a backup team of similarly clad and equipped SWAT troopers stormed the house and unleashed a snarling attack dog. Frank and Jerry watched through tear-filled eyes as they followed him inside, then contacted Bob in New York on the van's cellular telephone. "You're not going to believe this, but they threw a grenade in the house," Jerry reported, still laughing.

Bob dropped the phone.

Lieutenant Jerry Robbins was standing nearby. "What's going on?" he asked Bob.

Bob was too convulsed with laughter to answer. All he could manage was a few feeble snorts as he fumbled on the floor for the telephone. Finally he recovered sufficiently to relay the report to Robbins.

"They threw a *what*?" Robbins gasped. His eyes bugged out like they always did when he was excited.

"A fucking *grenade*," Bob managed weakly.

"You wouldn't have believed it," Frank recalled later. "The only thing I can compare it to was an incoming artillery barrage back in 'Nam. You could feel the concussion in your chest as the air molecules compressed against you. One of the neighbors came running out of his house screaming like a maniac. It was pandemonium out there."

Bob and Jerry Robbins drove out to Englewood in a hurry. "I couldn't believe my eyes," Bob related. "The floors were charred black, the doors were blown out, all the kitchen cabinets were dangling off the wall. It was like being in a battle zone. Thank God there were no kids inside. Too bad Lopez wasn't in there, though."

Frank eyed him quizzically. "Would we really have been upset if Lopez had been blown away in that explosion?" he asked with a half-smile.

They both nodded affirmatively; the answer was clear. Lopez had to be tracked and taken down by them, alive or dead but confronted face-to-face. It was the only way they could balance their account with Rock Solid.

Chapter Twenty-five

"In my mind I always saw this thing ending in a bloodbath on the Lower East Side . . . I just never saw us losing."

—BOB BARCHIESI

DESPITE its comic aspects, the Ridge Road raid turned into a bonanza. Two heavy-duty safes were discovered in the house: one sunk into the floor of a basement closet, and the second standing in the garage adjacent to the house, which Frank Bose immediately recognized as the same safe he had seen at the TriBeCa loft in August of 1985. It took a professional locksmith almost five hours to drill through the heavily reinforced floor safe, where police recovered ten thousand glassines of high-grade cocaine stamped ROCK SOLID and wrapped in forty-six individually numbered packages. The free-standing garage safe was found to contain two Interdynamic Tech 9 machine guns, magazines and ammunition, and a small amount of miscellaneous drugs. Fingerprints of some of the major Rock Solid operatives were obtained, as well as all of the signature rubber stamps that Lopez used to identify his products, including Rock Solid. A Sears electronic door opener in the garage proved to have the identical serial number as the hand-held activator found in Ricky Moreno's BMW.

Most importantly, a sweep of the Ridge Road premises uncovered most of the organization's records. A tightly wound cylinder resembling a piano-roll turned out to be ledgers listing thousands of drug transactions documenting dates, the names of dealers and customers, and the amounts of money received from each. Detailed examination of the confiscated ledgers disclosed one encouraging fact: that sales had been steadily dropping at the Eleventh Street location since late in 1985, the exact time Bose and Barchiesi had begun their non-stop harassment of the building. Just as significant was the discovery of a large quantity of new glassine envelopes stamped with the brand name LUCKY. Alejandro Lopez had complimented them in the only way a man of his unmitigated arrogance could. He had grudgingly admitted that their constant pressure forced him to change his logo. It was not the total victory they had been looking for, but it was a victory nonetheless. Rock Solid was dead. Lopez was next.

The raid and seizures made prime-time news throughout the metropolitan area. The following day, a solemn-faced Chris Borgen of CBS News stood in the jumbled living room of the Englewood Cliffs house, gave a brief summary of events leading up to the raid, and recounted the details of the operation: "The cops admit there was a downside to last night's operation," he intoned gravely. "The man they call the ringleader, Alejandro Lopez, got away. 'Only for the moment,' they add; 'only for the moment.' "

"It was a bitter, frustrating time," Frank remembered. "I suppose we shouldn't have counted on getting Lopez in Englewood, but I guess we did in spite of ourselves. Looking back on it, I know I must have, because I felt like somebody had kicked me in the chest. Bobby and I would sit in The Wicked Wolf night after night, trying to pump each other back up, trying to find a way to make something positive out of all of this, but it was really tough. It was hard to reconcile what we'd ended up with when we knew how close we came to taking him down.

"I tried to put it out of my mind when I was off-duty. My wife, Candy, worked on weekends when I was home, so I got to spend a lot of time alone with my daughter, Amanda. She was three or four then, you know, a really cute, important time for kids when everything's new, everything's an adventure. She was too busy finding out about life to be frustrated by it like I was at that point, so in that respect she was teaching me back then. We'd go off to the amusement park for the day and just hang out, more like companions than father and daughter; and for that short time I was almost successful in putting the Lopez thing away. . . . Almost, but not quite.

"We'd go to McDonald's on Sunday mornings. Amanda loves McDonald's, and it was a real treat for both of us. I'd find myself unconsciously seating us at a rear table with me facing the front door, and my nine millimeter close by where I could get it in a hurry. No matter what I was doing, there was a part of me that was thinking about Lopez, working on new strategies, letting my imagination get the better of me. If I couldn't get him in reality, I nailed him a thousand ways in my mind's eye.

"To be honest, guys on the job thought we were nuts to let this scumbag consume our lives the way he did, but I don't think we could help ourselves at that point. When we weren't mapping strategies on the job or in The Wicked Wolf, we were on the telephone, calling each other at home. I'd wake up at three in the morning with some crazy new idea, and I'd be on the phone with Bobby, tossing it around for the rest of the night. We'd go over the same ground a hundred times, looking for a new angle, a new tributary that might spin off and lead us in another direction. Maybe it had to happen that way. Maybe that's why we never really lost heart, even when things looked the blackest."

Bob Barchiesi nodded agreement. "You could never really forget about it altogether. It was just too much a part of your life. My family was really important to me during all of this, but I never brought my wife and children into it. I suppose Linda might have wanted me to tell her everything that was going on, the danger and all, but that's just not my style. If she asked, I'd just tell her that everything was okay. Maybe that was unfair, but it was the only way I could deal with it. A case like this consumes you, turns your life inside out. I was living in a pressure cooker every day, but I wanted them to have as normal a life as possible. I had to find ways to decompress by myself.

"I tried to lose Lopez in the gym or out on the running track. There's something about running with the sun beating down on your head and your eyes focused on your feet beneath you. . . . All I could hear out there was the beat of my feet hitting the surface of the track, and the sound of my own breathing. It had a kind of hypnotic effect on me. I could lose myself in the moment for a while.

"If you've ever tried to bench-press four hundred pounds in the gym, you know that you have to stay focused on what you're doing or you're not going to make it. You have to close your eyes and visualize every step in the process: your hands gripping the bar, your muscles tensing, the final split second when every ounce of energy you possess is propelled upward toward the bar above you. You have to be able to project that weight going up. If you let yourself think about failure, you're going to fail. It's that simple. Winning in any kind of sport means keeping a positive attitude.

"I'd like to think I brought some of that attitude to this Lopez investigation. No matter how bad things looked, I always projected us being successful in the end. I could visualize a thousand different scenarios but they always ended up the same way, with

Frank and me winning. Honestly, I always saw this thing ending in a bloodbath on the Lower East Side, and I suppose you could call that negative thinking, but it really wasn't. No matter how many times I played the tape in my mind, it always ended up the same way. I just never saw us losing."

The next step for Bose and Barchiesi was to make the most out of what they had, and the more they looked the more it began to appear that they had a lot indeed. Among the records, lists of drug operatives included telephone numbers, many in Puerto Rico, that they ran down with help from the Puerto Rican Telephone Company. They were soon receiving FAXed material from Puerto Rico almost daily, and connecting the names of individuals on the island with their relatives in the Rock Solid organization back in New York. Invoices describing shipments of furniture from the TriBeCa loft to a woman named Hilda Vasquez in Bayamón, Puerto Rico, surfaced, as well as the news that the shipments had been forwarded to a former US Air Force installation called Basa Ramie.

The precinct computer was available for motor vehicle and warrant checks, but it was insufficient to process the piles of raw material they were receiving from Puerto Rico. The walls of their already cluttered office at the Anti-Crack Unit were soon covered with hand-lettered poster-board charts listing telephone numbers, frequency of calls, individuals and locations, as well as a series of parallel grids and cross-references designed to forge an unmistakable link between the sites in Puerto Rico and the Rock Solid organization in New York.

As part of the overall strategy, Maria Salazar, the "Bunny Mother" of 507 East Eleventh Street, was targeted for arrest and furnished her captors with the information that Alejandro Lopez had fled to Puerto Rico and was running his cocaine empire from a small village on the coast. Heartened by this information, Bose and Barchiesi hit upon a strategy that was almost absurd in its simplicity. They would contact all of the individuals they had so far identified in Puerto Rico by telephone, as well as anyone in the vicinity who had a name remotely resembling "Lopez," and ask them if Tito was at home.

Frank and Bob knew they would be held accountable for all telephone calls made from their office to Puerto Rico, and they were not yet ready to have their investigation held up to departmental scrutiny, so they went downtown to the offices of Assistant

District Attorney Pat Conlon, and telephoned from there. A Spanish-speaking female police officer named Elisa Padron was enlisted to call, and began the painstaking task of dialing and questioning, hour after hour, day after day, until it began to appear that they might possibly be on the wrong track. Then, like wildfire, they hit pay dirt.

Elisa Padron dialed the number of a barber shop in Rio Piedras that was listed under the name Benito Torres, one of Lopez's associates. A female voice answered. "¿Hay Tito Alla?" Elsa asked routinely.

"He'll be back in a half hour," the woman replied.

Elisa's eyes went wide. "He's there!" she rasped, covering the receiver with her hand. "The woman says he'll be back in a half hour."

"Make sure it's the right Tito," Bob urged.

"I'm looking for Tito Lopez," she clarified.

"In a half hour," the woman said, annoyed, and hung up.

"Holy shit, it's him!" Bob stared at Frank.

Frank punched the empty air triumphantly. "Do you hear that, Mr. Lopez? We chased your ass all the way down there and we're coming down to bring it back!"

It was hard for Frank and Bob to contain their excitement. In the hours following confirmation that Tito Lopez was in Puerto Rico, they ran the gamut of their emotions, proposed and rejected dozens of schemes for getting to the island, and generally feasted in the glow of their success. They could take the information to their superiors, they knew, but there was no way they would be given authorization to travel to the island based on a single telephone call. They phoned McGuire Air Force Base and explored the possibility of taking a military junket to another Air Force base that was about an hour away from Rio Piedras, but discovered that most of the base had been turned over to the civilian population and that only a portion was still an Air Force installation. Finally, they placed a call to the United States Coast Guard and reached Special Agent Pedro Gonzales, who was assigned to the Puerto Rico Narcotics Task Force.

Gonzales listened to their account over the telephone and suggested that the best course of action for them to take would be to work through local law enforcement agencies on the island. He referred them to a Sergeant Pedro Morales of POPR, Police of Puerto Rico, in a small town on the coast of Puerto Rico called

Aguadilla. *Aguadilla*: It was the location they had pinpointed through records research and telephone checks as the native home to most of the New York members of Rock Solid.

"I know this Lopez," Morales told them flatly over the phone. "He has been associated with drugs for a long time in Aguadilla, and has been arrested along with one of our own former Narcotics agents. He once assaulted one of our policemen and has threatened others. We are *chomping at the bit* to get our hands on him down here."

Morales told them that Lopez was free on bail, awaiting trial on the Narcotics charges. Immediately Frank and Bob began a series of FAX transmissions between New York and Puerto Rico to establish for certain that they were talking about the same Alejandro Lopez. They included copies of all New York and New Jersey warrants as well as mug shots of other members of the Rock Solid organization who they hoped Morales would be able to identify.

Morales FAXed Frank and Bob a picture of Nelson Alphonso, whom he identified as a notorious hit man for local drug operatives, and who he said was awaiting trial in San Antonio, a suburb of Aguadilla, along with Tito Lopez on the drug and assault charges. They recognized him immediately as Lopez's New York bodyguard, the man whom Bobby Feliciano had told to furnish Frank with cocaine while he and Bob were still undercover at 507 East Eleventh.

"Frank and I discussed it, and decided that the smart thing would be to wait until Lopez and Alphonso appeared in court and snap them up then," Bob recalled. "But Morales insisted on taking them right away. He said it was too important to wait and that he would use the entire resources of POPR at his command to see that both men were captured and brought to justice. He told us he'd telephone back as soon as they were safely in custody."

"How can I explain what we felt?" Frank wondered. "Here we were at the end of the line. It had been over three years at that point, and everything we'd been working for was finally happening. Bobby and I were like lunatics. We wanted to get down there any way we could and lead the charge, but all we could do was sit there by the telephone with our hearts in our throats, waiting for the word from Morales. It took two hours for him to get back to us and I've gotta tell you, it was the longest two hours either of us had ever spent in our lives."

The telephone rang and Bob almost knocked it to the floor answering it. "Morales?"

There was a pause at the other end. "I'm afraid I have bad news, Sergeant," Morales intoned dolefully. "We went out to the farm where he was staying and found him there . . ."

"And . . . ?" Bob almost screamed into the receiver.

"And, I'm sorry to tell you that Lopez escaped on one of his horses."

Bob felt his chest cave in. "He escaped on a fucking horse?" he asked weakly.

"He has lots of horses," Morales replied.

"You went out with all of the resources POPR could command, and he got away on a *horse*?"

"These things happen."

Bob slammed the receiver onto its cradle.

"A *horse*?" Frank echoed, in disbelief.

Bob just sat there and shook his head. "Can you *fucking* believe that?"

"There is no way I will *ever* fucking believe that!" Frank snatched the phone, dialed Special Agent Gonzales at the Coast Guard base, and recounted the improbable tale. "Do *you* believe a bullshit story like that?" he demanded.

To Frank and Bob, Gonzales' silence on the other end spoke volumes, confirming what they already suspected. Something stunk in Aguadilla.

Chapter Twenty-six

THERE were a lot of questions that needed answering, and on an October afternoon in 1987 Bob Barchiesi was able to step back from the turmoil of the investigation long enough to put some of them into perspective.

"I suppose people might ask 'why?' Why did it take so long for the New York Police to get a bunch of drug dealers out of a New York City–owned building?" Bob reflected to an interviewer. "Why didn't they just charge in there, arrest everybody, and get it over with once and for all? Well, there really isn't any easy answer to that question, but to begin to understand it, you have to know a little bit about how the system works.

"Our laws stipulate that, in order for police to obtain search warrants to enter apartments, we have to be able to establish 'probable cause.' Now, that's a pretty ambiguous term, but to some district attorneys it means 'stay out altogether unless you want a pack of howling civil libertarians coming down on you.' That makes the cop's job a lot tougher. We can bust low-level dealers out on the street, but the major players are given privileged sanctuary behind closed doors to do whatever they want."

Bob smiled wryly at the incongruity. "Lopez knew that," he pointed out. "Lopez knew that as long as he kept the bulk of his supply indoors in various 'stash' locations, and conducted actual sales outside in the hallways and on the streets, and then only in individual small quantities, there was no way we could really penetrate his operation. The street people were his buffer; they got busted regularly, but street dealers are the easiest people in the world to replace. I could tell you that, based on my experience and my instincts, sixteen of the twenty-four apartments in 507 East Eleventh Street were used as stash locations, but if I tried to go inside and prove it, the DAs would be the first guys to start yelling 'foul,' followed by most of the politicians and half the special-interest groups in the city. It's like we're playing this game and we're supposed to play by the Marquis of Queensbury rules or we're not playing fair."

Bob shook his head, amazed. "Let's face it, if there were rules, they all worked in Alejandro Lopez's favor. Lopez was free to do just about anything he pleased, as long as he did it indoors where we couldn't lay a finger on him. Our hands were tied everywhere we looked. We couldn't expect any help from the job, and the people in the neighborhood were so terrified of him they just stayed indoors and kept their mouths shut. The building was owned by New York City and controlled by the Housing Preservation Department, but I couldn't get a key for the front door. The superintendent of the building, who was a city employee, was too scared to open his door and answer my knock. He had to live with these scumbags. If they thought for a minute that he was cooperating with the police, they would have ground him up for dog meat.

"The truth is, Lopez knew the system. He knew that the cops were afraid of the politicians and the politicians were afraid of the voters, and every time a citizen complained about being treated unfairly by the law it sent shock waves up and down the line. So he had his people calling their City Councilmen and Civilian Complaint Review Boards on a regular basis, screaming their heads off that their rights were being violated, whether or not anything was happening. It was an effective weapon for him. He came close to shutting down the investigation against him because people uptown were getting jittery about his rights. They never thought about the rights of the people he was killing.

"Lopez could never have gotten away with any of this if the NYPD had stepped in and taken a forceful position, but he knew they wouldn't do that," Bob asserted emphatically. "He knew he was dealing with a reactionary department, a department where career choices take precedence over strong law enforcement. It's not a policy that's written on some job description. It's more of an attitude, and it starts back in the police academy. Day after day, class after class, new recruits are told how limiting their jobs are going to be; what they *won't* be able to do, rather than what they *can* do as police officers. By the time they graduate, probationary patrolmen know all about covering their asses with paperwork but they haven't learned very much about being forceful and independent. The system stifles independence and initiative. Cops learn to wait until something happens, then look around for a supervisor to tell them what to do about it. They're afraid to make a move on their own for fear that somebody will pick up a telephone and report them to the CCRB or the IAD for breaking the rules.

"Lopez and his people loved the rules as long as they were working in their favor. They knew just how far they could stretch them and they got a lot of pleasure out of seeing the police hog-tied.

It was as if they figured they had this permanent franchise to go on doing business unmolested for the rest of their lives, and when the rules started working against them they became indignant. Martinez and Garcia were more outraged than scared when we walked in on them in the Holiday Inn. They didn't think we were supposed to do that; like it wasn't playing fair! What's this 'playing fair' shit anyway? Shouldn't the game be stacked in favor of the good guys? We're *supposed* to win, aren't we?"

Bob shrugged his shoulders. "Rules or no rules, the clock was running out on Lopez and I believe Frank and I were chosen to bring him down. I know it sounds crazy, but I have to believe everything that happened during that period happened for a reason. Call it 'divine intervention,' call it whatever you want. I'm not a regular churchgoer but I believe in a higher power, and I believe that higher power looked at Alejandro Lopez, saw that he was destroying lives, killing people, and said *'That's enough!'* Frank and I just happened to be there when he said it.

"And maybe we were being tested. We tried so many different things and we ran smack into so many brick walls, we found ourselves getting down in the dumps a lot, really frustrated. Then, just when we thought we had nowhere else to go, something amazing would happen, like spotting Juahito on the Cross-Bronx Expressway, and we'd get all pumped up again. It seemed like whenever we were way down in the valley, something like that would happen to pick us up and get us back on track again. To me, that's God telling me, 'Don't give up. You're going to get this guy. It may not happen the way you want it to happen, but it will all be for the best.' "

Bob took a deep breath and let it out slowly. "And it was," he finally went on. "Even the things we thought were defeats turned out to be victories in the long run. If we'd nailed Blondie and Juahito that night on the Cross-Bronx, we'd have only had them on New York State charges; but as things worked out, I just happened to spot a telephone number scrawled on a wall in the Bronx, and we got them out in New Jersey with all that money and narcotics, and they end up doing time for both, consecutive terms. Things like that just kept on happening, so I have to believe it was all a part of some master plan for us. Somebody else was calling the shots. In retrospect, I'd have to say it was all part of a cleansing process; cleansing for Frank and me, cleansing for the people of the Lower East Side. It crystallized our beliefs in ourselves and in each other. It reinforced our conviction that somewhere in all this insanity, somebody was looking out for the decent people, for the good guys."

PART THREE

"*Perseverance is more prevailing than violence.*"

—PLUTARCH

Chapter Twenty-seven

A NOISY argument in the hallway outside apartment 2 awakened John Lunievicz early on the afternoon of December 5. Disturbances were nothing new to him. If anything, the thirty-four-year-old drifter had become so desensitized to the sounds of conflict in the building at 507 East Eleventh Street that he was able to sleep through the worst of them. In the almost one year he had occupied his tiny first-floor flat, Lunievicz could not remember a day without the clamor of angry shouting matches, without screams, without gunshots. Most of the time he simply ignored them, or at worst cast a wary eye across his cluttered room to make sure the dead bolt on his front door was firmly in place. It offered him little reassurance. Lunievicz, even with his limited intelligence, was painfully aware that dead bolts were for apartments in safe suburban neighborhoods, not dope-infested tenements where even the children carried automatic weapons.

On this afternoon though, Lunievicz was grateful that the argument in the hall awakened him when it did. He sat groggily on the side of his bed and tried to focus his nearsighted eyes on the small desk calendar he kept on the nightstand by his bed. Under the date Friday, December 5, he had penciled the name "Brock" and the numeral 1 in a childish scrawl. Brock was the name of a man who had offered him a part-time loading job at a warehouse on Ninth Avenue, and one o'clock was the hour he was supposed to report to work. That meant he had a little more than an hour to dress and walk clear across town. Had it not been for the disturbance in the hall, he probably would have slept the afternoon right through and missed out on the job altogether, so for once he had the Rock Solid greasers to thank for something more than harassment and aggravation.

A ribbon of cold water trickled from the faucet when Lunievicz turned on the tap. He grimaced, splashed an icy handful on his face, brushed his teeth with baking soda, and combed his thinning brown hair in the milky, pockmarked mirror above the sink.

That would have to be it, he decided, as he changed into the only relatively clean shirt he owned and scooped a handful of loose change from the top of the dresser into his pocket. He had planned to stop at the YMCA and take his first bath in nearly a month before going to the warehouse, but there would be no time for that now. He would just have to hope that the work was outside, and that the thickness of his U.S. Army fatigue jacket would keep him from offending sensitive noses.

"Hey, man!" Lunievicz recognized the voice behind him in the corridor as belonging to the man called Jorge Romano. He pretended not to hear and continued on toward the front door of the building.

"Hey, man . . ." Jorge caught up with him on the sidewalk. "What you running away like that for? You and me never had no problem between us."

Lunievicz bristled. He had confronted Jorge only the day before to complain once again about the endless stream of traffic trudging past his apartment night and day to buy drugs. Or had he confronted Jorge's brother, the one they called Willie? There were so many of the spick bastards it was hard to tell them apart. "I gotta get across town," he muttered, continuing to walk. "I got no time to talk to you now."

"I got time." Jorge fell in alongside him and skipped a few paces until he matched Lunievicz's step. "See, man, I was in the army just like you. I learned how to march real good, know what I mean?"

"I wasn't in the army," Lunievicz replied.

"Oh, I thought the jacket . . ."

"I got it from the Salvation Army."

Jorge pondered it. "Hey, you ain't still pissed off about them guys busting up your place like that, are you?" he asked finally.

Lunievicz ignored the question. He knew that Jorge would deny that he had taken part in the burglarizing and trashing of his apartment a week before, but he wasn't certain whether Jorge knew that he had paid an angry visit to the Ninth Police Precinct, complained about the theft and destruction of his property, and offered to supply them with information about members of the Rock Solid organization in retaliation. It had been a brash and foolhardy act, he now realized; the act of a desperate man who had reached the end of his rope. Now he hoped the police would ignore his offer to name names and forget about the incident altogether.

"Hey, no hard feelings, man. You and me shouldn't have no bad blood between us," Jorge went on, continuing in lockstep cadence. "Look, I'll tell you what I'll do. You know the Barcelonita Club in the building? How about you and me have a couple of pops in there and patch things up between us, know what I mean? No reason bad shit should be going down between me and you."

"I got to go to work."

"So you come by the club after work. You'll see, man, it's real nice in there. Plenty of table-grade pussy hangs around that place too, no shit."

They crossed Broadway into a freezing wind and continued west along Eleventh Street. "How about it?" Jorge pressed.

"I never been in there," Lunievicz said hesitantly.

"Well, you're gonna be in there tonight." Jorge danced playfully in front of him and blocked his way on the sidewalk. "I'm telling you, man. You're gonna have a ball. Your money's no good in that place, everything's on me, you name it. And you see a pussy you like, you just point her out and she's yours. You're gonna fuck your brains out tonight, amigo. I shit you not."

Lunievicz looked nervously at his wristwatch and brushed past Jorge. "I got to go or I'll be late for work."

"But you'll come to the club when you get back, right?" Jorge yelled after him.

"Maybe," he murmured under his breath and continued westward down the sidewalk. The idea of spending time with Jorge and the rest of them didn't particularly appeal to Lunievicz, but the secret social club called Barcelonita that occupied half the entire first floor of the building next to his apartment had intrigued him since he first set eyes on it almost two years ago. He had heard the pulsating beat of Salsa music blaring nightly from behind the locked doors, and the excited high-pitched laughter of women who drank too much. Some nights he lay motionless in his bed, listening to the music and the laughter, envisioning the women. He pictured their smooth, supple torsos, swaying voluptuously in tight-fitting satin dresses to the Latin rhythms, their full red lips beckoning to him, seducing him, their brown, Latin bodies writhing sensuously beneath him, crying out in pain and ecstasy as he thrust deeper and deeper inside them. It had been a long time since he'd been with a woman, a very long time.

There had been a girl once back in Pennsylvania, but that seemed a lifetime ago, before the downward spiral of unskilled, low-paying jobs, tenement apartments, welfare hotels and shelters that had led him to Alphabet City. Her name was Elaine Figliusi and she was seventeen years old. John Lunievicz remembered the first time he saw her working in her parents' dry cleaning store, and the nervousness he felt when she had coyly flirted with him from behind the counter. He remembered his panic when he impulsively asked her if she would go roller-skating with him that evening, and his astonishment when she accepted. He also remembered her mother's stern disapproval. That was not to change throughout the seven months Elaine and he saw one another. Mrs. Figliusi called him "that Polack," and considered him a hulking, vulgar brute. He was not Italian, she pointed out to her defiant daughter, and had not even finished the fourth grade in his native Poland. Sensing that her protestations were falling on deaf ears, she finally made a novena to Saint Jude, Patron of Impossible Causes, asking him to intercede and put an end to their unprovidential union once and for all.

It worked. Although John Lunievicz was too slow-witted to grasp even simple theological concepts, he understood that when he was opposed by sacred heavyweights he was up shit's creek. Elaine must have sensed it too, because she began backing away before Mrs. Figliusi's last votive candle sputtered and died inside Saint Dominic's Church. The relationship ended as abruptly as it had started, and with it went John Lunievicz's last steady piece of ass. Since then it had been catch-as-catch-can, and the lower he sank on the social ladder, the leaner the catchings became. Now he had come to the point where almost anything looked good to him, especially the overpainted, hip-swinging *muchachas* who frequented the Barcelonita Social Club at 507 East Eleventh Street.

He arrived at the warehouse twenty minutes late and was forced to endure a harangue from the boss of the loading dock before beginning to haul packages of frozen meat into waiting refrigerator trucks, a task which was to take the next four and a half hours. It was grunt work, standing in the freezing wind, lugging icebergs of frozen filets, roasts, and cutlets until his hands turned blue and throbbed with pain. By six P.M. when all the trucks were loaded and he had been paid, his skin was numb and his wind-assaulted face had assumed a mottled, red flush. Cold and exhausted, he headed east toward Alphabet City when a Calvert whiskey window display in a nearby tavern caught his eye, and in a relatively short time he had spent his entire earnings for the day on one-ounce shots of Calvert's whiskey and chasers of cold draft ale. It was almost nine o'clock when, drunk and disheartened, he returned to his apartment and found a prostitute named Sonia Perez waiting for him in the hallway.

"*Buenas noches*," she brushed up against him and touched his well-muscled chest with her fingertips. "You looking for a date tonight?"

Lunievicz's mouth went slack. "I got no more money."

"You don't need no money when you're with Sonia," she cooed seductively. "Jorge told me to take you back to the club and be good to you. You want that, don't you? You want Sonia to be good to you?" She circled his waist with her arm and inserted her hand beneath his shirt, softly massaging the tightened muscles. "Jorge tells me you lift weights. I like a man with a good build."

It was too much for Lunievicz and in an instant he began to hyperventilate. Each sucking gasp of air he took resounded through the darkened hallway like the sound of air escaping from a child's balloon. "I don't feel so good," he managed to stammer.

"Let Sonia make you feel better." She led him toward the rear of the building, and obediently he followed her through an interior passageway to the back entrance of the Barcelonita Social Club.

"*Saludos!* Welcome to our little *cantina*," Jorge Romano answered her knock, ushered them inside with a flourish and pointed to a well-stocked bar. "You look like a man who's had a rough day. What's your pleasure?"

Lunievicz squinted into the dimly lit room, its few bare wooden tables still unoccupied due to the early hour. With the exception of a billiards table and several video games set along the opposite wall, the club's spacious interior had a drab, hollow look; more like a bus station waiting room than a saloon. He recognized the bartender as a man called "Mello" and another man standing nearby as Leonardo Carreon. Two other women, whom he did not recognize, were seated at the far end of the bar. They noted his entrance with disinterest before returning to their drinks and hushed conversation.

"I got scotch, gin, vodka, good Puerto Rican dark rum," Jorge said grandly, pointing to the stacked bottles of liquor on the back bar. "You can have anything you want, as much as you want, no charge."

Mello glanced at Sonia hanging on Lunievicz's arm and winked conspiratorially. "Take the rum, man. Rum's an aphrodisiac, know what I mean?"

"Hey, my man don't need no fucking aphrodisiac," Jorge guffawed. "My man here is strong as a horse. They're gonna have to jerk him off four or five times after he's dead just to get the coffin lid shut."

Lunievicz agreed to a glassful of dark rum but declined Jorge's offer of cocaine. "Hey, man, this here's first class Colombian blow, guaranteed to put you in the mood," Jorge said, scooping up a small amount of the white powder with his pinkie nail and snorting it with relish. "We got a direct pipeline from Medellín. Whenever we run low we give them a blast on the horn and they Federal Express us a new batch." He cackled at the incongruity of his joke.

"I don't take drugs," Lunievicz told him. "Drugs ain't no fucking good for your body."

Jorge carefully laid out six evenly spaced cocaine lines on the bar with a single-edged razorblade. He inhaled one with a slender glass pipette, then passed it to Sonia before pouring Lunievicz's drink from the bottle Mello had left on the bar. Lunievicz accepted the drink with a nod, drained his glass in a single gulp, and took the bottle.

Jorge observed Lunievicz throughout the remainder of the evening as the social club filled with regulars and their guests, astonished at his capacity for alcohol. Knowing he was drunk to begin with, Jorge assumed he would be incapacitated after three or four healthy shots of the hundred-proof rum, but Lunievicz refused to cave in. Drink after drink, he stood giggling like an adolescent as Sonia teased and challenged him; stumbling awkwardly in a vain attempt to match the Latin rhythms when she coaxed him onto the dance floor. Four hours later, after finishing off one entire bottle and the better part of a second, he was still on his feet.

"How you doing, man?" Jorge asked.

Lunievicz belched.

Jorge nodded to Sonia, who leaned closer to Lunievicz, cupped his face in her hands, and whispered, "You're looking so good to me now, baby. I think you and me should get it on while you can still make it."

Befuddled as he was, Lunievicz was not insensitive to her husky, whispered entreaty, the touch of her wet lips on his earlobe, the tantalizing smells of her breath and her perfume. He felt her ample hips grinding into his side and understood that if he did not act now, he would soon be unable to act at all. Jorge watched him and understood what was happening. He alerted Leonardo Carreon, who was standing by the door, and together they steered Lunievicz into the hallway with Sonia following until they reached a spot in the corridor where Jorge had secreted a length of lead pipe under the staircase. Allowing Leonardo to assume the burden of steadying their almost unconscious companion, Jorge signaled for Sonia to leave, retrieved the pipe and creeping stealthily behind him, swung it with sledgehammer force into the back of John Lunievicz's head.

The blow shocked Lunievicz back to sobriety, but he was unable to keep his legs from buckling beneath him. Still not comprehending what was taking place, he crashed to the floor of the vestibule and reached back where the pipe had impacted and split his head open like an overripe melon. He felt a jagged edge of bone, and warm blood pumping through his calloused fingers. A milky cloud descended, then lifted with jarring impact as a second blow grazed his chin and landed full-force on his shoulder. Blinded by blood streaming into both his eyes, he felt for the floor and struggled to get back onto his feet.

"*Kill that Polack motherfucker!*" Leonardo screamed as the mortally wounded Lunievicz lunged toward him in the narrow hallway. Jorge responded by swinging the pipe like a scythe into Lunievicz's kneecaps, driving him to the floor once again. Lunievicz made another halting effort to rise but his strength was nearly gone. He raised his elbows in a feeble attempt to ward off the torrent of blows that followed, one after another, crashing into his exploding skull with an almost monotonous cadence. Finally, inevitably, he succumbed to the savagery of the beating and allowed his body to go limp inside the shelter of the descending cloud.

When they were certain he was dead, Jorge and Leonardo dragged his body back through the corridor to his apartment. "Get some kids to clean up that mess," Jorge instructed Leonardo, indicating the grisly trail of blood, brains, and scattered slivers of bone in their wake. "It wouldn't be a good idea for the customers to have to walk through all this shit tomorrow morning."

Leonardo searched through Lunievicz's pockets, found the key to his apartment door, and unlocked it. A small man in poor health from years of obsessive cocaine use, he was winded from the effort of dragging the 250-pound Lunievicz. "How long do you wanta wait before we dump him?" he panted.

"He'll be okay here 'till morning," Jorge replied as they rolled the body inside the open doorway. "We'll get some garbage bags, wrap him up and dump him in Brooklyn like we did with that rat, Ralphie."

"That's good 'cause this fuck was a rat, too," Leonardo noted.

Jorge paused inside the apartment to catch his breath, then removed a pearl-handled gravity knife from his pants pocket and released the razor-sharp blade. "And here's what we do with rats . . ." He inserted the point of the blade into the soft flesh just below Lunievicz's chin and drew it slowly across the Adam's apple, right then left, as easily as if he was filleting a fish, until the throat was laid open from ear to ear. ". . . Everybody's gonna know what they get when they go to the cops." Then in a gesture that would be recognized on the street as a sign of contempt and disrespect, he punched the knifeblade through the open wound at half-inch intervals until the bloody neck resembled a crudely rendered zipper. "This'll show them what happens to anybody who fucks with The Rock."

Chapter Twenty-eight

"We always knew the answer was there, staring us in the face somewhere. We just had to focus in on it."

—FRANK BOSE

IN a voice choking with fear, Maria Salazar, the "Bunny Mother" of 507 East Eleventh Street, related the details of John Lunievicz's murder to Frank Bose the following morning.

"Hold on, Maria, okay?" Frank pushed the hold button on his desk telephone, retrieved the microcassette recorder from his bottom drawer, and signaled for Bob to pick up the extension. "Okay, Maria, I'm back."

"They killed him with a pipe," she exclaimed, almost hysterically.

"Calm down, Maria. Who killed who?"

"Jorge and Leonardo killed that Polack in apartment two."

"When did this happen?" Frank broke in.

"Last night. They got him drunk in the club before they killed him."

"You're sure about this, Maria?" Frank looked across the desk at Bob and shrugged.

"They killed him right downstairs."

"Where's the body now?"

Maria's voice lowered and became conspiratorial. "Oh, man, I'm dead if they find out I called you."

"Nobody's going to find out. Now, I can't do anything unless you tell me where the body is," Frank urged her.

Maria paused. "It's downstairs, in the apartment."

"Number two?"

"I think so . . ."

"Okay, you just sit tight and I'll have somebody out there in a few minutes."

"If they ask me, I don't know nothin'."

"It's all right, Maria. Just sit tight." Frank hung up the phone.

Bob called Ninth Precinct Homicide before the receiver landed on its cradle, found out that the homicide had not yet been called in to the police, and related the details of Maria's report. "They'll meet us there," he told Frank, who was waiting impatiently by the squadroom door.

Four Homicide detectives from the nearby Ninth were waiting outside of number 507 when they arrived. Outside the building, a single bloody footprint on the concrete landing attested to the carnage that had taken place the night before. Inside, someone had halfheartedly attempted to clean the floor and walls of the hallway, but streaks of dried gore still lined the edges of the chipped linoleum flooring and clung tenaciously in hollows and cracks. Nearby, beneath the metal stairwell, shards of splintered bone and blood adhered to the limp, moist fibers of a wooden floor mop.

The grisly trail led directly to Lunievicz's apartment in the back of the building. They tried the door and found it blocked from inside by his body. Carefully, they pushed the door inward until they were able to squeeze through the narrow opening one at a time.

Bob shook his head. "Either the poor son of a bitch put up one hell of a fight, or they were just beating on his dead body for the fun of it."

The smell of death was oppressive, hanging in the frigid air, thick, musty, unmistakable. The only noise was the tattoo of dripping water on the pitted surface of the sink. Wordlessly Frank and Bob made their way into the hallway and went outside, where a small band of curious onlookers had gathered on the sidewalk. The crowd milled about in the chill morning air, bundled against the ravages of winter, speculating in steamy whispers about the events inside as the Ninth Precinct detectives made their notifications and began to cordon off the area. Soon the crime scene was secured, and the desultory onlookers moved on to other things. Violent death was no novelty on East Eleventh Street.

For Frank and Bob, the murder of John Lunievicz brought the arrogance and brutality of the Rock Solid organization once again into sharp focus. They saw it at once as a defiant boast by Alejandro Lopez that, despite police interference, he still called the shots on East Eleventh Street, and a sobering reminder that they were yet a long way from their goal of capturing him. Early reports from the Ninth Precinct uncovered a rumor being spread across the Lower East Side neighborhood that Lunievicz had been killed for being an undercover policeman. Once again, members of Rock Solid had seized the moment to drive fear into the hearts of the already terrified residents of East Eleventh Street. They had witnessed what happened to informers; now they were being shown that even the police could not escape the awful avenging wrath of Alejandro Lopez.

Back at the Twenty-third Precinct Bob Barchiesi reported the Lunievicz homicide to Deputy Inspector Martin O'Boyle, stressing what Frank and Bob believed was the obvious link with the Lopez organization and requesting authority to expand their previous investigation of The Rock at 507 East Eleventh Street. O'Boyle went them one better. He authorized Bose and Barchiesi to work the Lopez case *exclusively*. From there on in, they would be permitted to spend all of their working hours on Rock Solid. It was a highly unusual move but O'Boyle was sensitive to the repercussions that had begun to echo from the media and the downtown brass. Lopez had become big trouble, and big news.

For Frank and Bob it was like a vote of confidence. Buoyed by the expanded latitude they had been given, they began by contacting the NYPD Management Information Systems Division (MISD) and obtaining a computer printout of every violent crime that had been reported in the three square block area encompassing 507 East Eleventh Street during the previous five years. The results were staggering, even to Bose and Barchiesi who were fully aware of Lopez's violent history: This tiny pocket of humanity, three small blocks on the map of Manhattan, consistently displayed crime rates thirty to thirty-five percent higher than the most notorious crime-ridden areas of the city. And of the thousands of burglaries, robberies, muggings, stabbings, shootings, and homicides that had been logged since 1978, there were few that could not be directly attributed to the Rock Solid cocaine empire.

"Sometimes the links were obscure, but there was never any doubt that Lopez was responsible," Frank Bose recalled. "If he had never set up shop on East Eleventh Street, there would never have been the enormous numbers of related crimes in that area. If Alejandro Lopez had never come through his mother's womb, this area wouldn't have festered the way it did."

They began the painstaking task of once again drawing up organizational charts, mapping the structure of the Rock Solid organization from top to bottom. At the top, all power flowed from

Alejandro Lopez down through a baffling array of confederates, building and street managers, dealers, lookouts, steerers, and runners. Where mug shots or surveillance photos of individuals were available, they were affixed to their corresponding box on the charts, down to the most insignificant street dealers. They knew that when the time came for them to testify against Lopez, they would be called upon to provide documentation of their charges, and so they burned the midnight oil, night after night, referencing and cross-checking until their minds clouded over from the sheer volume of information they were forced to absorb.

"Undercovers bought up people on the street at the same time," Bob related. "New faces, kids we'd never seen before. We figured they were being shipped up through the pipeline from Aguadilla. Every time we busted one of them we'd ask them to pose and snap their picture for our collection back at the precinct. They could've told us to 'go to hell' and refused, but most of them just puffed out their chests and mugged for the camera. I guess it made them feel important."

By now Frank and Bob were bringing paperwork home with them, when they got home at all. Frank would rise two hours earlier than usual and work out new programs on his home computer. He and Bob read and reread the programs, covering the same ground over and over, concentrating on every tedious detail in an effort to find that one glaring omission in their thinking that would open yet another door for them. When they were not rummaging for figurative doors, they were knocking on real ones; practicing good old-fashioned foot-pounding detective work; questioning everyone or anyone in the neighborhood they felt might provide a new perspective, a new piece of the puzzle. The answer was there, they were convinced. Somewhere in the harrowing piles of paperwork, the files, forms, arrest records, photo montages, and computer printouts . . . somewhere in the minds and hearts of witnesses who remained too terrified to come forward was the final, unassailable piece of information that would lead to Alejandro Lopez's final destruction.

The legwork paid off. On the evening of January 9, 1988, as they were making their customary swing through East Eleventh Street, they spotted a male Hispanic named Ricky, known to them as "Truck" because he had once been a professional truck driver. Although Frank and Bob had no reason to believe that Ricky was intimately associated with the Lopez operation, they knew he had been involved in drug activities before and suspected that he might have information about the Lunievicz homicide. They approached him as he spoke with two other male Hispanics in an open doorway and asked them all to return to the Ninth Precinct for questioning.

The three were debriefed by members of the Ninth Precinct Squad and released without having provided any significant new information. As he was about to leave the precinct, Ricky veered off into a private office:

"I want to talk to you guys in private," he confided once he was out of earshot of the others. "Downtown on Twelfth and Second in an hour, okay?"

"What's it about, Ricky?" Bob asked.

"In an hour." Truck turned and left the precinct.

Frank and Bob were there at the appointed hour, in time to observe Ricky pacing nervously beneath a sidewalk lamp post on Second Avenue, his already battered face twisted with fear. Frank edged the car carefully to the curb as Bob rolled down the window.

"What's up, Ricky?" he asked warily.

Ricky's animal eyes raked the periphery. "Let me in the car," he rasped.

Frank and Bob had their service revolvers drawn, resting between their legs on the vinyl car seat. Truck scanned the street one last time as Bob reached behind and unlatched the rear door, then plunged headlong into the backseat and curled on the floor of the car. "Get the hell out of here!" he yelled hoarsely.

Frank drove while Bob searched Ricky for a weapon. "Okay, whatta you got to tell us?" he asked once he was satisfied that Truck was unarmed.

"That Tito Lopez is no good. He's a piece of shit," Ricky said fiercely.

"We *know* he's no good," Frank broke in. "What's your point?"

"He's no good in the heart," Ricky repeated, pounding his chest with his closed fist. "We grew up together, Tito was my best friend, and he came to my house and put a gun to my head in front of my wife and said he was going to blow my brains out."

"Why did he do that?"

Ricky shrugged. "I dunno. He said I owed him fifty dollars."

"He was going to kill you for fifty bucks?"

"Like I said, he's no good in the heart."

"So what does this have to do with us?" Frank broke in impatiently.

"I know you guys picked up money from Bobby Feliciano."

Bob shot a glance at Frank. "Yeah, what else do you know?"

Ricky went on to furnish explicit details of several meetings between Bose, Barchiesi, Feliciano, and other Rock Solid confederates. The disclosures took Frank and Bob by surprise. They hadn't known that Truck was so well connected within the Lopez organization.

"So what're you telling us?" Frank prodded. "We already know Tito is in Aguadilla."

"He's in the fuckin' Bronx, man," Ricky corrected him. "I seen him there a couple of times."

"Seen him *where* in the Bronx?"

"They got a club up there on Westchester and Evergreen avenues. I seen him driving his brown Buick Le Sabre up there."

"You sure about this, Ricky?" Bob asked.

"Why should I lie to you guys? I seen him at the club and I seen he got a Mac Ten machine gun sitting right in the back of his Buick." Ricky's voice became hushed. "You two better be careful. He said if you two ever tried to take him, he'd kill you both. He said he's got a bullet just waiting for each one of you."

Threats were threats, and there had been a lot of them, but they never got any easier to take. Frank and Bob had learned to live with the idea that they and their families were targets, and that they might be blown away from ambush at any moment of the day or night. The knowledge had honed their instincts, made them super-sensitive to sounds and images and the feelings in their gut. On the job they took every unexpected movement as a sign of imminent danger. At home both of them slept fitfully, alert to sounds and movements in the night.

Ricky's warning resounded in Bob Barchiesi's head as he drove home that night. It was almost 4:30 A.M. when he arrived at his quiet tree-lined block. The street was dimly illuminated by an almost full moon and wreathed with shimmering ice-blue stars that penetrated the overhang of denuded tree branches and danced across his windshield like tracers. He was exhausted but he knew he would not sleep. Jumbled images of the investigation would come in the dark to haunt him, and as much as he needed to dismiss it, Ricky's whispered admonition would remain.

He passed a car that was parked diagonally across the street from his house with its headlights on and motor running. Instinctively he glanced into the front seat as he drove by and caught the silhouette of a single male driver sitting motionless behind the steering wheel. The car began to move slowly as he pulled into his driveway, edging across the street toward him. Bob was out of his car instantly, his gun drawn and pressed against his right thigh. He could see the car moving toward him through the steam of his own heavy breathing, and hear the steady drone of its approaching motor above the pounding of his heart. He stiffened, his index finger tightened on the trigger as the car drew even with him at the entrance of his driveway.

"Thanks, you saved me the trouble of stuffing it in your mailbox." The friendly face of a young man appeared through the partially rolled-down window of the car. He reached across the front seat and handed Bob a rolled copy of his daily newspaper. "Have a good day," he grinned and drove away.

Chapter Twenty-nine

ACTING on Ricky's tip, Bose and Barchiesi ran down a social club at Westchester Avenue and Evergreen Avenue in the Bronx called Diviertase, and discovered that Hilda Vasquez, Alejandro Lopez's sister-in-law, was listed as one of the principal owners. This disclosure, coupled with Ricky's assertion that he had recently seen Lopez in the club, were all they needed to conclude that the Bronx connection was too significant to ignore. It was evident that a major surveillance of the location would have to take place and the sooner they were able to set it in motion the better chance they would have of spotting the elusive drug kingpin.

Frank had been kicking an idea around for months, and he decided it was time to bring it to Lieutenant Jerry Robbins at the Anti-Crack Unit. Frank knew that Robbins had a technical background like himself, and that he was known around the unit as a gadgeteer and an expert scrounger. Whatever the item, however scarce or impossible to come by it may have been, Jerry Robbins was the kind of guy who would bust his balls to get it, and he usually did, especially if he was presented with a challenge or a dare.

Frank's plan was to build a customized surveillance vehicle, using electronics items purchased with drug forfeiture money, pirated from other unused police vehicles, or simply scrounged wherever and whenever the opportunity presented itself. Jerry Robbins liked the idea and from that moment on, Frank knew he had him hooked. He suggested to Robbins that there was probably no way they could lay their hands on the type of vehicle they needed, and in a few days Jerry scrounged a blue-and-white police vehicle which they repainted. Frank had a shopping list of electronics equipment he needed to complete the project. Once again he suggested to Robbins that there was no way they could come close to getting it all, even with the five thousand dollars of drug forfeiture money Robbins had managed to obtain. Jerry took it as a personal assault on his initiative. In a matter of days he came up with everything Frank had requested and more.

Working by hand in the downstairs garage of the Anti-Crack Unit, Frank and Jerry Robbins, along with Detectives Paul Van Eyken and Tommy Lohmann, brought Frank's plans and diagrams to life. They worked on their own time, weekends and evenings, each contributing his own area of expertise until the project was completed. The finished project was a masterpiece. It was fully soundproofed, carpeted, rigged for still, film, and video photography with super-sensitive listening devices, recording mechanisms, and microphones front and back. An ultra-sophisticated VCR system was linked to the video surveillance camera and equipped with a hard-copy photoprinter that produced instant photographic images seconds after they had been shot. Operated with a special battery system, its cameras were sensitive to ultra-low light conditions, able to read license-plate numbers in total darkness for up to eight hours at a stretch. Nothing the NYPD had in its inventory could come close to matching it for high-tech effectiveness.

Now the Bronx surveillance could begin in earnest. Hour after hour, day after day, Frank and Bob and the rest of the Rock Solid team sat in the van and filmed the Diviertase social club. There was little doubt that drug activity was taking place inside, but the volume of sales was a trickle compared to drug activity on East Eleventh Street. More importantly, nothing was seen of Alejandro Lopez or any of the other major Rock Solid operatives. It was beginning to look like a dead end.

If the Bronx social club was an unproductive lead, things were beginning to heat up on other fronts. "Bunny Mother," Maria Salazar, had become a consistently reliable informant since the Lunievicz murder, filling some of the gaps in their knowledge of the Rock Solid organization. A young woman named Toni Menendez dealt cocaine in The Rock, she told Frank and Bob. Toni Menendez could tell them a lot about the operation and about Alejandro Lopez, Maria asserted, and if they could get to her she probably would. She had a big mouth.

Maria was right. A police undercover named Gabe Galliano had little trouble in establishing contact with Toni and winning her confidence. Before long she was taking long rides in Galliano's undercover car and bragging to him about her contacts within the Rock Solid organization. She was close to Lopez she told him, suggesting that there was more to their relationship than business. Tito Lopez had important friends in the Medellín, Colombia, drug cartel, she said. They, as well as The Man, would protect her if the police tried to cause her trouble. Gabe took it all in with interest. So did Frank and Bob, who were following in their customized surveillance vehicle. Gabe was wearing a wire and every word Toni spoke was being recorded.

They followed the pair to a location at 2175 Cedar Avenue in the Bronx where Toni led Galliano to a sixth-floor apartment. Inside, Galliano purchased an eighth of a kilo of cocaine from Leonardo Carreon and Raul Garcia "Goggles" Feliciano, the lookout they'd busted on a murder rap back at the warehouse. Although the surveillance team was unaware of it at the time, Carreon had fled The Rock at 507 East Eleventh Street after he had participated in the murder of John Lunievicz. Feliciano was the lookout who had impersonated a blind man outside of Alejandro Lopez's TriBeCa warehouse three years earlier.

They continued to make cocaine buys at the Cedar Avenue apartment throughout the following weeks, as well as monitor several other locations that Toni Menendez and Gabe Galliano led them to until they were satisfied they had enough evidence to make arrests. Warrants were obtained but just as they were about to be served, a fight broke out in the Cedar Avenue apartment over a spilled glass of water. In the fray, Leonardo got stabbed eight or nine times in the chest and abdomen with a switchblade knife and was sent to the Bronx Lebanon Hospital emergency ward in critical condition. It screwed up the surveillance team's plans. The warrants had to be rewritten.

On February 18, the team hit three locations in the Bronx simultaneously: an apartment on Morris Avenue, a restaurant on East 183rd Street, and the 2175 Cedar Avenue apartment occupied by Goggles Feliciano and Toni Menendez. While Detective Bobby "The Goose" Geis arrested Leonardo Carreon in Bronx Lebanon Hospital, Frank and Bob led the assault on Cedar Avenue, along with Lieutenants John Fahey and Jerry Robbins. Using a pneumatic battering ram on the door of the sixth-floor apartment, they stormed inside with shotguns and assault rifles, surprising Toni Menendez as she watched television in the front living room. Frank went into the rear bedroom where Goggles was sleeping and pressed the barrel of a shotgun under his nose. "Up, scumbag!" he ordered.

Maria Salazar had told Frank and Bob about threats that Goggles had made against them to his drug associates. "How about it, Raul?" Bob asked, backing Goggles against the wide-open bedroom window overlooking Cedar Avenue six floors below while both lieutenants waited outside in the living room. "We hear you've been telling everybody you're gonna blow us away with a machine gun. Is that true?"

"Who told you a thing like that, man?" Goggles's eyes went wide. The ominous sounds of traffic drifting upward from the street behind him magnified the terror he already felt. He had heard stories about these two *loco* cops before. "You know, life is a precious thing. I got great respect for life."

Bob stifled a smile. "Hey, if life is such a precious thing to you, how come you carved your buddy Leonardo up like that?"

"No, no. There must be some mistake!" Goggles was sweating profusely in spite of the cold air blowing through the open window. "I would never threaten men like you."

Wordlessly Frank and Bob lifted the smaller man by his elbows and sat him on the windowsill with his back to the street below. "I know you'd never be dumb enough to threaten me and my partner," Bob started speaking in a low voice as Frank began to rhythmically clap his hands together. "Because if you did, you'd probably end up out there on Cedar Avenue. Know what I mean?"

The tempo of Frank's handclapping increased like the beat of bongo drums, punctuating Bob's remarks like a bludgeoning metronome: two claps of his hands together, two slaps of his thighs, followed by two menacing thumps of Goggles's heaving chest.

"We'd really hate to see that, Raul," Bob continued above the throbbing beat of Frank's grim pat-a-cake charade. "Being that life is such a precious thing to you and all . . ."

Clap, clap; slap, slap; thump, thump. Frank was not smiling.

Bob removed Goggles's Coke-bottle lenses. "You see Raul, unless we're satisfied here that you didn't really mean those things you said, the only thing that won't be cracked on you will be your glasses."

Goggles swallowed hard. "Hey, man, you don't want to do this thing . . ."

"What we want is Tito Lopez," Bob broke in. "We know you know where he is."

Clap clap; slap, slap; thump, thump.

Goggles's animal eyes darted back and forth between them. His breathing came in shallow, labored gulps.

"Tito Lopez," Bob repeated evenly. "After you have landed we will put these intact eyeglasses back on your shattered body and confound the coroner . . ."

Clap, clap; slap, slap; thump, thump. The force of Frank's palms on Goggles's chest pushed him to the brink. His eyes were pressed closed, his sweat-soaked face tightened in anticipation of the awful final thrust that would send him hurtling to the sidewalk below. Still he remained resolutely silent, as if this violent, cataclysmic death was preferable to what he knew awaited him if he gave up Tito Lopez.

"This is your last chance . . ." Bob warned.

Goggles stiffened. His right hand shot upward in a jerky motion as if he was crossing himself before uttering a final, desperate prayer.

Bob turned away disgustedly. "Alright, let's take this scumbag downtown."

"Yeah, I know." Frank slapped the cuffs on Goggles's wrists. "Life is a precious fucking thing."

Chapter Thirty

"We had made up our minds that if Lopez got either one of us, the other would take him down no matter how he had to do it, and to hell with the job."

—BOB BARCHIESI

As a result of the Bronx raids, fifteen people were arrested for sale and possession of narcotics, three pounds of cocaine and 335 vials of crack were seized, along with weapons and several thousand dollars in cash. Goggles refused to make a deal to furnish information about Tito Lopez and faced charges on an A-1 felony with jail time equivalent to the sentence for first-class murder. All in all, Bose and Barchiesi were satisfied that the operation had been productive since it provided yet another layer of pressure Lopez would have to deal with in the coming months. Inch by painful inch, Lopez was watching the underpinnings of his empire beginning to fall apart. His preening aura of invincibility crumbled with every new arrest and seizure. Every busted drug confederate sapped his strength a little more, and increased the steadily mounting body of evidence that was accumulating against him. Day by day the noose drew tighter.

As more and more records on Lopez began to surface, Frank and Bob reached out to police departments throughout the country in an attempt to cut off every possible avenue of escape left to him. The woman named Hilda Vasquez had been identified as Lopez's sister-in-law, and by monitoring her telephone records they discovered a large volume of calls being made from Puerto Rico to locations in Gastonia, North Carolina, and Portland, Maine. Bob placed a call to Sergeant Edwards of the Gastonia Police Department and informed him of the telephone calls as well as New York's ongoing investigation into Lopez and Rock Solid. Edwards was impressed. The law enforcement officials and citizens of Gastonia did not tolerate people of Lopez's stripe, he

189

informed Bob. If Lopez was anywhere nearby, New York could rest assured he would no longer be a problem to them or anyone else.

The telephone calls to Maine had been made to the NCO residence quarters of an active naval base. Frank phoned the base provost marshal's office and secured a promise that the location would be investigated and the results made known to him. The navy wasted no time. Frank received word in a few hours that the premises had been raided and the occupants, a woman who later proved to be Hilda Vasquez's sister was evicted on the spot. The message had to be getting through to friends, relatives, and associates that it was not a healthy thing to be associated with Alejandro Lopez.

Records seized from the Englewood Cliffs raid disclosed that Lopez had a daughter, Nina, who graduated from one of the most expensive private schools in New York and was currently attending Harvard University in Cambridge, Massachusetts. Photos, warrants, and records were FAXed to the Harvard campus police detailing Alejandro Lopez's criminal past and requesting any information about him they might possess. While his daughter was not suspected of complicity in any of the Rock Solid dealings, it was certain that word would filter back to her father that the Harvard police had joined in his pursuit.

"We were in high gear now," Bob recalled. "Everything we did was calculated to push him into a tighter and tighter corner. In the beginning we'd been reacting to Lopez: He'd make a move and we'd respond to it. Now the tables were turned. Everywhere he looked we were pressing in on him. He had to believe that he couldn't trust even his closest friends at that point; that he couldn't have a private conversation or make a telephone call without it getting right back to us. Wherever he was he was sweating, and he knew he had to do something to get us off his back."

What Lopez did was offer them a sacrificial lamb. On February 21, a message was sent to New York from the police department in Aguadilla that Nelson Alphonso, Lopez's bodyguard and enforcer, had been arrested in Puerto Rico and was being held for extradition back to New York. Frank and Bob were suspicious of the communication, especially since they believed that some of the Aguadilla police had by that time been thoroughly corrupted by Rock Solid money, but also because a one-week time limit had been arbitrarily set for Alphonso's extradition. It was obvious to Bose and Barchiesi that Sergeant Morales did not want New York police nosing around Aguadilla for any extended period of time.

The one-week time limit pressed NYPD's lumbering system of paperwork and procedures to the limit. In order to obtain the proper authorization for an overseas extradition, Frank had to hand-carry the innumerable forms required from department to department, sidestepping the tedious system of protocols that was usually observed. He accomplished in less than three days what usually took weeks and by February 24 he was fully authorized to travel to Puerto Rico and pick up Nelson Alphonso.

NYPD regulations prevented Bob from going, the theory being that supervisors were needed at home and too valuable to spare for what they saw as a mopping-up exercise. Both he and Frank were disappointed since their underlying reason for wanting to make the trip was to gather information on the possible whereabouts of Alejandro Lopez. By now they were both used to functioning as a team. Having to proceed alone was, for Frank, like entering the arena with one arm tied behind his back.

Still, it was the break they had both been looking for, and on Wednesday, February 25, he and Detective Louie Torrellas took an afternoon flight to San Juan and went immediately to POPR in Caguas where they reported to Major Miguel Castillo of the Fugitive Extradition Unit. Castillo, a robust, full-bearded caricature of a banana-republic dictator, was resplendent in crisply starched fatigues that glistened with rows of campaign medals. He offered them a cup of coffee and stretched behind his ornate wooden desk: "Your prisoner will be ready for you to take back to New York on Friday," he informed them with a smile. "Have a good time while you're here. Go to your hotel and relax on the beach. When you leave on Friday, we'll have him waiting for you at the airport."

It was all taken care of. Frank had less than two days to try and locate Lopez so there was no time for the beach. He left Louie Torrellas at their hotel and took a cab to the FBI regional headquarters at Hato Rey, where he contacted Special Agent Bram Carper, whose radio handle was "Agent Surf King." Not expecting much help from local police, Frank and Bob had worked to involve the FBI in the Lopez case back in New York. Assistant District Attorney Pat Conlan had obtained a fugitive warrant for Lopez's arrest and transferred it to Hato Rey. Now, after meeting the clean-cut FBI agent for the first time, Frank was concerned:

"He started out by telling me all the problems he had finding out about Lopez," Frank remembered. "He said he'd had trouble disseminating the information we had sent him from New York, and that he'd had no luck verifying the phone records we'd sent him through the local telephone company. I thought that was strange, since Bob and I had gotten everything we'd asked them for. We'd found they were more than willing to help."

Frank shook his head. "It was pretty obvious to me from the beginning that if we left it to the FBI, we'd never run Lopez down. When I asked Carper whether a Department of Motor Vehicles check had been done he told me it had been run under the name Alejandro Lopez. *That was it*, nothing more; it hadn't occurred to anyone to run Lopez under his mother's name, Garcia. Here was a bureau that was supposed to be expert in Latin American affairs and no one stopped to think that Spanish people often use a matronymic. Lopez could have been calling himself Alejandro Lopez *Garcia* or Alejandro *Garcia* Lopez. No one thought of that."

Frank suggested that they begin by driving out to Rio Piedras and questioning Natalia Torres, the wife of one of Lopez's close associates. Carper agreed and volunteered the information that he had been out to Rio Piedras several times before but had not been successful in locating Natalia or her residence.

Agent Surf King's difficulties notwithstanding, they located Natalia Torres's residence almost as soon as they arrived at the supermarket they had been directed to. Their knock was answered by a middle-aged woman who identified herself as Natalia. Carper, who spoke excellent Spanish, began to question Natalia, but it soon became apparent to Frank that this was not the kind of interrogation he was used to. Maybe it was the difference between Spanish and English, maybe it was 5,000 miles or three and a half years of hunting Lopez. Whatever the reason, the questions seemed rambling and not to the point. If the questions followed a pattern, Frank couldn't see it. If the questions were meant to lead to meaningful conclusions, Frank couldn't find them. Finally, Frank stepped in and took over the questioning.

As it turned out, Natalia spoke almost perfect English and the interview proceeded smoothly. While she was not ready to give up Lopez entirely, it was obvious through her answers that she was aware of the pressure being applied to members of Lopez's family and had no desire to provoke the authorities further. Lopez had visited her some months earlier and had stayed in a spare bedroom for a few days, Natalia allowed, but she did not know of his present whereabouts. She related that he had recently visited his father and that he had been seen walking some of his pet pit bull terriers, and through Frank's skillful questioning, dropped several unintentional hints that Lopez was still somewhere on the island.

On the trip back from Rio Piedras, Frank concluded that he'd rather depend on himself than on the FBI. While he had not expected Carper to share his own intensity over Lopez, he assumed the FBI agent would at least respond with interest. To Frank, Carper seemed less interested in pursuing the fugitive druglord than he was in keeping track of his expenses. Every few miles, the pitted road back to town was punctuated with ramshackle tollbooths and Carper would ask for a receipt at every one. They would wait interminably while a slow-moving government functionary hand-scribbled a receipt, which the Surf King would tuck into his expense ledger. He told Frank that he never spent a nickel on the job that wasn't vouchered to the Bureau.

They drove to the town of Isabela, where Lopez's father was reported to live. Carper had a plan: They would locate the local postman in an attempt to ascertain Lopez's whereabouts. Frank suggested that they might get better results by simply going to the local post office and questioning the postmaster. Surf King reluctantly agreed. They arrived at the Isabela Post Office and located the postman who was responsible for mail delivery in the area where Lopez had reportedly been seen. Carper immediately began to question him in flawless Spanish: "My associate does not speak your language," Frank understood him to say smugly. The postman eyed them both inquisitively. "Then why don't we speak English?" he suggested with barely an accent, relating that he had retired and returned to Puerto Rico after having spent most of his adult life working in Brooklyn.

Carper again began his interrogation, this time in English, but even in English his questions sounded rambling to Frank's impatient ear.

"Have you ever seen any of these men?" Frank broke in, placing an array of six photographs in front of the confused mailman.

The mailman scanned the array of portraits, all Hispanic males with the same approximate features. "Sure, I saw this man this morning," he replied, pointing with certainty to the mug shot of Alejandro Lopez. "He was right here in this building."

Frank felt his chest tighten. "Are you certain? Look at the photograph again."

"That's the man," he asserted. "He was with a young girl and a baby. He had a pit bull dog on a leash."

"Was he driving a vehicle?" Frank asked excitedly.

"A tan van with sliding doors. They were parked right in front of the cafeteria down the street."

It was too good to be real. Lopez's father lived in a house next door to the cafeteria. "How can you be so certain of these things?" Frank asked him.

"I know everyone in Isabela," the mailman responded proudly. "This man was a stranger."

Back at FBI headquarters, they ran a DMV check and found that a tan van was registered to an Alejandro *Garcia* Lopez. "That rips it," Frank said resolutely to Carper. "Let's go back to Natalia, force her to tell us where he is, and take him now."

Surf King turned ashen. "Let's not do anything hasty here," he cautioned. "This is a dangerous fugitive. We can't just go charging in there. I'll have to notify my superiors. There's an inspection coming up. This will require some careful planning. We'll have to assemble SWAT units . . ." the list went on.

Frank returned to his hotel, disheartened. "Lopez is down here, *definitely*," he told Bob over the telephone. "But there's no way we're going to get much help from this FBI asshole, Carper. If we're going to get him, you and I are going to have to come down here by ourselves and do it. There's no other way."

Major Miguel Castillo was waiting at the San Juan airport on Friday morning with Frank's prisoner as he had promised. Handcuffed during the entire flight back to New York, Alphonso suggested to Frank and Louis Torrellas that he had been set up; that Lopez had put a gun to his head and threatened to kill him, and that he was now prepared to cooperate with the police and testify against his former boss. Frank listened to Alphonso's account halfheartedly. His mind was back in Puerto Rico, back in the rutted streets of Isabela where Alejandro Lopez walked freely with his pit bull dogs on a leash. The events of the past three years swirled kaleidoscopically in his mind and slowly coalesced into a single, unalterable conviction:

He and Bob were going to Puerto Rico and they were coming back with Tito Lopez or they were coming back dead.

Chapter Thirty-one

WHILE Frank was still in Puerto Rico, Bob was assigned to supervise a Queens, N.Y., task force that was pursuing the killers of Edward Byrne, a young New York City patrolman who had been gunned down by members of the Pappy Mason drug ring. Byrne's assassination was a stark reminder to every other member of the force that the new breed of drug criminals respected no uniform, badge, or credential when it came to protecting their interests. They were now prepared to gun down a policeman as easily as they would gun down a drug confederate. In New York City, all-out war had been declared by the druglords and cops were now fair game.

The message was not lost on Frank and Bob. Although they had never questioned Alejandro Lopez's capacity for violence, the brutal execution of Edward Byrne underscored the grim reality of the threats Lopez had made against them and their families. If either of them had ever harbored a secret doubt that Lopez was fully prepared to kill them and mutilate their children, that doubt was forever washed away as the final drops of Patrolman Edward Byrne's young life spilled out on a dusty Queens street.

Cops die. It never gets any easier.

Frank and Bob discussed it over drinks at The Wicked Wolf as they laid out plans for their return to Puerto Rico. In Aguadilla they would be on Lopez's turf. They could expect no protection from a police department if it was on his payroll. It was almost a certainty that he knew they were coming and would be ready for them. He knew they had tracked him for more than three years and that they would not quit now. Frank and Bob had no idea how far his tentacles reached, but the thought that they might never make it off the airplane was not beyond believing.

Still, there was never any question about whether they would go, only when, and what procedures they would follow when they went. They discussed the possibility of trying to obtain police permission to travel to Puerto Rico and make the arrest, but it was immediately obvious that there was no way the department would sanction it. A police department that was too timid to enter an apartment in a New York City—owned tenement to arrest drug dealers inside was certainly not going to authorize a highly speculative trip to an overseas jurisdiction. If they were going, they were strictly on their own.

They had crossed an invisible line, and there was no turning back. What they knew they had to do contravened almost every rule of police protocol. New York City cops did not stick their necks out without departmental sanction if they wanted a steady job on the force. They did not make unauthorized trips thousands of miles away and shove their noses into the affairs of other police jurisdictions where they were not wanted. They certainly did not dig into their own pockets and spend their life's savings on a venture that was likely to end their careers and possibly their lives. Frank and Bob were prepared to do all of this, and more if they had to. Their obsession with capturing Alejandro Lopez was total.

Jerry Speziale told them it was right, but he also told them in a hundred subtle ways that it was not smart. Jerry had come in on the Rock Solid operation during the latter part of the investigation after the threats against Bob's and Frank's families, and if they had reason to believe that anyone would take it to the mat with them, that person would have to be Jerry. But Jerry backed off. Without actually coming right out and saying so, he made it clear to them that he had enjoyed the train ride for as long as it lasted, but that he was getting off before it crashed. He was simply not willing to put his career on the line for a scumbag like Alejandro Lopez. He wished Frank and Bob well and they both understood, but it still hurt.

The major sticking point was whether or not they would go to Puerto Rico armed. Plainly, they would be leaving themselves dangerously vulnerable if they went unarmed. Lopez had guns and the will to use them, and there was no guarantee that they would be given weapons by the FBI in Puerto Rico if the need arose. But carrying weapons into another jurisdiction was technically illegal, and they themselves risked the chance of being arrested by the Puerto Rican police, or worse. As far as Frank and Bob were concerned, the police in Aguadilla were at the very least inept and at the worst corrupt. Frank and Bob had no reason to suspect that POPR would treat them kindly if it was discovered they were carrying illegal weapons.

The argument went on for a week, sometimes hot and heavy, lasting into the small hours of the morning in The Wicked Wolf. "We kept the place in business," Frank recalled with a smile. "The waitress, Maureen, got to know us better than her own family. I think if a night had gone by without us coming in she would have missed us. Bob and I fought like hell about this thing. I told him that I didn't give a shit about the job or the POPR. I wasn't going to leave myself out in the open like that where Lopez could take his time zeroing in on me. All I wanted was an equal chance. I wanted to take the nine millimeters down there even if it meant smuggling them onto the island. I pointed out that we would have already crossed the line as soon as we stepped off the plane in San Juan. Our careers were probably down the toilet anyway. What the hell did we have to lose?"

Bob argued with equal conviction that even more than the possibility of arrest by local police, by carrying illegal weapons they would be running the risk of being shot and killed in Puerto Rico without justification. Men carrying unlawful handguns could be reasonably accused of any crime and there was little anyone could say in their defense, whether or not they were New York City policemen. In fact, a case could be made that since they had once received bribes from Lopez, they had gone to Puerto Rico to resume their business relationship. Bob remembered Inspector Thomas Gallagher's dire warning of three years before: that the time would come when nobody would remember it had been a police operation. All that would be remembered was that two cops had once been on the take.

Frank finally relented, and the last hurdle had been overcome. They made a joint decision that, rather than be accused of running a totally clandestine operation, they would notify everyone and anyone who was not in a position to stop them. That translated to anyone outside of the job who did not have the will or the authority to sabotage their plans. They informed members of the District Attorney's office in New York and the US Attorney's office in Puerto Rico, Judge Leslie Snyder, and the FBI. Frank spoke at length with Agent "Surf King" on the telephone and told him to expect them any day. Surf King was not overjoyed at the prospect but he could do nothing to prevent them from coming in an unofficial capacity.

"We planned it out right to the last detail," Bob remembered. "We didn't want to be seen as a couple of hothead bozo cops charging in there with our guns blazing. Not that we didn't think about it. Frankly, we talked about blowing him away with a high-powered rifle and throwing the gun in the Caribbean, but all it was was talk. We're professionals and we knew for this thing to work it had to be a thoroughly professional operation, no matter what we felt in our gut. We went out of our way to notify everybody that we were only going down there to assist the FBI in their operation and to provide information, period." Bob grinned. "Nothing could have been further from the truth, but that was what we told everybody. You do what you have to do, right?"

"I would have had no qualms about killing Lopez," Frank admitted. "I would have taken my chances with any grand jury in America; just walked up to the witness stand and sworn that I truly believed that my little girl was going to die unless I stopped this man. And I did. I believed then and I believe now that it would have only been a matter of time before Lopez made good on his promise. Maybe the grand jury would have found against me, but at least Lopez would be gone and my family would be safe . . ." Frank pondered it. "It would have been a pretty interesting case, don't you think?"

They arranged for a week of vacation time each, and on the morning of March 12, 1988, after withdrawing most of their personal savings from the bank, they drove to Kennedy Airport and boarded a plane for San Juan. For both of them, the idea that they were finally getting a shot at the man who had consumed their lives for so long was like a dream they had not dared to believe. They had spent almost every working hour together and most of their free time for more than three years planning for this very moment. They had followed every lead, pursued every avenue available to them for as long as they had known one another in an obsessive, relentless search for a single New York druglord: Alejandro Lopez, a man who had committed the crime of infesting the Lower East Side with lethal poison and the fatal blunder of thinking he could buy, bully, and terrorize Frank Bose and Bob Barchiesi.

Lopez had come to stand for everything Frank and Bob hated, but he was no longer a symbol; no longer a photograph on the precinct wall for them to puncture with darts, no longer a name whispered in trembling voices by terrified residents of Alphabet City, no longer a larger-than-life abstract who seemed forever beyond their reach. Somewhere below, cowering in the dense

Caribbean foliage, Alejandro Lopez waited for their arrival with anticipation and fear. They could see his contours in the billowing clouds beneath them, hear the rasp of his heavy breathing in the drone of jet engines, smell his nervous sweat filling the antiseptic confines of the airplane as it drew them closer and closer to their target.

Lopez was real, and he was finally theirs.

Chapter Thirty-two

T HE plane coasted to a smooth landing in San Juan, and they both breathed a sigh of relief. Frank reached above him to remove his carry-on bag from the overhead compartment and felt a stabbing pain. His back had gone out. It was an old job-related injury that never seemed to get any better. Whenever he stood too long, or sat too long, or simply reached out in the wrong way as he had now, his back went out and it hurt like hell.

"You okay?" Bob asked, noticing his discomfort.

Frank grabbed the bag and stepped into the crowded aisle. "My back," he winced. "What a fucking lousy time for this to happen."

"You going to make it?"

Frank looked at Bob like he was out of his mind. "Are you kidding? It'd take a lot more than a bad back to stop me at this point." He made his way resolutely to the front of the plane and out into the terminal.

After renting a car at the airport, they drove to the Howard Johnson Hotel in San Juan where they deposited their bags in the room and continued on immediately to Aguadilla. It was dark by the time Frank had negotiated their way to Rio Piedras and located Natalia Torres's house once again. They drove past, then on to Lopez's father's house in Isabela, where they again made a drive-by surveillance. They had no intention of questioning anyone that late at night but Bob wanted to familiarize himself with the terrain. They had only a short time to do what they had come to do. The fewer surprises they would have to confront later on the better.

They drove to FBI headquarters on Monday morning to meet with Agent Carper and were forced to cool their heels in the reception room for nearly an hour before they were finally issued hand-passes and Surf King granted them entry into his pine-panelled office. Frank was in real pain, practically immobilized by the long wait, and was in no mood for friendly chit-chat when they entered and found him sitting alone at his desk. "What happens if we don't get one of these?" he asked sarcastically, displaying the cardboard hand-pass. "Does a special FBI laser beam come shooting out of the wall and cut us in half?"

Carper ignored the barb. "I can give you both a few hours," he said laconically. "Do you have any special destination in mind?"

"We want to go out to Rio Piedras and see Natalia Torres," Frank replied in obvious pain.

"Why don't you go back to the hotel?" Bob suggested. "You're not going to be any good to us unless you rest that back for a while."

Frank reluctantly agreed. They drove back to the hotel, dropped Frank off, and Bob continued on to Rio Piedras in Carper's car. The trip, which had taken three hours the night before with Frank driving, took almost four hours due to Surf King's insistence on obtaining receipts at every toll stop. "I want to interview Natalia when we get out there," Bob told Carper on the way out, aware that he was there in a strictly unofficial capacity and that the FBI man could refuse permission for the interview.

"Sure. *Un recibo, por favor.*"

"I understand she told you that Lopez had stayed at her place for a while in a spare bedroom," Bob said.

Surf King nodded. "I went out there after your partner left and checked the place out. The air conditioner in one of the bedrooms was running while I was out there. Maybe he was there then."

Bob almost choked. "Did you go in to see if he was there?"

"I had no authorization to conduct a search," Surf King replied.

"Weren't you worried that he might come out of there and shoot you? You *are* a law enforcement officer. You do have the right to go back there and secure your own safety."

"*Un recibo por favor . . .*"

It was mid-afternoon when they arrived at Rio Piedras. Surf King knocked authoritatively on Natalia Torres's door and Bob immediately stepped in front of him and flashed his shield when she answered. "I'm Sergeant Barchiesi of the NYPD," he told her. "Maybe you heard about me. I'm one of the guys who put a lot of Tito's people in jail."

Natalia took a step backward. She had heard about the two *loco* cops who were nailing nearly anyone who had anything to do with Rock Solid and were still relentlessly tracking its boss, Alejandro Lopez.

"I'm down here with my partner," Bob went on. "And guess what? We're not going away. We'll stay here until we nail Tito.

We'll go to Brazil or Argentina or Antarctica if we have to, but we're not going back to New York without him." He looked deeply into her eyes. "We're prepared to do whatever we have to do to get Tito; to take down whoever we have to take down to get at him, understand? If that means you have to take the fall, that's the way it'll go down. It won't mean a thing to me or my partner."

Natalia's dark eyes darted nervously between Bob and Carper. It was obvious that she was not prepared for the kind of trouble she saw coming. "I don't know nothing about Tito . . ."

Bob followed her into the house. "Before you say any more you ought to know I have some documents here that might prove interesting to the authorities back in New York." He opened a manila folder he was carrying and displayed Natalia's financial records. Natalia had applied for welfare assistance, claiming that she had an income of only $150 a week while her bank receipts showed monthly deposits of more than $10,000. "I think this shows that you've been laundering money for The Rock," Bob told her matter-of-factly. "In case you didn't know, that's a crime. I should probably arrest you right now."

He believed that Natalia was ready to break, but he also knew that however strained her allegiance to Lopez might have been, she would not be persuaded to betray him on the strength of threats alone. Natalia was steeped in the traditions and behaviors of a drug society, a society that left no doubt as to the fate of informers. Bob realized that all of their careful planning, all of the pressure that they had exerted on Lopez's family and associates in New York, Maine, and North Carolina could prove fruitless unless he was able to tap into that strain of emotion that motivated her most deeply, that made her less afraid of informing on Tito Lopez than living the kind of life he had forced upon her.

Years of interviewing suspects and witnesses had honed Bob into a skillful questioner. He understood that in the most fundamental terms an interrogation is a fencing match with both participants probing for openings and weaknesses. Everything is important; an inadvertent slip of the tongue, an unguarded moment of discomfort, a reflexive blinking of the eyes, can send a subtle message that might mean the difference between success and failure. Most importantly, a skilled questioner knows that his subject needs to come away from the encounter with something more than they had when they began. In Natalia's case, Bob suspected that what she wanted most of all was a little peace of mind.

He spotted a frightened child cowering in a rear doorway as

they spoke. "To be honest, we don't really care about you, Natalia. You already have more trouble than you need. Your husband's left you and if you go away, who's going to take care of your kids?"

Natalia's shoulders slumped. The air seemed to go out of her and Bob pressed his advantage: "You see, Natalia, the thing of it is, we'll put you away if we have to but that's not our objective. We want Tito Lopez and we think you can lead us to him. We're certain you know where he is, and you have to believe you'll be better off with him out of your life, right?"

Natalia nodded resignedly. "I got a call from some Colombian who threatened to kill my children because Tito ripped him off for some dope. It's just not fair."

She went on to relate how Lopez, watching the demise of his cocaine empire resulting from constant police pressure and desperate for product to pull himself out of the hole, had stiffed a Colombian druglord for millions of dollars. He needed working capital to get moving again and he needed product to generate the capital. It was an endless, plunging spiral, Bob knew, like the last futile gasp of a dying man, paying the interest on his Visa card with his BankAmericard, and the BankAmerica interest with his American Express. Sooner or later the interest was bound to come due.

"Unfortunately, Lopez is affecting everybody's life," Bob pointed out. "But until we get him, it's just going to get worse for you."

Natalia swallowed hard. "I think I know a place where he's been staying."

"Okay, do you want to show us where it is?"

"No, no . . ." She shook her head vehemently. "I'm afraid of Tito. He'd kill me if he knew I was even talking to you."

Carper sat impassively in a chair by the window during the questioning, staring out onto the parking lot of the supermarket. He did not seem at all annoyed that Bob had shut him out of the questioning or that events seemed to be proceeding without his participation. Surf King seemed to have his mind on other things and that was just fine with Bob. The last thing he needed was an overeager Fed screwing up his good work.

"Can you tell me where Tito's place is?" Bob asked Natalia.

She jerked her head to the right. "It's a big farm down by the water, with lots of horses and pit bulls. I'm not saying he's definitely out there, but that's where he goes when he has problems. His wife and kid stay out there."

"I need directions, Natalia."

"You have to drive down a big hill to get there . . ."

"Street names," Bob interrupted her.

"Calle Esmerelda, Prado . . ." She choked the words out, as if each painful disclosure might prove to be her final undoing. "There is a street, *calle de una sola dirección*, called Septimo, I think." Her directions were scattered and Bob understood little of what she was telling him. He assumed that Surf King was absorbing most of it and could identify the places she was referring to. He was satisfied that she was telling him the truth; at least as much of the truth as she dared tell. He had questioned too many subjects in his career not to be able to tell when someone was being evasive or outright lying. Natalia Torres was terrified of Tito Lopez, but the constant turmoil her life had become because of him was forcing her to the brink of desperation.

It was evening by the time Bob had finished questioning Natalia, too dark to search for the farmhouse. Carper drove him back to the hotel, where he recounted the afternoon's events to Frank. The news was like a shot in the arm to Frank. His increased flow of adrenaline made him momentarily forget about the pain in his back, but only momentarily. He was still hurting but that was not going to stop him from joining the search for Lopez. Bad back or no bad back, he was going out there the following morning, he told Bob. He would go out there if he had to go out in a wheelchair. He hadn't come this far to be a spectator.

By the time they got to FBI headquarters in Hato Rey the following morning, he was feeling a bit better. They were joined by Special Agent John Galindo, the assistant SWAT team commander for the district, who drove with Bob in a special undercover car while Frank went out with Surf King. There was no communication between the vehicles. As diplomatically as he could, Agent Galindo told Bob that Surf King had never mastered the art of using the FBI's short-wave radio out in the field. He always transmitted on the wrong frequency when he was far from his home base.

They stopped along the way for breakfast and called Natalia Torres from a pay telephone. There was no answer. "Weren't you supposed to set it up for Natalia to be there when we called?" Bob asked Carper, who was standing by the telephone booth.

"Me?" Surf King looked astonished.

Agent Galindo stood speechless for a moment. "Are you telling me you didn't even call before we left?" he finally managed to ask the confused Carper.

"Why is this my responsibility?" Surf King asked.

"Because you're supposed to be a federal law enforcement agent, you asshole," Galindo howled. "Because you're supposed to have some inkling about what the fuck is going on around here!"

"You wrote down Natalia's directions, didn't you?" Surf King asked Bob weakly.

Bob cast a sidelong glance at Galindo whose face had assumed a mottled red flush. "What was I supposed to write down, Bram? I don't know a goddam thing about this island. Practically everything she said was Greek to me. This is your territory, I just naturally figured you were listening to her and knew what the hell she was talking about."

It was fast becoming a Keystone Kops episode. Carper assumed a pose of aggrieved innocence, climbed back inside his car, and took off with Frank after Galindo and Bob. By now, everybody knew they had no alternative but to search for the farmhouse utilizing what Bob remembered of Natalia's disclosures and Galindo's knowledge of the area. They followed several unproductive routes before Galindo finally maneuvered the FBI vehicle down a rutted dirt road that seemed to match Natalia's description. Bob noted several landmarks she had said were on the road, and could smell the tang of salt air rising through the matted canopy of trees and foliage ahead.

Suddenly it was there before them, just as Natalia Torres had described it. Nestled in a grove of grass and stately palmetto palms, the ranch stretched below them: a compound of wooden outbuildings bracketing a white stucco main house that overlooked a broad expanse of shimmering blue-green Caribbean sea. Dozens of sleek Parsefino stallions gamboled on the carefully manicured lawn, and fifty to sixty small wooden structures formed a sentry barrier that ran around the periphery.

They were in luck. A US Navy solar observatory stood on a hill above the ranch, offering an unobstructed view of the location. Galindo accompanied Frank and Bob to the gate, flashed his FBI credentials, and asked permission for them to come onto the base for purposes of observing the property below. Bob held his breath while the request was considered. It was anything but a sure thing that they would be granted access to the base. They had no military reason for being there and Naval authorities did not seem overly impressed that they were on the trail of a notorious drug-lord.

After a hushed discussion between members of the base establishment, Bob and Galindo were finally granted entry and established a surveillance position at the edge of a one-hundred-foot cliff overlooking the ranch. Sharing a pair of long-range binoculars, Bob and Agent Galindo alternately held onto each others' ankles as they dangled perilously over the precipice, observing the activity beneath them. They spotted several vehicles parked on the property: a tan van and a black Cadillac sedan identical to the one Lopez's brother, Eduardo, had been driving when he was arrested in New York the year before. Galindo ran the plate numbers over his car radio and they both came back registered to Alejandro Garcia Lopez. There was no longer any doubt.

Closer inspection of the strategically placed wooden shacks revealed a pit bull in each, resting just out of the penetrating sun, their senses alert for alien sounds and smells and movements outside the compound. "What do you make of that?" Galindo handed the binoculars to Bob.

"*Holy shit*. Anybody who tried to get through that would be torn to pieces," Bob replied.

"The man's not taking any chances," Galindo agreed.

Frank and Surf King took the other car and approached the ranch from a dirt access road that wound from the base of the cliff to the ocean. They passed the ranch several times before Frank noticed the figure of a man in a floppy straw hat, standing in the midst of the playful stallions. He wiped the sweat from his eyes and squinted through the dust that had accumulated on the car's window, making sure that he was seeing what was really there and not simply what he wanted to see. The overhead sun shaded most of the man's face beneath his wide straw brim, allowing capricious dots of light to dance across his features as he moved among the horses, providing tantalizing glimpses that disappeared with every turn of his head. Then, in an instant, the shadows receded and Frank could plainly see his eyes, his nose, the haughty thrust of his jaw.

The man was Alejandro Lopez.

Chapter Thirty-three

"WHAT do we really have here?" Carper sat behind his desk at FBI headquarters and cocked his head like an inquisitive spaniel.

"We have Tito Lopez, the guy we came down here to get!" Frank tried unsuccessfully to control the mounting anger in his voice. "We'll never have a better chance to take him than we do now."

Carper leaned back in his swivel chair. "We have no proof that it's even him."

Frank groaned. "*Proof*? I was sitting there looking him square in the face. Nobody knows that face better than me. I've been throwing darts at it for the past three years. What do we need here? Does the guy have to wear a sign on his chest saying he's Alejandro Lopez before we can go in there after him?"

Carper stared vacantly across the spacious office. "I shouldn't have to point out to you that we find ourselves at a severe tactical disadvantage here."

Frank shot a glance across the office at Galindo, who was averting his gaze embarrassedly. "How's that, Bram? At the very least there's four of us and one of him."

Carper fidgeted behind his desk. "We don't know that Lopez lives at that location. How can we draw up a warrant if we're not sure that's his place of residence?"

"Wait a minute!" Bob broke in angrily. "Let's lay it all out. What do we really have here? We have prior information going back years describing the ranch in detail, right down to the horses and pit bulls. We have Natalia, who corroborated that description and who told us how to get there. Based on her information we went out to the location and obtained a positive visual identification from a police officer who's been tracking him for the past three years. And finally, we've positively identified two vehicles on the premises as belonging to Alejandro Lopez. What more do we need?"

Carper cleared his throat nervously. Frank, Bob, and Galindo could see his mind racing. "We'll need further verification," he said finally. "I'll drive out there tomorrow with Natalia Torres and get her to positively ID the place. As soon as I can arrange it, we'll take a chopper out there and make an aerial reconnaissance of the location; take some photographs . . ."

"That could take weeks!" Bob moaned. "We don't have weeks. What happens if Natalia gets cold feet and warns Lopez that we're down here?"

Surf King shook his head somberly. "There are procedures that have to be followed here."

Bob looked across the room at Frank who was barely able to conceal his anger. Galindo had left the room. "You *are* aware that we have to be back in New York by tomorrow," he pointed out.

Carper folded his arms. "Relax. Everything will be taken care of."

Frank and Bob could not relax. Their return trip to New York was three and a half hours of recrimination and rage. Neither of them had any confidence whatsoever that Surf King had the will or the savvy to arrest Lopez, and they knew that every minute of delay diminished the chances of taking him by surprise. Any major surveillance operation such as the one Carper planned was sure to arouse the interest of local police who were probably on Lopez's payroll. Natalia was shaky. There were a thousand reasons for consternation and very few for optimism, but their hands were tied. The upshot of three and a half years of their lives would have to be left to the not-so-tender mercies of FBI Agent Bram "Surf King" Carper. It was not a cheery prospect.

Carper had given them assurances that as soon as he was satisfied that proper precautionary procedures had been followed, the FBI would lead a SWAT team assault on the Lopez ranch. The thought gave them little comfort. As much as they both liked Agent Galindo, both Frank and Bob had serious doubts about the FBI SWAT team's approach. Their operations were highlighted by ninja-black-clad assault forces, Galindo had bragged to Bob during their trip out to the Lopez ranch. One of them carried an acetylene tank on his back to cut through the steel barrier. When Bob pointed out the obvious danger of such a procedure—that one shot from a high-powered rifle hitting any of the tanks would blow their entire assault team to smithereens—Galindo had just shrugged.

Back in New York, Frank and Bob stayed in constant telephone contact with Carper, agonizing over the interminable delays, making suggestions that they realized would probably never be followed. They suggested strongly that Lopez be processed through the federal system and transferred to a federal facility in Manhattan once he was arrested, since they had good reason to suspect that the local authorities in Aguadilla might be corrupt and that he might once again escape on a horse, or something equally implausible. There would be no problem doing that, they pointed out, since the warrant against him had been issued in the district of New York. Surf King was non-committal.

Despite their constant prodding, Carper's preparations took another week. Finally, at 6:15 on the morning of March 27, battle-clad FBI SWAT troops swooped down on the location carrying assault rifles, explosives, and flamethrowers. Staying low behind protected thickets on the surrounding hills, marksmen with high-powered rifles shot out the tires of every vehicle they could see, and trained their telescopic gunsights on the farmhouse below. Special commando units crept within a few hundred yards of the ranch and shouted through an electronic bullhorn for Lopez to surrender. Awakened inside the house, Lopez heard the roar of an airplane directly overhead and decided to give up rather than become the victim of an aerial bombardment. Lopez remembered the grenade that had been thrown into the house at Englewood Cliffs. He had no reason to doubt the police would use similar force to flush him out. In fact, what seemed to be an assault from the air was merely a heavily laden Coast Guard PBY that was taking off from a nearby base, but the roar of its motors above Lopez's roof provided a bit of unexpected bounty for the assault forces. Half-dressed, Lopez staggered out onto the grounds and gave himself up without a fight.

Standing haplessly in his underwear outside the house, surrounded by growling pit bulls and thoroughbred stallions, Alejandro Lopez hardly resembled the fabled drug czar who had held a terrified neighborhood hostage for so many years. He cowered in the glare of spotlights, seemingly awed by the firepower that had been arrayed against him, waving his arms frantically and crying, "*I surrender, I surrender!*"

FBI records from that morning show that Lopez admitted his identity, as well as his guilt, while being transported to jail in San Juan. After the initial shock of his arrest, his bearing again became egomaniacal: "I'm no angel," he haughtily admitted to FBI Agents William Ramos and Bram Carper. "I know I'm guilty but I never killed nobody, I never raped nobody, and I never sold dope in

Isabela, never near my farm. You don't shit where you eat. I've got plenty of money, you know that. I could have gone to Brazil if I wanted to, but this is where I belong. This is the headquarters where I was going to build my empire."

Bose and Barchiesi had been forewarned of the exact time the raid was scheduled to take place, and on the morning of March 27, Frank waited by his telephone with almost uncontrollable anxiety for news from Carper while Bob waited at home for him to relay the results. The ordained hour came and went, and another hour slipped by without any word from Carper. The ominous ticking of the office clock punctuated the silence and measured Frank's labored breathing. Hour by hour, he watched the hands of the clock advance until he had endured as much as he was willing to endure. He snatched the phone off the hook and dialed FBI headquarters at Hato Rey.

Surf King answered. "Hey, guess who's sitting right next to me in my office?" he asked breezily.

"Don't play games with me, Bram." Frank's voice was a low snarl.

"Your boy Alejandro is sitting right here at my desk." He laughed a high-pitched, laugh.

"You have Lopez in custody?"

"Sure, he's not ten feet away. You want to speak to him?"

Frank felt his eyes growing wide. "Did the operation go off on time?"

"Six-fifteen, like clockwork. We caught him in his skivvies . . ."

All the rage Frank had been building up over the preceding weeks, all of the snubs and indignities and interminable delays he and Bob had been forced to suffer coagulated in his mind and exploded into the receiver: "*Why the fuck didn't you call me?*" he screamed. If he could have reached through the telephone wire he would have pulled Carper back to New York by his scrawny neck and gleefully beaten him to death with his bare hands.

"You know how these things are," Surf King responded lamely.

"Yeah, I know how they are." Suddenly Frank was exhausted. He felt like he had just gone fifteen rounds with the heavyweight champ of the world and taken the decision, but was too beat up to climb off his stool. He allowed the receiver to fall back onto its cradle and dialed Bob at home.

"We got him," he said in a low voice.

There was silence on the other end. "You mean they've got him," Bob replied finally. "He's not here yet."

Chapter Thirty-four

BOSE and Barchiesi wanted to be the ones who brought Alejandro Lopez back to New York for trial, but as was the case in the extradition of Nelson Alphonso, it was highly unlikely that Bob would be allowed to go. Supervisors were simply not spared for that kind of operation, irrespective of time invested or emotional involvement. Irritated by the department's inflexibility, Bob decided to give it one last shot. While Frank filled out the proper forms requesting funds and authorization for the trip, Bob went to the office of Deputy Inspector Martin O'Boyle and asked him to make a telephone call and personally intervene on his behalf.

O'Boyle thought about it. By now it was common knowledge that Frank and Bob had made an unauthorized trip to Puerto Rico, and as the word filtered upward through the layers of bureaucracy as it most certainly would, there were bound to be repercussions. O'Boyle was a book cop, and he knew that Bose and Barchiesi had thrown the book out the window. They had flaunted every rule and convention, taken chances cops were not supposed to take in order to bring a fugitive to justice, chances that in the long run could cost them their jobs. But O'Boyle was also a fair cop. He realized that what Frank and Bob had accomplished was at the very least a remarkable feat of investigative tenacity and personal bravery that deserved to be rewarded. He made the call.

Frank began the routine of obtaining the signatures necessary for the extradition, tediously hand-carrying the paperwork upward through layers of police officials until he finally arrived at the office of Chief Joseph Demartino, a recent transferee from the Internal Affairs Division. The chief scanned the request and placed an angry telephone call to Martin O'Boyle:

"What's going on down there?" he demanded. "Do you have enough sergeants down there that you can spare one for this kind of bullshit?"

"Sergeant Barchiesi and his partner are primarily responsible for the capture of this individual," O'Boyle told him.

"So what're you doing, rewarding him?"

"I guess you could say that," O'Boyle replied.

Frank's final stop on the ladder was the office of Police Commissioner Benjamin Ward, where he was waylaid by a civilian clerk who informed him that he could not procure the commissioner's signature on any document that was printed on computer paper. Ward signed only documents that were printed on rag-bond paper, she told him matter-of-factly. It was a hard and fast rule.

"Are you kidding me?" Frank couldn't believe his ears. "Are you telling me you're running the risk of having a dangerous fugitive escape while we're splitting hairs about paper quality here?" He turned his back on the startled clerk, went to the elevator, and punched the "Up" button.

"You can't go up there alone," she protested.

"Who's going to stop me?" Frank challenged.

Reluctantly, the harried clerk accompanied him upstairs to Commissioner Ben Ward's office; that rarified stratum called "God's level" by police officers who are rarely, if ever, admitted to its august corridors. He waited impatiently in the outer chambers while the clerk went inside with the request and returned shortly with Ben Ward's signature and approval. Apparently the commissioner had been too busy with other matters to check the rag content of the paper.

Finally the papers were signed and the resulting shock waves began to register throughout the department. A lieutenant named Joe Lisi, who was reported to be an expert on extradition, as well as a lot of other stuff, called O'Boyle and pointed out the impropriety of his action. O'Boyle reminded Lisi that he was a deputy inspector and that Lisi was a lieutenant. Lieutenants didn't second guess deputy inspectors, he reminded him. If Lisi didn't like what was going on, he could turn it into a personal crusade and they would see who won, the deputy inspector or the lieutenant.

Lisi was self-important but he wasn't dumb. Trying to salvage at least a little bit of his authority, he sought Bob out in the precinct hallway: "Hey, Bobby," he called jovially. "You know we're friends. I really don't blame you for this situation, I blame O'Boyle." He fell in easily alongside Bob and walked with him down the hall. "Sure, we'd all like a nice trip to Puerto Rico, but rules are rules, man. We just can't have sergeants taking off on every junket that comes along."

Bob accompanied Lisi to his office and shut the door behind him. "Let me tell you something, Lieutenant," he began formally, refusing to participate in the artificial glow of familiarity Lisi had created. "I deserve to go down there and put the cuffs on this bastard and I'm going, with the sanction of the job or without it. I'll go down there on my own time, I'll spend my own money, I'll do whatever I have to do; but one way or another I'll be there when he walks out of that cell!"

On April 6, 1988, Frank and Bob again stepped off a plane in San Juan, Puerto Rico; this time authorized to be there and armed to the teeth. They went immediately to the offices of Major Miguel Castillo who was in charge of Puerto Rican extraditions and whom they had met on their earlier trip. Castillo, resplendent in starched fatigues, his chest bristling with shining campaign medals, smiled broadly at them as they entered. "Hello, my friends. You're here for Lopez, sí?"

"That's right," Bob replied.

"You can't have him."

"What's that?" Bob thought he had heard the major incorrectly.

Castillo shrugged. "There's nothing I can do. He's wanted back in Aguadilla on local charges."

Frank and Bob stood stunned. They both remembered their admonition to the FBI that Lopez not be allowed to fall into the hands of any corrupt local authorities. Now they felt betrayed; as if the rug had been pulled out from under them and they had been left bleeding on the ground.

"What do we have to do to get him back?" Frank finally stammered.

"You're not getting him," Castillo replied.

"Do we need the signature of the President of the United States?" Frank went on. "We'll go to the fucking White House if we have to, but we're not leaving without this prick!"

Castillo grinned condescendingly. "Go have a good time. Avail yourselves of the pleasures that San Juan has to offer. I cannot help you in the matter of Alejandro Lopez."

They had come too far to quit now. Both of them were determined to get Lopez no matter what it took: "We were losing it at that point," Frank admitted. "When we left Castillo's office we were talking about breaking into the jail, kidnapping Lopez at gunpoint, renting a private plane, and forcibly taking him off the island. We had visions of a Mexican standoff at the airport with the POPR. It was all crazy but we weren't thinking rationally. We were really desperate. Nothing mattered to us but getting Lopez; not the job, not the danger. Nothing."

They stopped at FBI headquarters on their way to their hotel and confronted Special Agent Thomas Alba, Surf King Carper's boss, and the man directly responsible for having released Lopez to the Aguadilla police. "I just wanted to tell you that everything we warned you about has just taken place," Bob told him through clenched teeth. "We told you there might be improprieties between Lopez and the POPR, and you wouldn't listen to us. Now they've got him where we can't get at him and in all likelihood he'll be gone in a couple of days."

Alba shrugged disinterestedly. "It wouldn't be the first time we had to re-arrest somebody. It won't be the last."

Bob's blood was boiling. "Well, while you're thinking about that, here's something else for you to think about. This thing doesn't end here. We've been after this guy for more than three years and now it looks like he's going to slip through our fingers. If that happens, we're holding you personally responsible. If the story comes out in the press, *and it's sure to do that,* you personally and the FBI in general are going to look like the biggest bunch of assholes in the history of law enforcement. You'll be the laughing-stock of the whole fucking country!" He turned and accompanied Frank out of the office.

Bob's harangue must have had some effect. By the time they arrived at their hotel room there was a message for them to call an FBI agent named Bill Pitts in New York. Pitts was more than deferential when he came on the line:

"Just tell me what you need and it's yours," he informed Frank. "Call me at the office, call me at home. If you need me in Puerto Rico, I'll fly down there today. You name it, you got it."

Encouraged by Pitts's reaction, Bob placed calls to ADA Pat Conlon and to Judge Leslie Crocker Snyder in New York, both of whom responded without hesitation. Telephone calls were made, people were notified. Throughout the lumbering bureaucracy wheels began to turn. Soon the hotel telephone began to ring off the hook with offers of assistance from various law enforcement agencies. Special Agents Art Barnes and Joe Menendez from the Drug Enforcement Agency called, on direct orders from Bob Stutman and Kevin Gallagher of the DEA. They had been told to offer Frank and Bob every possible assistance, they said. The integrity of the DEA depended on Lopez being captured and returned to justice. Finally, they were told that the offices of Senator Alfonse D'Amato had been apprised of the situation and was closely monitoring events.

The following day, Frank and Bob were given an office at the Hato Rey headquarters of the DEA. A helicopter and a full-time agent were assigned to them, and they were told that any reasonable request they had would be granted, no questions asked. The offices of the Governor of Puerto Rico were applying pressure on local police to release Lopez, the DEA told them. Somebody from Washington had mentioned that $5 billion in yearly aid to the island could be jeopardized if Lopez was not returned promptly.

All of a sudden, Frank and Bob's isolated three-and-one-half-year quest was becoming a *cause célèbre* among people with clout. Everybody was looking to hold everybody else responsible for the abysmal state of affairs, and everybody was tripping over everybody else to set things right. Where before they had trouble getting the right time of day from local officials, they now found themselves treated like visiting royalty. There would be absolutely no problem with placing the local charges against Lopez in abeyance, the prosecutor from Aguadilla fairly gushed when they spoke to him on the telephone. He would be placed in their custody without delay, and they would be allowed to take him anywhere they wanted to.

Finally Surf King Carper telephoned Bob at his DEA office and offered his assistance. "How many men will you need, how soon do you need them, and where do you want them to be?" McDonald asked purposefully.

Bob hesitated. He knew it was a time to be magnanimous, to show Carper that he and Frank were above petty vindictiveness and retaliation. He swallowed hard and looked at Frank.

"Fuck you, Bram," he said with utter satisfaction.

Chapter Thirty-five

"This is a test: The date is April 8, 1988. The time is ten fifty-five A.M. I'm Detective Frank Bose, shield number 1491, assigned to the Special Anti-Crack Unit; present with Sergeant Robert Barchiesi at the state penitentiary in San Juan, Puerto Rico to take charge of the prisoner, Alejandro Garcia Lopez, for the purpose of his extradition to New York. This is the end of the test."

THREE years and eight months to the day after they had arrested Anna Ruiz at 507 East Eleventh Street and begun their Rock Solid odyssey, Frank and Bob stood inside the administration building of the gothic stone San Juan Penitentiary and waited for Alejandro Lopez to be delivered to them by prison guards. It was an incredible moment for both of them; a blend of sheer exhilaration and lingering apprehension. All of Major Castillo's difficulties had seemingly been overcome, but they were both painfully aware that anything could still happen. Lopez's money and influence reached deep within the system. It was not beyond the realm of possibility that he might pull off a last-minute coup and once again slip through their fingers.

Fifteen minutes passed, then twenty. It seemed to them both as if the entire span of time from the beginning of their investigation until now had been compressed into those agonizing final moments, as if the rest of the world had suddenly shifted into slow motion while they hovered somewhere beyond the speed of light. Uniformed guards and prison personnel materialized in open doorways like sluggish ghosts, appraising them, wanting to catch a glimpse of the two madmen who had traveled all this way to retrieve the prisoner they knew as "The Man," Tito Lopez.

Frank's patience was stretched to the snapping point. He raised his .35mm camera and in a gesture of frustration began to snap their pictures. Suddenly he saw locked inside the viewing frame of the camera what could only have been an outrageous mirage.

"Holy shit! Do you see what I see?" he gasped to Bob.

"I don't fucking believe this!" Bob stared through the security gate, where a uniformed guard stumbled across the stone courtyard of the prison, carrying two enormous, fully packed suitcases. Strolling leisurely behind the struggling guard, he saw an impeccably groomed and tailored Alejandro Lopez, sniffing the stale prison air with a look of regal disdain. Despite his arrogant bearing, Lopez seemed strangely shrunken inside the immensity of stone and steel, swaggering like a pitifully inept Charlie Chaplin getting ready for a pratfall.

Lopez approached them with a twisted smile fixed on his face. "Hey, you guys did a helluva job!" he exclaimed. "Which one of you is Bose?" He extended his hand.

"Don't you try and shake my hand!" Frank wheeled him around and slapped on the cuffs. "I've been waiting a long time to do this."

Lopez's smile remained fixed. "So you're Bose, huh?"

"I'm *Detective* Bose and this is *Sergeant* Barchiesi," Frank corrected him.

"And you're under arrest, scumbag," Bob added. "You're going back to New York to face charges of Criminal Possession of a Controlled Substance in the First Degree and Conspiracy to Distribute Narcotics in the Second Degree."

Lopez seemed unimpressed. "I gotta tell you both you done a good job," he repeated.

"You also have charges against you pending in New Jersey," Frank reminded him. "As soon as we're finished with you, they're going to want a piece of you."

Lopez nodded and docily followed them to a waiting car. They drove back to DEA headquarters, secured their prisoner in a holding cell on the premises, and requested that they be put on the earliest possible flight. Everything that could possibly go wrong had gone wrong and they weren't taking any chances. The sooner they were off Puerto Rican soil, the safer they would feel. The DEA was more than cooperative. Within an hour they had been driven to the San Juan airport and placed aboard a Lockheed 10-11 jumbo jet bound for New York.

Although his handcuffs were never removed, Lopez was effusive on the trip back, expounding on subjects ranging from his early childhood in East Harlem, New York, to the threats against Frank and Bob: "If I really wanted to kill you, you'd both be dead by now," he asserted. "But I got nothing against you. You were just doing your jobs. We need law enforcement. Without guys like you everything would be chaos."

Frank and Bob exchanged quizzical glances. "I don't understand that," Frank said. "Your whole life has been contrary to that. If you really believed that philosophy, you would never have done the things you did."

"You don't understand. I did what I had to do," Lopez responded.

"You're a pretty intelligent guy. You probably could have done a lot of other things," Bob suggested.

Lopez nodded. "Sure, maybe I could've been a lawyer or something but I never got the opportunity. Where I came from in Harlem they weren't prepared to teach Latin kids. They had a European system; you know, Dick and Jane and all that shit. At my house we spoke only Spanish, so it was tough."

"Listen, you chose to do what you did," Bob reminded him. "You lived a pretty good life for a while but you had to know this day would come sooner or later."

"You must have known that there was someone out there who wouldn't give up until they caught you," Frank added.

Lopez stared at them vacantly. Obviously he had never considered the possibility. He had naturally assumed he could bribe them into turning their backs, or frighten them into abandoning their relentless pursuit of him. He shrugged nonchalantly. "Hey, I just gotta face what I gotta face. I don't regret nothing. I done alright; I got a daughter in Harvard and my conscience is clear. Drugs were there when I was born and they'll be there after I'm dead. You guys know that."

"That doesn't make it right," Frank pointed out.

"You guys just can't understand, can you?" Lopez shook his head. "A man can't survive without money. When I was a kid my parents worked their asses off and they never had nothing. I was raised on welfare and all my brothers and sisters became junkies. Then one day I finally said, 'What the hell, let them kill me' and I walked away from all that. I pulled myself up from the gutter and I'll never regret it. I know you guys hate me but I can't help that. There are plenty of people who love me for what I did."

"We don't hate you. We got to find you," Frank corrected him. "We consider ourselves professionals."

"That female judge hates me," Lopez asserted. "So I guess I'll just have to go back to New York and put on an act for twelve people."

"Nobody hates you. Maybe they just hate what you stand for," Bob pointed out.

Lopez lapsed into a brooding silence. "That female judge is gonna get me no matter what," he said finally. "I'd rather that you guys kill me now and get it over with."

"No, no. We want you nice and healthy so you can stand trial in good shape." Bob said. "We haven't busted our balls for the last three years so you could get off as easy as all that."

Lopez thought about it. "Three years, huh?"

"Closer to four."

He cupped his chin in his manacled hands and stared upward to the ceiling. "You guys know I raise pit bulls to fight in the ring," he said finally. "But what you don't know is I never fight them to kill one another. It's a sport, just like any other sport, with a doctor and a referee. You just let them fight until one of them turns his head and you know he's beaten. Then the fight is over." He looked them both in the eye. "For three years now we've fought each other, and neither one of us would turn our heads. That's something, huh?"

Speaking with Lopez in the intimacy of the plane, both Frank and Bob began to understand a little of why he had reached the pinnacle of his profession. "I know it sounds crazy, but the guy can be really charming," Frank related. "There's something almost seductive about him. I found myself listening to him and actually wanting to like him. I had to physically get up and walk to the rear of the plane just to get my head back on straight. I had to remind myself that this guy was a punk, a coke-sniffing coward who had somehow managed to get himself into a position of power with his charm and wit, then hold onto that power through sheer terror. I had to remember the cold-blooded murders; that he'd threatened to cut my little girl up into little pieces and mail her to me in a shoebox."

The plane landed on time. Driving home on the parkway after Frank and Bobby Geis had taken Lopez to Central Booking, Bob watched sentry rows of emerging maple and willow trees speed past his open window, and inhaled the lightly scented air of early spring. He had anticipated this moment for almost four years: the heady glow of final victory, the thrill of celebration, the intoxicating feeling of having finally been vindicated after a lonely, wearying struggle; but all he felt was empty, as if someone had unplugged him from the wall and left him dangling in empty air.

"I found myself thinking that I was really sorry it was finished," Bob admitted. "After almost four years of walking a tightrope, of experiencing all the uncanny things that happened, all the excitement and anticipation, the adrenaline highs, the obsessiveness of it all, I realized that it was finally over. I knew right then that there would never again be anything in my life that could come close to matching this experience. No matter how many more years I stayed on the job, no matter how many more busts I made or how many kilos of dope I seized, I would never be able to recapture the sheer excitement of Rock Solid. I had reached the top and it was all downhill from there. It was a feeling of unbelievable sadness. I felt empty."

Frank Bose remembered standing in Central Booking as they took Lopez away to his cell and thinking, "Oh my God, it's 1968 all over again. Where the hell do I go from here?"

The following day Frank and Bob removed Alejandro Lopez's dart-punctured portrait from the wall in their Twenty-third Precinct office and drove downtown to 507 East Eleventh Street. A neighborhood teenager stood nearby and watched as they ceremoniously hung the photograph on the front door of Lopez's former stronghold with the word APPREHENDED stamped boldly across its front. The youth's eyes went wide with shock when he recognized the fabled druglord's portrait hanging on the door. He turned and bolted down the sidewalk, shouting the incredible news to everyone he passed: *"They got Tito! They got The Man!"*

Chapter Thirty-six

"There will be a lot of fighting now. More of me will come, and they'll be a lot worse."

—ALEJANDRO LOPEZ

L OPEZ'S ominous warning, made to Frank and Bob during his extradition back to New York, was to prove prophetic, starting with his own family in Puerto Rico. Barely a month after Lopez's arrest, FBI agents from Hato Rey contacted Frank and Bob in New York to inform them that Ernesto Lopez, Alejandro's father, had been kidnapped by unknown persons and was being held for ransom. Frank and Bob could only speculate that the kidnapping had been carried out by angry members of the Medellín, Colombia, cocaine cartel to whom Tito Lopez was heavily in debt. That conclusion seemed to be borne out when on June 17, 1988, Ernesto Lopez was found stabbed to death, his body dumped in the middle of a busy highway.

As Lopez awaited trial in the Tombs holding facility, his heirs began a bloody struggle for control of his cocaine empire. On August 8, 1988, Roberto Padillo-Sosa, a Puerto Rico–based money courier for Alejandro Lopez, and Angel "Kato" Jiminez, a drug dealer who ran a crack operation on Third Street, were gunned down by a fusillade of machine-gun fire in front of 507 East Eleventh Street. Detectives from the Ninth Precinct Homicide Squad, knowing that Frank Bose and Bob Barchiesi had intimate knowledge of drug operations on East Eleventh Street, notified them of the shooting and asked them for assistance.

Frank and Bob were enraged when they were told of the renewed warfare. They were not naive enough to believe that the capture of Alejandro Lopez would end drug trafficking in Alphabet City altogether, but they had hoped it might have effected some change on East Eleventh Street. Now it was clear they had been wrong. The Rock, with its reinforced steel doors, webwork of interconnecting passageways, and underground tunnel system, had become a cocaine Mecca, a magnet for drug purchasers throughout the Northeast corridor. With or without Tito Lopez, it represented an incredibly rich, ready-made market for illicit narcotics that was just sitting there, waiting to be taken over by whatever druglord proved to be the strongest and most ruthless.

Jerry Speziale had a brother-in-law who owned a heavy equipment business. "Jerry, do me a favor and have him flat-bed a bulldozer down to 507 tomorrow morning, okay?" Frank Bose asked Jerry. "If Bobby and I can't get this city to do something about what's happening, we're going down there and flatten that building to the ground."

Jerry looked at him like he was nuts. "I mean it," Frank emphasized. "We'll lose our jobs but we'll close down that operation once and for all. Lopez is not going to win now."

Frank and Bob phoned Bob Drury and Richard Esposito of *New York Newsday* and related their plans for the building. They told the reporters that they could have the exclusive story if they showed up at 507 East Eleventh the following morning with a *Newsday* photographer. It was a calculated gamble. Although Frank and Bob were perfectly willing to go through with the demolition at that point regardless of the consequences to them, they felt that the power of the press would be a far more destructive weapon than any bulldozer.

Rich Esposito proved them right: "Don't do anything crazy," he cautioned after he had heard the story. "Meet Bob and me for dinner tonight and let's talk about it. Maybe we can come up with something more effective."

Frank and Bob met the reporters at Gleason's restaurant that evening and repeated their threat to bulldoze the building into heaps of rubble. Drury and Esposito listened with fascination as they recounted the violent history of The Rock, the Lopez organization, and the seemingly endless pattern of inaction that had brought them to this point. They were mad and they were convincing. By the time they had finished, the two reporters were certain that they meant to carry out their threat.

"Why not let us be your bulldozer?" Drury suggested. "Give us documentation of everything you're telling us, and we'll write a story that will set this city on its ears!"

And so they did. Under a prominent photograph of Bose and Barchiesi standing inside a graffiti-covered hallway and a banner headline stating, "*Drug Fortress 'The Rock' Holds City Block*

Hostage," the August 22 issue of *New York Newsday* related the
sordid drug history of the building and the Lopez organization:
". . . A violent drug gang that police have linked to at least nineteen murders has forcibly taken over the twenty-four-unit city-
owned building," the article began. "Detectives say it is a virtual
Gibralter of fortified apartments and secret drug caches."

Citing Frank and Bob's single-minded four-year obsession with
The Rock, the threats against them and their families, and their
eventual capture of Alejandro Lopez, Drury and Esposito painted
in graphic detail a grim portrait of official malaise and bureaucratic inertia. Assistant District Attorney Patrick Conlon, who had
obtained fifty convictions against the Lopez organization, was
quoted as saying: "As a prosecutor, this is the most frustrating
case I have ever come across. I know we're not winning the [drug]
war, but I would like to think we could win the battle for this one
little building. But when the murders keep happening, I know it's
not over yet."

Nineteen murders. Frank and Bob had painstakingly studied
the Ninth Precinct Homicide Control sheet and pieced together
the evidence linking Lopez with at least that many. "I went
down the Homicide Control list and it just made me sick," the
article quoted Frank as saying. "Some weren't killed in the building itself, but they were all killed in the area; in front of the place,
down the block, and all of them were Rock Solid related in one way
or another."

Carmen Leandry: shot through the mouth by Rock Solid operatives. *Ralph Rodriguez:* murdered for speaking to Frank Bose and
Bob Barchiesi. *Victor Cruz, Gregory Polleck, Julio Torres*: gunned
down during drug disputes at 507 East Eleventh Street. *John
Lunievicz*: beaten, stabbed, and mutilated for complaining to police about drug activity in The Rock. The list went on, a grisly
compilation of human beings who had been slaughtered to ensure
Alejandro Lopez's rise to power and to cement his viselike grip on
the drug trade of East Eleventh Street. The saddest homicide of
all was that of little Daisy Rios, just two years old, who had been
blown apart by an errant .44 caliber slug fired by a Rock Solid
dealer during an argument over drugs.

The *Newsday* article produced exactly the effect Frank and Bob
had hoped for. Suddenly Rock Solid was a media event, and their
telephones at the Anti-Crack Unit and at home began to ring off
the hook with requests for interviews from all of the major TV
networks. In turn, Frank and Bob informed them that they could

only give interviews with proper departmental authorization. Personal TV and press coverage was not, after all, what they were after. They wanted the story of The Rock, and the city's dismal failure to deal with it, brought to public attention. Knowing full well that the police department of the city of New York was almost pathologically sensitive to press criticism, they hoped the media furor would spur them to action.

It did, but in a way that Bose and Barchiesi had not envisioned. When Mike Callahan, Managing Editor of NBC News, sought permission from the department for a series of interviews to be conducted by Channel 4 reporter, McGee Hickey, he was at first put off entirely by the department's Deputy Commissioner of Public Information in the hope that the news would become stale and he would eventually lose interest. When Callahan persisted, he was informed that the interview would not be possible since public exposure might jeopardize Bose and Barchiesi's value in future undercover operations.

There was no way the department was going to allow Bose and Barchiesi to go on camera and tell the story of Rock Solid. Too many people were bound to be embarrassed. Too many sensitive toes up at "God's level" would be stepped upon. Two inevitable questions were bound to be asked: Why had Frank Bose and Bob Barchiesi been forced to use their own money to capture Lopez, and what, if anything, had been done to help their families? They were questions that nobody in the police hierarchy wanted anything to do with, questions that could never be adequately answered. Clerks and staffers at One Police Plaza were put on overtime pulling and checking Frank's and Bob's stats from the time they had entered the department in an effort to uncover something that might discredit them. When no incriminating material was found, they were tersely informed that the department would not prevent them from granting interviews with the press and TV, but that they strongly recommended against it. Frank and Bob both knew what that meant.

Deputy Inspector Ronald Thrash, who had been assigned to check into Bose's and Barchiesi's personal statistics, learned from the department's Public Information section that they had been nominated for the *Daily News*'s Centurion award for personal heroism and valor, a citation that carried a small monetary prize for the recipients' families. Thrash informed Frank and Bob, and Deputy Inspector Martin O'Boyle, their boss at Anti-Crack, personally saw to it that the necessary paperwork was set in motion and that the proper personnel endorsed it. They were a lock for the award, O'Boyle told them confidentially, and from what he knew about it, they deserved it.

The paperwork got as far as Chief Raymond Jones, who refused to sign it. When representatives from the Centurion Foundation inquired about his refusal, Chief Jones said simply: "We have a problem with these guys." That was it. No further explanation was forthcoming.

Recalling the incident later, Frank said, "I don't know whether the guys from the paper got the message, but Bobby and I certainly did. When cops talk about having a 'problem' with other cops, it means that those cops are dirty. This son of a bitch was telling them that we were suspected of being dishonest cops." Frank shook his head. "I don't know about Bobby, but that was what ripped it for me. That's what took me over the edge. I said to myself, 'If that's all I can expect from this job after all these years, then this job can go to hell.' "

Bob and Frank went to Deputy Inspector Thrash and asked for an explanation. Thrash was at first wary when they came into his office: "This smacks of Batman and Robin," he said, eyeing them both speculatively. But as they recounted the entire story of their involvement with Rock Solid to him, he became more and more conciliatory. They told him about the undercover controlled pad, and the threats against their lives and the lives of their families. They told him about going to Puerto Rico on their own time, using their own savings, and about the capture of Alejandro Lopez and what it had meant to them. They told him about The Rock, and about how much it tore them up inside that nothing was being done to make it safe again. And finally, they told Deputy Inspector Thrash how they felt about their treatment by the police department. They hadn't expected to be treated like conquering heroes, they told him; only like good cops who had done their duty as they had seen fit. They had never expected they would be treated like pariahs.

Thrash listened quietly. "How are your families?" he asked them when they were finished. "Can I do anything for them?"

The question stunned both Frank and Bob. Never during the four years of their Rock Solid involvement had anyone from the department thought to ask about their families' welfare, much less offered to do anything to help. They had both logged numerous threat reports with the NYPD's Intelligence Division Threat desk and they had disappeared into that black hole of municipal paperwork where reports went to die and never be seen again. They had become so calloused to inattention and desensitized to slurs and innuendo that they found themselves speechless at his offer.

"Thrash was really a good guy," Bob reported. "We could see that he genuinely cared. But it just goes to show you how out of touch they are at headquarters. Before we spoke with him, Thrash had a completely tainted picture of what had happened. We could see his expression changing from hard and tight to compassionate as we talked. It was like he was hearing it for the very first time."

"Would you like to talk to Chief Hall?" Thrash went on, referring to Chief Francis Hall, Commander of the Narcotics Division. "I can't promise it'll do you much good, but maybe you'll feel better."

An appointment was arranged and they met with Chief Hall in his offices that afternoon, accompanied by Thrash and Lieutenant John Fahey. Their conversation was distinctly one-sided: "I sense that neither of you are venal people," Hall lectured them from behind his ornate wooden desk. "But I have to tell you both that if this thing doesn't go away you could get hurt. You would not be the first police officers in the New York City Police Department who had good intentions and got hurt in spite of them." He eyed them both speculatively and pointed to the telephone on his desk. "Do you see this?" He lifted the receiver and banged it down. His eyes went wide and the veins on his forehead protruded angrily. "*This is a booby trap!*" he screamed. "Every time it rings it can explode on me, and right now I can hear it ticking."

Frank shot a sidelong glance at Bob, who was trying to avoid Chief Hall by staring into the empty air. In a flash both of them realized that they had the same "take" on what they were hearing. To them Chief Hall's outpouring sounded like the response of an overworked bureaucrat who saw threats behind every door.

"It's like I'm the manager of a major-league baseball team, and you two are my clean-up hitters," Hall went on, almost recovered from his outburst. "If I tell you to take the pitch and you ignore me and hit the ball out of the park, what am I supposed to do, lavish praise on you or kick you off the team for disobeying orders?" He leaned across his desk and narrowed his eyes until they became slits. "*I have to think of the team,*" he enunciated slowly. "If the press does not stop bothering me, if this thing does not go away immediately, your careers will suffer."

Chapter Thirty-seven

O N October 25, 1988, Alejandro Lopez stood before Judge Leslie Crocker Snyder in her eighth-floor courtroom at 111 Center Street, Manhattan, and pleaded not guilty to one charge of Criminal Conspiracy to Distribute Narcotics and one charge of Criminal Possession of a Controlled Substance. Judge Snyder, who had presided over the Pony-Pak trial two years earlier, was in no mood to grant Lopez any opportunity for escape and she refused his attorney's application for bail without hesitation.

"It was an interesting moment," Judge Snyder recalled. "I remember being astonished by Lopez's demeanor when he first walked into the courtroom. He was smiling at me, and winking. I thought to myself, *'This guy is trying to come on to me!'* Can you imagine that? I got the feeling that he thought the whole thing was some kind of joke."

The joke ended when Judge Snyder denied bail. No longer playing the role of a charming Casanova, Lopez hardened at the news and became once again the belligerent thug who had dominated the drug trade on East Eleventh Street for so many years. It was vintage Lopez. Just as he had first sought to tempt, then intimidate Frank Bose and Bob Barchiesi, he now attempted to alternately enamor and bludgeon Judge Leslie Snyder. Having risen to power with the absolute belief that everyone could be charmed, bullied, or bought, he was incapable of acting in any other way, even though it was clear by now that the strategy was no longer working.

Lopez was represented by noted criminal attorney, Irving Anolik. Anolik, a Harvard-educated ex-Marine in his middle fifties, presented a marked contrast to the bellicose Valerie Vanleer-Greenberg who had defended Irma Garcia and Raphael Martinez in their 1986 Pony-Pak trial. Where Vanleer-Greenberg had been openly contemptuous of police and the government's case, Anolik was courteous and restrained. Where she had charged at the prosecution's witnesses like an angry bulldog, he presented his client's defense in measured, forceful terms, presenting an effective counterbalance to the brooding, mercurial Lopez.

The gist of that defense was that his client, Alejandro Lopez, was the victim of mistaken identity. He established early on in the proceedings that he intended to discredit eyewitness identification of his client as based on error rather than vindictiveness. He was careful to portray Bose and Barchiesi as outstanding police officers who had simply been mistaken in identifying his client. Finally, he sought to show that Alejandro Lopez had been victimized by friends and relatives who used his name and reputation to line their pockets.

"We believe that the prosecution's witnesses will be exclusively, or almost exclusively police or law enforcement witnesses," he told the jury in his opening statements. "I am going to ask you to consider whether a particular police or law enforcement officer had the ability to observe what he claims to have observed." Hammering home his contention that the case against his client was largely circumstantial, he stressed, "I do not believe that the prosecution will be able to produce any television pictures of my client. I do not believe that the prosecution will be able to produce any electronic tapes of conversations with my client. I do not believe that the prosecution will be able to establish that my client was ever observed selling cocaine.

"Ladies and gentlemen, you will find that my client was not arrested in New York, but in Puerto Rico," Anolik pointed out. "We expect to establish that Mr. Alejandro Lopez was being used because of the fact that he was away in Puerto Rico most of the time; that they decided to use his name as a front. When the police were spoken to, they felt he was a good guy to use as a scapegoat. He can't deny it. [The police] can't verify anything through him. Let's call him 'the boss.' "

Anolik's argument that there was no ironclad evidence showing Alejandro Lopez in the act of selling drugs was incontestable, but the prosecution's case against him, even though circumstantial, was overwhelming. One by one, Assistant District Attorney Patrick Conlon presented police witnesses who frustrated Anolik's attempts to discredit them. When the defense attorney challenged Jerry Speziale's testimony that he had seen Alejandro Lopez outside of the Edgewater, New Jersey, house, suggesting that he had confused Alejandro with his brother Eduardo, Jerry shot back that he had identified both brothers standing together, only a few feet apart.

As the days of the trial progressed, testimony against Lopez became more and more damaging. Police officer after police officer took the stand to testify about their participation in the Rock Solid investigation and when the time came for Patrick Conlon to unveil his main witnesses, a substantial foundation had already been laid. On October 25, the district attorney called Frank Bose to the witness stand.

Painstakingly, Pat Conlon took Frank through every step of his and Bob's investigation, starting from their initial contact with Anna Ruiz through the raid at the TriBeCa warehouse, the controlled pad, the Edgewater and Englewood Cliffs operations, and the Puerto Rican trips by both of them that ended in Lopez's eventual capture. The jury heard tapes of the entire bribery sequence, and Pat Conlon questioned Frank extensively at the end of every tape, emphasizing certain points about Lopez's stewardship of the Rock Solid organization that Bobby Feliciano had inadvertently disclosed. With every new disclosure, Conlon added another dimension to the emerging picture of an ongoing, organized, systematic, high-profit drug cartel that could only have been built and held together by Alejandro Lopez.

Then it was Irving Anolik's turn. Point by point, he retraced every word of Frank's direct testimony in an attempt to catch him in an inconsistency or an outright lie. Holding the typewritten transcript in his hand, Anolik analyzed it for subtle shades of meaning and rephrased the same questions over and over, trying to elicit different responses and to wear down Frank's defenses. He had a knack of drawing the witness's attention away from the jury with clever subterfuges, and almost lulling the entire courtroom to sleep with his tedious repetitions. Then without warning, he would pounce on a reply like a hungry cat on a cornered mouse, and drive a small but significant point home to the suddenly aroused jurors.

"I'll have to say that being on the witness stand is one of the most exhausting things I've ever had to go through," Frank related. "You can never let down your guard, even for a split second. These attorneys are trained to grind you down until you can hardly think straight, then throw you a curve when you least expect it. It's not just that you have to answer the same questions in the same way; you have to use exactly the same words or it will read differently on the transcript and that could be grounds for an appeal. I sat on that witness stand for seven straight days and my stomach was in knots at the end of every day. By the time it was all over I felt like I'd had open heart surgery."

Again and again, Anolik pounded away at Frank's credibility, suggesting that he had a personal vendetta against his client and was hardly an unbiased witness. It was a point that might well have been objected to by the prosecution, but Pat Conlon allowed Anolik to continue with his line of questioning, hoping against hope that he would open a Pandora's box from which there would be no escape.

Anolik obliged. In a cynical reference to Frank's trip to Puerto Rico in March of 1988, he suggested that it may have been more pleasure than work: "Was this one of your more disagreeable functions, having to go to Puerto Rico in the winter?" he asked.

"I didn't refuse to go, sir," Frank replied.

"Then you went down there again at *taxpayers' expense* in March, is that correct?"

Frank shot a glance across the courtroom at Pat Conlon, who was attempting to stifle a smile, then looked heavenward and muttered a silent *"Thank you, God."*

"Yes, I went down, but it was not at the taxpayers' expense," he answered slowly and audibly.

"You paid your own way?"

"Absolutely."

"You didn't get reimbursed?"

"No, sir."

Anolik eyed Frank incredulously. "Was this some sort of vendetta you had?" he demanded.

"No sir. *I was concerned for the safety of my family.*"

Anolik had opened the door during his cross-examination and prosecutor Pat Conlon charged inside. "Detective, can you tell the members of the jury about the threats that were made against you and your little girl that resulted in your going to Puerto Rico?" he asked during redirect.

Anolik was on his feet in an instant. "Your Honor, I ask for a withdrawal of the jury and a mistrial!"

Judge Snyder overruled, pointing out that Anolik had himself opened up this line of questioning.

"Were these threats made personally against you and your family?" Conlon persisted.

"Yes, sir."

The courtroom was in an uproar. Irving Anolik was again screaming for a mistrial, and Judge Snyder was angrily ordering him to take his seat. Frank felt his tension begin to evaporate, as if an iceberg was beginning to melt inside his chest. For the first time since he had started his testimony his fists slowly began to unclench.

"Can you give us the substance of the threats made against you and your family?" Conlon continued his questioning.

"I was told that Mr. Lopez was going to have a man with a machine gun come in from Aguadilla to kill Sergeant Barchiesi and myself. In addition to that, I was told that my little girl would be cut up and sent back to me in a shoebox," Frank replied shaking, his voice choked with emotion.

A hush fell over the courtroom as he struggled to regain his composure. "It was a moment of high courtroom drama," Pat Conlon reflected. "Frank was visibly shaken and the jury was really moved by it all. The only conclusion I can draw is that Lopez hadn't been straight with his attorney. It's almost inconceivable that an experienced trial lawyer like Irving Anolik could make a dumb mistake like that, but for whatever reason, he did. We had discussed the possibility that there might be an opening in the questioning where Frank could bring out the threats, but we never in our wildest dreams imagined that the defense counsel would blunder into such a dangerous area. It played right into our hands. The faces of the jurors turned white. It wasn't just another cop testifying against another drug dealer up there anymore. Now it was personal. It was life and death."

"Lopez was like stone, he didn't bat an eye," Frank recalled. "It was as if it was more important to him to show everyone that he had that kind of power than to deny it. I looked at the jury and saw it in their faces. They'd heard enough. The trial lasted almost three more weeks, but as far as I'm concerned, Pat Conlon could have rested his case right then. Lopez was finished."

Bob Barchiesi followed Frank to the stand. In response to Pat Conlon's careful questioning, he explained for the jurors the function of a Narcotics supervisor, the description and violent history of the building known as "The Rock" at 507 East Eleventh Street, and the internal structure of the Rock Solid operation. He outlined his team's operations against the organization in detail, stressing the amounts of confiscated drugs, cash, and weapons that had been seized during the various raids. At each disclosure, ADA Pat Conlon paused to produce a sample of the contraband being described. Bob would be given sacks of cocaine that had been marked into evidence which he passed among the jurors, and automatic weapons which he displayed in front of them and dramatically slammed the bolts open and shut.

"Most of what goes on in a courtroom is boring as hell," Bob asserted. "Probably the hardest job a prosecutor or an attorney has is keeping the jury awake and focused on the proceedings. After a while they begin yawning, their eyes get glassy, and it's not unusual to see one of them start to nod off. Having the jurors pass huge bags of cocaine among them doesn't really mean anything as far as enhancing the evidence, but it gives them something to do besides just sit there. When I'd stand and rack the slide of a Tech 9 machine gun it would make a helluva bang in the courtroom. You could see their eyes click open."

Throughout Bob's testimony, Lopez countered every new presentation of evidence with winks, smiles and uncaring shrugs, playing up to female jurors who he felt might be captivated by his fatal charm. Either on his own or on the advice of his lawyer, he had shaved his ever-present moustache and closely cropped his hair in an effort to alter his appearance for the trial and cast doubt on the testimony of witnesses who had identified him. The effect of this physical transformation seemed to encourage his sense of unreality, his innate sense of drama. A paid-up member of the Screen Actors Guild, he put on a performance for the jury. Like an imperious Shakespearian actor immersed in a role, he postured and preened to the amusement of the prosecutors and the consternation of his defense counsel.

Alejandro Lopez did not take the stand in his own defense, and after sixteen days of police testimony against him the prosecution rested its case. In his summation to the jury, Irving Anolik again stressed his contention that his client had been nothing more than an unwilling dupe whose name had been used by unscrupulous friends and relatives, and that police officers had mistaken him for his brother Eduardo or other Hispanic drug gang members with similar features:

"Ladies and gentlemen, I don't know if any of you have ever seen those shows where they have Elvis Presley lookalikes. I've seen maybe thirty people who claim they look just like Elvis Presley. Maybe they do, maybe they don't. But remember that when police officers went to 63 Ridge Road [Edgewater Place] on February 26th and 28th, 1987, they had a picture of Alejandro Lopez and they expected to see Alejandro Lopez, if he was there."

Anolik allowed the point to sink in, hoping to create a spark of doubt in the jurors' minds. "Yes, there are family resemblances between Eduardo Lopez and the defendant, Alejandro, so if these officers saw someone similar they were going to say it was Alejandro."

Anolik's summation was lengthy and impassioned. "Please, ladies and gentlemen," he pleaded upon closing. "I ask you to view the evidence, and I think I have a right, without appealing to your prejudice or to your sympathy, to say to you that there is not sufficient evidence in this case to convict this man of any crime. Certainly not of Possession, certainly not of Conspiracy beyond the reasonable doubt that any citizen of this country is entitled to. I ask you to return a verdict of not guilty in this case. Thank you for your patience and indulgence."

In her closing charge to the jury, Judge Leslie Snyder meticulously explained what the charge of "constructive possession" entailed, and what elements were required to convict on such a charge:

"A person who does not have actual possession of an item may have constructive possession. Constructive possession occurs when a person has the ability to exercise dominion and control over an item or items, even if he doesn't have actual physical possession. As long as the item is under a person's substantial control, he may be considered to possess it under the law."

Citing examples of constructive possession, Judge Snyder went on to define what was meant by circumstantial evidence, explaining that in many instances a circumstantial case can be stronger than one with direct evidence, if the weight of that evidence was commanding and well documented. Although Judge Snyder did not say so directly, it would have been almost impossible for jury members not to have reached the conclusion based on the testimony of the past four weeks that an overwhelming circumstantial case against Alejandro Lopez had been presented. Finally, thanking the jury members for their patience and attentiveness during the grueling month-long trial, she sent them to deliberate.

Frank and Bob sat in the courtroom as the jury filed out and eyed each other uncertainly. Suddenly both of them realized for the first time since they had begun their four-year campaign against Alejandro Lopez that things were entirely out of their hands. Everything was about to be decided by twelve men and women they had never even met.

Chapter Thirty-eight

THE Lopez jury deliberated for two and a half days but to Frank and Bob it seemed like centuries. Every hour that passed without a verdict added to their growing sense of apprehension that they had somehow failed to make their case, that somehow Alejandro Lopez would slip through their fingers once again. They reviewed their testimony with one another endlessly, searching for a word, a phrase, a missed opportunity that might have turned the tide against them. No matter how ironclad the evidence against Lopez seemed to be on paper, they were unable to shake the pervasive feeling of doom that pressed in on them.

"Nobody was popping champagne corks at that point," Frank remembered. "We were pretty sure we'd established a prima facie case against Lopez, but juries can be quirky. Despite Judge Snyder's charge to them about circumstantial evidence, we could never be sure it sunk in. We thought about the possibility that he'd be let off, but I don't think we discussed what we'd do if that ever happened. Now we don't even want to think about it."

They didn't have to. The jury rendered their decision at 2:37 on the afternoon of November 26, 1988: Guilty on two counts. To say that they felt relief would be an understatement, but it was a tentative, probing, uncertain kind of relief that bordered on emptiness. "When you let the air out of a balloon, there's nothing left inside but a vacuum," Bob Barchiesi observed. "Lopez had been such a dominant part of our lives for such a long time, that I guess neither of us had given much thought about what would happen once he was gone. Now he was gone, and that took some getting used to. Someone we had really hated was out of our lives, but so was all of the passion we'd built up hating him. It's hard to describe what that feels like."

On a rainy December afternoon, Alejandro Lopez again appeared before Judge Leslie Crocker Snyder for sentencing. After a final plea for leniency by Irving Anolik, ADA Patrick Conlon stood before Judge Snyder and recapitulated the case against Lopez, taking pains to introduce into the proceedings the staggering profits he had realized from his Rock Solid operation: "In August of 1986, from the first of the month to the thirty-first, he sold three hundred eighty thousand dollars' worth of Rock cocaine," he related. "In September of 1986, he sold two hundred sixty-three thousand dollars' worth of Rock cocaine . . ." The litany went on, month after month, an astonishing testament to the unbelievable amounts of money that could be made from the sale of drugs. Conlon pointed out that in only the last five months of his operation, Lopez had sold more than one and one-half million dollars worth of Rock cocaine, and that he had been doing that volume of business for the previous *ten years*.

Finally, he summarized the threats against Bose and Barchiesi, and against their families, and the patterned violence that had been Lopez's trademark since he had first arrived on East Eleventh Street and set up shop in The Rock at number 507: "Violence was a way of life in that building, Your Honor," he reported somberly. "There were shootings and stabbings, like the death of Daisy Rios, a two-year-old baby shot inside apartment nine, and the homicide of John Lunievicz who was beaten to death in apartment two."

Conlon asked Judge Snyder to impose the maximum penalty allowed under law; a three-million-dollar fine and a jail sentence of thirty-three and one-third years to life. Then Defense Attorney Irving Anolik asked to be allowed a final statement:

"I would like to point out, Your Honor, that I have never indicated that the detectives in this case were anything but heroes in the type of work they did on the Lower East Side. They exposed themselves to danger every day of the week to protect the citizens." He went on to repeat his claim that, although Bose and Barchiesi had acted heroically in smashing a major drug ring in Alphabet City, they were mistaken in presuming that his client was a part of that ring. "I have no quarrel with the arresting detectives," he said in closing. "They are excellent police officers, but even the best police officers make mistakes. Cases are reversed all the time."

The court clerk then turned to Alejandro Lopez and asked him if he wanted to make a statement before sentence was imposed upon him. Lopez stood defiantly, his mouth fixed in an angry snarl: "When I first came here, and the first words you told me was, 'I've been waiting for you a long time,' I knew I wasn't going to get a fair trial." His jaw jutted forward contemptuously.

"Understand, I was raised in East Harlem and came to the Lower East Side when I was seven years old. Drugs was there before I was born and they will be there after I'm dead. So I must have been a conspirator from the day I was born, because [drugs] was always around me, in the streets, next door, in the yards, everywhere. Out of fifty guys that I grew up with, maybe two or three made it, okay? Most of them are dead, some are in jail. It took forty years for me to go to jail and I lived pretty good compared to them. I don't regret that.

". . . Yes, I made money," Lopez said proudly. "I have money, and I have credibility compared to my brothers and friends. I do have credibility; maybe not compared to Your Honor or to maybe these great cops you have here, maybe not compared to them. But where I come from, I do have credibility." He nodded with satisfaction. "And who raised me? Who was my father? Welfare, that's who raised me!" He glared angrily at the judge. "That's all I got to say. Do what you want with me now."

Judge Snyder looked down at the seething defendant, and addressed him in a clear, uncompromising tone: "One good thing about our American system of justice is that it affords everybody an opportunity to be heard," she began, "no matter how absurd or phoney and unbelievable what they say may be. One of the most significant aspects of this case, which cannot be emphasized strongly enough, is that the evidence clearly and overwhelmingly has established that this defendant was not an addict, was not a street-level seller or possessor of cocaine like many of the defendants who come before this court. No, he was a businessman motivated by only one thing: greed and the desire to make money.

"I am sorry I am not a psychiatrist, because I am certain that one could afford an interesting analysis of this defendant's personality. It is fascinating that in front of the television cameras he attempts to portray himself as a poor, unfortunate victim of society, when in fact he has been one of the biggest victimizers of this society, of the police, of the residents of the Lower East Side."

Judge Snyder turned her attention to the attorney for the defense. "Yes, Mr. Anolik, your client is an amazing combination of characteristics: Stupid enough to put all of his assets in his own name, yet sophisticated enough to distance himself from the street operations of this massive, victimizing narcotics operation; smart enough not to be where he could be witnessed on any kind of sale level, and brazen enough to be convinced that he could outwit all law enforcement efforts to apprehend him. And he almost succeeded. Had it not been for the extraordinary efforts of several police officers who remained courageous despite threats to them and their families, threats to cut their children up and send them home in shoeboxes, a major narcotics operation would still be flooding the Lower East Side with narcotics and poison.

"507 East Eleventh Street was a nightmare," she went on. "It was a nightmare not only for those in the building but for everyone in the area; a nightmare for any honest citizen. I am not sentencing this defendant for the bribery and murdering, only for conspiracy and the possession of narcotics. But there is widespread evidence in the records showing how violent this conspiracy had become, and how anybody who dared to cross it risked everything.

"So why should I show any sympathy or mercy for this defendant? He didn't show any for his victims. We will never know how many people became addicted because of Alejandro Lopez. We will never know how many children, teenagers, and adults became addicted for life because of Alejandro Lopez, or how many people fed their habits on his cocaine. We will never know how many families were destroyed by his cocaine, or how many people have died because he sold it. Nor will we ever know how many police officers have been injured, maimed or killed in their battle against the violence that his poison created. All we do know is that every police officer in this city risks his or her life when they go out on the streets to fight what has become this war on narcotics."

Judge Snyder looked across the courtroom at Frank and Bob who were seated in the first row of the gallery. "And I have to say a final word about the police officers in this case. I have alluded to this, but I want to make it absolutely clear that I have never seen more dedicated or courageous officers than the team in this case; Sergeant Barchiesi and Detective Bose in particular, as well as others who worked tirelessly with them. Without their devotion and their determination to clean up this drug organization by getting to the source of the drugs, to the root, the head of the operation, this poison could not have been eradicated. It is only because of them that this defendant was brought to justice.

"We have only begun to see the enormous personal costs to the police fighting this war; far too many have been killed or injured. But it is the courage and dedication of officers like the team we have had here who acted heroically despite the overwhelming danger, that gives our society the hope that our law enforcement efforts might someday succeed. We all agree that our war on drugs has barely begun. We need a master strategy, national and local, and far more resources on all levels. We need more law enforcement, more rehabilitation and drug education. Hopefully we will see more of these efforts soon. Meanwhile, punishment will have to suffice."

Judge Snyder threw the book at him: Eight and one-third to twenty-five years on the Conspiracy charge, and twenty-five years to life on the Possession charge, terms to run consecutively, one after the other. Alejandro Lopez would be seventy years old before he could ever hope to walk the streets a free man again. Frank Bose went home, unloaded his 9mm and put it away in a drawer.

Frank and Bob took their wives out to dinner that night and celebrated the end of Alejandro Lopez, and the revelry helped to fill the void left by his departure. There were champagne toasts and self-congratulations all around, and they rejoiced and decompressed until early in the morning. And when they were properly drunk and exhausted they went home to quiet tree-lined streets and slept a peaceful sleep, knowing that their families were out of danger at last. Families were forever. The empty feeling would be filled with their childrens' laughter.

Chapter Thirty-nine

AFTER his trial, Alejandro Lopez proved to be entirely adaptable to his new situation. Incarcerated in the New York Downstate Correctional Facility prior to being sent to a maximum-security prison, it was immediately apparent that his reputation had preceded him. Collecting newspaper accounts of his infamous life, his trial, and conviction, Lopez bragged about his exploits and, in a prison society where bombast, swagger, and notoriety are synonymous with manhood, he was easily able to surround himself with a cadre of loyal hangers-on. They listened to his endless boasting with awe and admiration, saw to his every whim, and helped provide what small luxuries there were available to an imprisoned felon. Although Judge Leslie Snyder had branded him as an escape and bribery risk based on his past conduct, he managed to gain unrestricted and unsupervised control of the prison telephones in only a few weeks.

By the end of December, Bose and Barchiesi learned that Lopez was still playing havoc with their lives. A police informant inside the prison code-named "Joseph," who had proved to be entirely reliable in the past, got word to the Intelligence Division that the druglord had openly discussed plans to have his arresting officers, ADA Patrick Conlon, and Judge Leslie Snyder killed as an act of vengeance. Frank and Bob did not treat the information lightly; neither did anyone else. Too much was known about Lopez's history of brutality to dismiss the threat as empty bluster.

"We'd put Lopez to bed," Bob related. "Frank and I really believed at that point that he was somebody else's problem for a change. Our families were safe, so far we'd managed to stay together. We thought we could get on with living normal lives after nearly four years. Then this thing surfaced and we were right back in the thick of it. Neither of us doubted for a minute that he was crazy enough or angry enough to do it, and we knew he still had the resources to get it done."

On January 6, 1989, a debriefing was held at the Manhattan

DA's offices to discuss the threats. Among those present to hear Joseph's account were Sergeant Michael McKeon from the NYPD Intelligence Division's Threat Analysis Module, Detective Julio Rodriguez from the Manhattan District Attorney's Squad, Lieutenant John Fahey, and Frank Bose. Fahey had balked at letting Frank attend the meeting, concerned that he was too personally involved and too emotional to remain objective, that he might fly off the handle and do something he would later be sorry for. Frank had laid it on the line: Either he would be allowed to sit in on Joseph's debriefing or Fahey could have his gun and shield and he would go to the press. Frank went to the meeting.

At the meeting, the informant known as Joseph again related the particulars of Lopez's threat, pointedly mentioning that he had never observed Lopez reading newspaper articles about himself or his trial, but that he had always enlisted the aid of another inmate to read the accounts to him. It was a significant disclosure, adding greatly to Joseph's credibility as an informant. Outside of Frank, Bob, and a few others in the police department and on the District Attorney's staff, nobody knew that Alejandro Lopez could not read or write. Lopez had always been ashamed of his illiteracy, they knew, and had gone to great lengths throughout his life to conceal it. Certainly there was no way he would have revealed it to another convict whom he barely knew.

Detective Julio Rodriguez, who conducted the interview with Joseph, gave him ample opportunity to lie about events and to embellish his relationship with the notorious druglord, but the informant remained convincing, stating on more than one occasion that he was only a casual observer of the events he was reporting. He disclosed that Lopez seemed pleased at the newspaper accounts linking him with nineteen homicides, but went on to relate that Lopez had admitted to having committed only four of the murders himself and ordering the rest.

Everyone was convinced that Joseph was telling the truth, but it was clear that there would be no significant response by the DA's office or the police department. In a written memorandum on the debriefing with Joseph, Assistant District Attorney Jonathan Soroko stated: "No response will suffice which would absolutely insure the safety of SNC personnel in all circumstances, and any response which remotely approached that, would be prohibitively expensive. By the same token, this does not justify no response at all. While it is clear that threats against line assistants are not of the same importance as threats against e.g., Mr. [Special Narcotics Prosecutor Sterling] Johnson, they are certainly of enough importance not to be ignored."

Soroko's memo was a part of the record, and for many in the law enforcement system of the city of New York that was response enough. It was not enough for Frank Bose and Bob Barchiesi. Both of them understood that the NYPD had no workable mechanisms in place to deal with threats to police officers, and that if anything was going to be done, they would have to do it themselves. They were not certain whether or not Lopez was serious. There was always the possibility that the threats were simply more of his *macho* bragging, but they could not take the chance. This was a man who liked to murder people. His record in and out of jail bore that out.

Bob remembered an informant named Raymon Salizar, a heroin addict he had arrested and sent to jail a year earlier on the request of his own family, who felt he would be safer there than out on the streets where he would surely kill himself with drugs. Bob, Frank, and ADA Pat Conlon traveled to the Downstate Correctional Facility where Salizar was incarcerated, and offered him a reduction in his sentence as well as a monetary reward if he would become an undercover informant against Alejandro Lopez. Salizar flatly refused; convict's bonds run deep.

"Look, Raymon. This has nothing to do with money, it has nothing to do with getting you out of stir," Bob told him. "Lopez crossed the line. He threatened to kill us and our families. He said he'd chop our children up and send them to us in shoeboxes. Now we hear he'd put a contract out on us from jail, and we have to find out if it's real or if he's blowing smoke. You can get that information for us."

Salizar agreed. Not for money or reduced time, but because he was basically a decent man who believed there were limits that should not be overstepped, even among convicts. It was arranged for him to be placed inside the same cell block as Alejandro Lopez, where he began to function as an informant. As an additional precaution, Pat Conlon arranged for the prison telephones to be wiretapped and for all of Lopez's outside conversations to be monitored.

The steel spring that had wound so suffocatingly tight during the three-and-one-half years of their Rock Solid investigation, and only just begun to unwind, was tightening again. Uncertain about the extent of the danger to them and their families, Frank and Bob knew they could do nothing but prepare for the worst and hope for the best. They knew they would have to tell their wives what was going on.

"I went home and took Linda aside where the kids couldn't hear us and told her that it wasn't over," Bob Barchiesi related. "I told her that from now on she had to walk our son James to the school bus and wait there with him until he got on. NYPD Intelligence had asked the local police to check our house from time to time, so I told Linda not to be alarmed if she saw a patrol car waiting outside or if officers knocked on our door. I can't describe how frustrated I felt. Here I was after spending four years of my life tracking down this son of a bitch and putting him behind bars, back to square one, no better off than I was back in 1985."

Frank concurred: "I had to take my daughter out of the school she was attending and enroll her in a private school. I told the authorities from the new school what was happening and gave them a list of people who were authorized to pick Amanda up. They were sympathetic, but they were also very apprehensive. They were afraid to let Amanda play in the schoolyard with the other children because it might pose a threat to them.

"My wife, Candy, is probably the most gentle, most benign individual I have ever met in my life. When it comes to this job, she's always had an air of unreality about it, as if it would all go away if she just didn't think about it. But when she saw how tense things were becoming, she asked me for a gun to protect her and Amanda. *A gun!* This from a woman who carries mosquitoes out of the house and sets them free. I remember looking at her and thinking, 'My God, what's happening to all of us?'"

They decided to see Captain Kenneth O'Brien, Commanding Officer of Manhattan North Narcotics, and lay it on the line. "Captain, my partner and I spent four years of our lives getting Lopez, and if I'd known in the beginning what I know now, I would have hunted him down and blown him away then, rather than go through all the heartache and the bullshit," Bob told him. "The NYPD doesn't mean shit to me anymore. My family comes first. Unless something is done about this, you can have my shield and my gun."

"What do you want me to do?" O'Brien asked them both.

"We want somebody to take this seriously," Frank said.

"Well, I take it seriously," O'Brien told them. "I'm going to see that your wives are given police short-wave radios so they can report the slightest sign of trouble as soon as it happens." He lifted the phone on his desk. "And I'm instructing that your home telephone numbers be programmed into the Communications Division's 911 number. I'll follow this up with a written request and make sure it's updated and reevaluated on a month-to-month basis. I want it done, and I want it done now. Call any time, night or day if you have a problem."

Linda Barchiesi received a call from school that their eldest son, James, now in kindergarten, was behaving in an unusually disruptive manner. When he was questioned by his teacher, James had said that he wanted to stay at home with his mother, that he was afraid some harm would come to her. Bob was like a lunatic when he heard the news. He and Linda had done their best to shield their own anxiety over the Lopez threats from little James, but their best had not been good enough. James had heard something, or sensed their tension, and now feared for his mother's welfare. Bob realized at once that he could not simply tell school officials the reason for his son's behavior since they might ostracize him from the rest of the school population for the other childrens' safety, but he also knew that he could not sit by and watch things get worse. He had to do something, short of breaking into Lopez's cell block and blowing his head off with a machine gun.

Every bulletin board in every police precinct in every borough in the city of New York carries a prominent poster emblazoned with the legend: *"Are you or any member of your family under stress? Problems with alcohol or drugs? Do you know another police officer in need of help? Call the NYPD Stress Unit 24-hours-a-day for help and help eliminate a problem before it becomes a problem!"* Bob agonized over whether or not to call the special 800 number listed on the poster and talk to a Stress Unit counselor. Finally he took it to his boss, Lieutenant John Fahey.

Fahey listened sympathetically while Bob recounted the problems he was having at home. Offering to help personally in any way that he could, he called a lieutenant at the Stress Unit, outlined the situation over the telephone, and handed the receiver across his desk to Bob: "Don't tell me your name, this is strictly confidential," the lieutenant began as soon as Bob came on the line. "Before you say anything, let me tell you what we do in situations like these. Before we talk to your son or your wife, we'll want to interview you to determine whether or not you have a problem. And let me tell you this up front: If we perceive that you do have a problem, I'm afraid our relationship will be no longer confidential. *When you leave our office, you will be placed on modified assignment and your weapon will be taken away from you."*

Bob sat dumbfounded. For the first time, he understood the magnitude of his mistake. Not only had he believed that the NYPD Stress Unit might offer some small relief for his beleaguered family, but he had allowed himself to be lulled into thinking that the unit was there to benefit cops in the first place. The realization hit him like a Magnum slug right between the eyes. The NYPD Stress Unit didn't give a shit about cops or their problems. The NYPD Stress Unit was there to head off cops who might embarrass the department!

"Both of us should have known we couldn't expect any help from the department but we kept on hoping," Frank Bose asserted. "I'm proud to be a cop, proud of what I do and the way that I do it, and I know I would never have been given the opportunity to go after Alejandro Lopez if I hadn't been a New York City Policeman. But still it hurts. It hurts to think they cared so little about us personally; that they care so little about cops in general, that they'd rather throw them to the wolves than risk hurting their image. Everything is image to them. Cops don't count for anything compared to headlines.

"I went out and bought myself a new fourteen-shot, nine millimeter automatic pistol and a great big, noisy dog. If the dog barked in the middle of the night, I was prowling the grounds with the nine millimeter, an extra magazine in my hand and a police radio in my back pocket. Sounds crazy, doesn't it?"

An incident that happened shortly after he bought the pistol made it seem a lot less crazy. A tall, thin Hispanic male appeared at the door one evening while Frank was at work and Candy was home alone. When she denied the man entrance, he pushed against the partially open door and tried to force his way inside. Candy managed to get the door closed and locked, but the intruder ran to the back of the house and attempted to force open the rear door, which was securely bolted.

Terrified, Candy at first called the New York Central Dispatcher on the police short-wave radio that Frank had given her, and pleaded for assistance. Her call was routed onto a common police network and was heard by every sector car in the city of New York, but because the transmission was hysterical and the vernacular was not professional, her plea was ignored. Remembering Frank's directions after his meeting with Captain Kenneth O'Brien, she quickly dialed 911 Central and told the answering operator that she feared for her life.

The operator refused to believe her. Near panic, Candy still had the presence of mind to call Frank at the precinct. Frank immediately contacted the 911 supervisor, identified himself as a police officer, and asked that a 10-13 response, code for "*An Officer in Trouble*," be given to his wife's call. Again, the supervisor refused, demanding further verification of Frank's credentials, suggesting that he might be a criminal. Somehow he was finally able to convince her, but by the time a radio car in his sector had been notified, almost a half hour had passed, more than enough time for any self-respecting assassin to have done his work and leisurely departed.

"I called up a lieutenant at the Intelligence Division Threats Unit the next morning and let him have it with both barrels," Frank reported. "I asked him what the hell good a radio and a 911 computer hookup were doing me when it took a half hour to get a car out to my neighborhood? Do you know what his response to me was? He said, 'You really didn't expect that was going to help, did you? Giving your wife that radio was just supposed to be a *placebo*.'"

Chapter Forty

I N time, some of the hurt wore off, and Frank and Bob were able to discuss their careers in the police department with a measure of detachment. One day in early 1990 they returned to The Wicked Wolf and tried to put some of their thoughts into words.

"I'll never regret having become a New York City Police Officer," Bob Barchiesi related. "I have nothing but respect and admiration for anyone who puts on that blue uniform and goes out into the streets every day. They do the most difficult job in the world, in the most difficult city, under the most difficult and maddening bureaucracy that ever existed in law enforcement. And they do a helluva job in spite of it. When I leave I'm going to miss the work, the camaraderie of the people I've worked with and had a chance to become close to. Will I miss the job? No."

Bob paused, then went on to clarify: "The job creates a climate where it's really impossible for police officers to work effectively. They come on the job young and enthusiastic, just like I was, and after a while they just get worn down by all the bullshit. They start to realize that it's a lot easier just to go along rather than make waves, even if that means not upholding the law the way they swore to uphold it when they graduated from the police academy. They become complacent because the job encourages them to become complacent.

"In other cities in America, they recognize that the cop's job is to enforce the law, and they do their best to see that he gets the tools to do just that. They don't hand him a badge and a nightstick and a gun and then try and turn him into a social worker. Cops aren't social workers. That's not to say cops are insensitive to social conditions, or that they don't have compassion. Cops have as much compassion as anybody else, but unlike social workers they have to be brave every day. Every day they have to walk into situations where their lives are placed in extreme danger. It's hard to think about the environment that caused someone to go bad when they're coming at you with a knife."

He became thoughtful, his voice was tempered with emotion. "I've been a New York City cop for more than eleven years. I've been in a lot of precincts, run a lot of Narcotics teams as a sergeant, and in my opinion these guys are the best cops in the world. They function every day knowing that the decisions they make out on the streets won't be judged on their merits, but how popular that decision is viewed on Monday morning by the press. After a while they have to figure that courage and enthusiasm don't count for much. What counts is keeping your nose clean and not embarrassing anyone higher up. Aggressive cops send shock waves up the system and they bounce back. Any rookie on the NYPD who thinks he can beat the system is in for a lot of heartache because the system is rigged. But if he wants more out of life than a safe, comfortable existence, this is a damn good way to get it, even with all the bullshit. I've made a lot of friends. It's been a privilege to serve with them. I'm going to miss them."

Frank Bose nodded agreement. "I spent the first fifteen years or so of my life screwing up. So, I guess you might say I've spent the rest of it trying to make up for that, starting with the Marine Corps. I'm no psychologist but it helps to sometimes try and figure out what drives me to do things. I worshipped my father and watched him die when I was seven years old, a time when I really needed a father. To be honest, it still hurts a lot. I still see that man through seven-year-old eyes, eyes that can't remember imperfection, so I guess that over the years his image has become almost godlike." He shrugged. "Maybe I was looking for a father when I joined the Marine Corps.

"Both my sons were taken away from me by my first wife at a time when I needed to be a father. I bankrupted two successful restaurant franchises battling her for custody, spent every cent I had, and when it was all over I was convinced I'd never see my sons again. So I just walked away, started a new life in the police department, married Candy and inherited a great stepdaughter, Edith, and had another child. I totally sublimated my feelings in work and, more than anything, I think that was what saved me in the long run.

"I came to the police force with the same ideal I had when I joined the Marine Corps, so it was a rude awakening to me when I finally realized that they were more interested in maintaining the bureaucracy than enforcing the law for the people of New York. The ideal was crushed, just like the conception I'd had about the Marine Corps had been crushed as soon as I landed in Vietnam.

All of a sudden I was face to face with the realities of survival. Randolph Scott and the Marine Corps band weren't going to march into Da Nang and save my ass."

Frank smiled at the relevance of his metaphor.

"In a way, Lopez saved my ass. He saved me from becoming the kind of cop I saw around me every day; cops who'd been so ground down by the system that they were afraid to do their jobs, or worse still, had become indifferent to them. Lopez was able to do what the Police Department of the City of New York was unable to do; to focus my enthusiasm and my rage. He told me that he was going to take away my little girl, and something inside of me snapped. I knew I could never survive another loss like that.

"The other thing that saved my ass was hooking up with Bobby. It was a blend that could never happen again on the NYPD in a thousand years, each of us filling in what the other one lacked, each of us bringing our own strengths and expertise into the blend. I know that we each had different reasons for becoming obsessed with Alejandro Lopez, but we both knew instinctively that once we started there was no turning back, and that no matter how it ended our lives would never be the same. Both of us knew that the day would eventually come when we would have to leave this job."

Frank hesitated, swallowed hard.

"I was thirty-two years old by the time I became a policeman, and I had to fight like hell to get this job. I had to take on men ten or more years younger than I was, and prove I was better than they were just to win the privilege of putting on that blue uniform. And even with all the aggravation, I was never prouder than when I put it on, day after day, every day. It would be nice to think that every cop felt that way. I know a lot of them still do.

"Now I feel clean, and very tired. I know that I have to let go, and I don't want to. It's like being cut from the umbilical, but there's nothing left on this job for me. Most cops will spend their entire careers running around the base of the mountain and never even try to climb it. Bobby and me, we got to the summit and we know what the view is like from there. I feel sorry for those other guys."

Afterword

O N a bleak February morning in 1989, Alejandro Lopez, shackled hand and foot, was put on a prison bus that would take him to maximum-security Shawangunk Penitentiary in Wallkill, New York, where he was slated to spend what would probably be the rest of his natural life. Two New York City cops and their families felt a little bit safer. In Alphabet City, things returned to normal, or at least as normal as things ever got in that unloved part of the world. The name of Alejandro Lopez was no longer whispered in frightened tones; in fact, it was rarely heard at all as younger men moved in to fill the gap left by his imprisonment. Drugs continued to be sold, though not as openly as before, and teenage lookouts with street names like Chepo and Spanky and Campeon began to appear once again on the dust-blown sidewalks and alleyways. The few members of the Rock Solid drug family who remained in the building called The Rock were evicted by the city of New York.

Workmen from the city came to 507 East Eleventh Street, broke through the reinforced steel barriers inside, and plugged up the labyrinthine system of escape tunnels that Lopez and his confederates had built between apartments and underground. The doorway to apartment number 2, which had been sealed like a sepulcher with a concrete slab after the murder of John Lunievicz, was reopened and a new door was installed, as were others that had been destroyed by police battering rams or raked with gunfire. Hallway floors were swept and an attempt was made to wash away the layers of grime and graffiti that had accumulated on the inside walls. They painted the exterior of the building brown.

A televised press party was held. Frank Bose and Bob Barchiesi were not invited. Police brass and politicians came, stood proudly in front of the newly refurbished building, and spoke into the eyes of television cameras about how successful they had been. A spokesman for the newly formed Police Housing Preservation Unit pointed out for the media that the city had begun to move homeless families into the apartments, and that uniformed patrol-men had been assigned to make daily inspections of the premises to insure that no drug activity was taking place inside. Citizens' groups endorsed what was being done, and spoke guardedly about recapturing the streets from the druglords, building by building, block by block, until New York was a decent place to live and raise families in once again.

Then, as suddenly as they had come, everyone went away and a brooding silence descended on East Eleventh Street. Like an old woman left alone, staring helplessly into a mirror and overlaying the memory of past conquests on her wrinkled reflection, the reality sunk in that all of the speeches, all the promises and hoopla were empty seductions; all the paint and glitter, like streaked mascara, were cruel deceptions. Nobody cared. Alone, stripped bare in the light of day, all that remained was an unloved, decaying shell.

Nobody had the strength to stem the decay because nobody really knew how it had started in the first place. It was the niggers and the spicks, some said, and corrupt, uncaring politicians. It was the times; a generation raised without values, without re-spect. It was drugs. Whatever the reason, everyone knew deep down that what had been could never be again. In their sorrow and their pain, they saw, like a frozen slide on a stereopticon screen, the day a crack appeared in a wall and went unfilled, a window latch that fell off and was never replaced, a crumbling concrete step that went unrepaired. Somewhere, on a particular day in the history of East Eleventh Street, someone said, "It's just not worth the bother." And on that day the neighborhood died.

So they waited for whatever was to come next: the junkies and the vagrants, the pimps and whores and sellers of dreams, the final cleansing sweep of the wrecker's ball.

"Maybe they'll tear it all down and build yuppie condos like they did over by Tompkins Square Park," Elizabeth Calabrese specu-lates from her second-floor flat at 512½ East Eleventh Street. "It wouldn't bother the junkies or the drug pushers none. All they'd do is move downtown a block or two, but what would happen to people like me, to good people? Nobody from the city ever cared what happened to this block, not the TV people, not the politi-cians, not the cops, nobody."

Her face is a mask of incomprehension when she hears the names Frank Bose and Bob Barchiesi. "Cops." She shakes her head knowingly. "They're all the same."

Anna Ruiz was arrested in the summer of 1988 and spent time in jail for Possession of Narcotics. Her current whereabouts are unknown.

Bobby Feliciano is currently serving a term of eleven years in jail for Parole Violation, plus an additional three years for Bribery.

"Little Tito" Garcia served time based on a term of four to twelve years in jail for Firearms Possession. He has been paroled.

Lisette "Vivian" Mazzola pled guilty to Conspiracy to Sell Narcotics and served time in prison. She has been released.

Eduardo Lopez is currently serving a term of eight and one-half to twenty-five years in Attica State Prison for Conspiracy to Sell Narcotics.

Ricky Moreno (aka Javier Padillo-Sosa) is currently serving a term of five to fifteen years in jail for Conspiracy to Sell narcotics. His brother, Roberto, was gunned down in a machine gun melee in front of 507 East Eleventh Street.

Nelson Alphonso pled guilty to Conspiracy and Bribery, and served a term of four and one-half to nine years in prison. He has been paroled.

Eddie Raul Garcia Feliciano ("Goggles") plea-bargained from First Degree Sale of Narcotics and is currently serving a term of six years to life. He was never prosecuted on Homicide charges.

Leonardo Carreon stood trial for Criminal Sale of Narcotics and was convicted. He received a sentence of fifteen years to life. He is currently appealing his conviction from jail.

David Lopez was found to be mentally deficient and unable to stand trial. He was placed in a psychiatric facility where he is currently undergoing treatment.

Maria Salazar (Bunny Mother). All charges against her were dismissed in return for her cooperation with authorities. Her current whereabouts are unknown.

Angel (Kato) Jiminez, was wounded in a shootout at 507 East Eleventh Street and is paralyzed from the waist down.

Carlos (Pito) Zapata pled guilty to Narcotics Sale in the First Degree and received a sentence of six years to life.

Jose (Joey) Cuadrato pled guilty to Narcotics Sale in the First Degree and received a sentence of six years to life.

Aaron Davilla (J. D. Gordo). Whereabouts unknown. He is believed to be working in a gas station in Aguadilla, PR.

Ricky ("Truck"). Whereabouts unknown. It is believed that he lives somewhere on the streets of the Lower East Side.

Willie Gonzales disappeared.

Natalia Torres was evicted from her home in Rio Piedras, PR. Her current whereabouts are unknown.

Irma Garcia ("Blondie") and **Raphael Martinez ("Juahito")** served three-and-one-half to seven-year sentences in a New Jersey prison resulting from the Fort Lee Holiday Inn arrest. Their drug conviction for activities at 507 East 11th Street were reversed on appeal in New York. Their related weapons convictions were upheld on appeal. At this writing they are waiting to be sentenced.

Alejandro "Tito" Lopez was convicted of Criminal Conspiracy to Distribute Narcotics and Criminal Possession of a Controlled Substance. He was fined $3 million, all of his assets were seized by the FBI, and he received a prison sentence of thirty-three and one-third years to life. Currently serving his sentence in Shawangunk Penitentiary in Wallkill, New York, he will not be eligible for parole until the year 2013. He filed a notice of appeal, which was never perfected.

Chief Francis Hall is retired from the New York Police Department and is currently lecturing about the police bureaucracy.

Deputy Inspector Martin O'Boyle was promoted to Inspector, and received the *Daily News* Centurion Award in recognition of the outstanding work done by the Anti-Crack Unit.

Deputy Inspector Ronald Thrash was promoted to Inspector and is the current Commander of the NYPD Auto Crime Division.

Chief Raymond Jones has retired from the New York Police Department.

Inspector Thomas Gallagher was promoted to Assistant Chief and is currently the Commander of Brooklyn North Patrol.

Lieutenant Joe Lisi was promoted to Captain. He can be seen occasionally in minor roles on TV police shows.

Lieutenant Gerald Robbins has retired from the NYPD and is now a consultant on piracy to the record industry.

Lieutenant John Fahey has been transferred to the detective bureau.

Lieutenant John Sullivan retired from the NYPD. He is currently an Adjunct Professor of Criminal Justice at Penn State University.

Sergeant Mike Barron was promoted to Lieutenant in 1989, retired, and is currently a Special Assistant U.S. Marshall for the Federal Eastern District of New York.

Jerry Speziale was promoted to Detective and transferred to the DEA Task Force.

Bobby Geis (Goose) was promoted to Detective and transferred to the Thirty-fourth Precinct Squad.

Gabe Galiano was promoted to Detective and is now working in Manhattan South Narcotics.

Louie Torrellas was promoted to Detective and is currently a member of the Thirtieth Precinct Detective Squad.

Joe Alvarez was promoted to Detective and transferred to the Detective Bureau.

Elsa Gonzales was promoted to Detective and is currently with the Department of Investigation.

Special Agent Bram (Surf King) Carper still works for the FBI.

Special Agent John Galindo resigned as the Assistant SWAT Team coordinator for Hato Rey, Puerto Rico. He still serves as an Investigating Special Agent in the Puerto Rico office.

Special Agent Bill Pitts was transferred to the Atlanta office of the FBI.

DEA Special Agent Art Barnes was reassigned to Washington, DC, Headquarters and has since retired.

Assistant District Attorney David Molton resigned from the District Attorney's office and went into private practice. He now defends accused drug dealers, handles their appeals, and has proved as adroit at defending criminals as he once was at prosecuting them.

Special Prosecutor Ed Boyar is now an assistant district attorney in Brooklyn. He prosecuted the Howard Beach and Bensonhurst trials.

Special Prosecutor Charles Joseph Hynes is currently District Attorney for the County of Kings (Brooklyn), New York.

Assistant District Attorney Roy Sweetgall resigned from the DA's Office and went into private practice. His current whereabouts are unknown.

Richard Esposito was promoted to City Editor of *New York Newsday.*

Bob Drury left *New York Newsday*, authored the book *Incident at Howard Beach,* and cohosted the TV series *The Reporters.*

Judge Leslie Crocker Snyder is currently serving a second term as Acting Supreme Court Justice of the New York State Supreme Court.

Assistant District Attorney Patrick Conlon was promoted to Deputy Chief of the Special Narcotics Prosecutions Investigations Section. In 1989 he entered private practice in New Jersey.

Assistant District Attorney John Soroko left the Special Narcotics Prosecutor's office.

"Maureen" still serves drinks and food at The Wicked Wolf.

*   *   *

Frank Bose was transferred in 1989 to the Drug Enforcement Administration of the US Department of Justice where he currently serves as a Detective Investigator in the Group 86 Narcotics Task Force. He was awarded custody of his two sons in 1990.

Bob Barchiesi is Special Agent in Charge of Criminal Investigations for the Virgin Islands Department of Justice.

THE authors wish to acknowledge the outstanding career and heroic sacrifice of Sergeant John McCormack, who was shot and killed in the line of duty on April 27, 1988. John was a partner and a friend. His support during the bribery phase of this investigation was invaluable. His loss is our loss, and a loss to all of the citizens of New York City whom he served so valiantly.